To my husband

BILL LUNNEY

and to the memory of our son

DAVID

CONTENTS

The Revels Plays
COMPANION
LIBRARY

E. A. J. HONIGMANN former editor
J. R. MULRYNE, R. L. SMALLWOOD and PETER CORBIN general editors

For over thirty years *The Revels Plays* have offered the most
authoritative editions of Elizabethan and Jacobean plays by
authors other than Shakespeare. The *Companion Library*
provides a fuller background to the main series by publishing
worthwhile dramatic and non-dramatic material that will be
essential for the serious student of the period.

Marlowe and the popular tradition

MANCHESTER
UNIVERSITY PRESS

THE REVELS PLAYS COMPANION LIBRARY

Marlowe and the popular tradition
INNOVATION IN THE ENGLISH DRAMA BEFORE 1595

RUTH LUNNEY

Manchester University Press
Manchester and New York

distributed exclusively in the USA by Palgrave

Published by
Manchester University Press
Oxford Road, Manchester M13 9NR, UK
and Room 400, 175 Fifth Avenue, New York, NY 10010, USA
http://www.manchesteruniversitypress.co.uk

Distributed exclusively in the USA by
Palgrave, 175 Fifth Avenue, New York,
NY 10010, USA

Distributed exclusively in Canada by
UBC Press, University of British Columbia, 2029 West Mall,
Vancouver, BC, Canada V6T 1Z2

British Library Cataloguing-in-Publication Data
A catalogue record for this book is available from the British Library

Library of Congress Cataloging-in-Publication Data applied for

ISBN 0 7190 6118 0 *hardback*

First published 2002

10 09 08 07 06 05 04 03 02   10 9 8 7 6 5 4 3 2 1

Typeset in Sabon
by Action Publishing Technology Ltd, Gloucester
Printed in Great Britain
by Bookcraft (Bath) Ltd, Midsomer Norton

GENERAL EDITORS' PREFACE

Since the late 1950s the series known as The Revels Plays has provided for students of the English Renaissance drama carefully edited texts of the major Elizabethan and Jacobean plays. The series includes some of the best-known drama of the period and has continued to expand, both within its original field and, to a lesser extent, beyond it, to include some important plays from the earlier Tudor and from the Restoration periods. The Revels Plays Companion Library is intended to further this expansion and to allow for new developments.

The aim of the Companion Library is to provide students of the Elizabethan and Jacobean drama with a fuller sense of its background and context. The series includes volumes of a variety of kinds. Small collections of plays, by a single author or concerned with a single theme and edited in accordance with the principles of textual modernisation of the Revels Plays, offer a wider range of drama than the main series can include. Together with editions of masques, pageants and the non-dramatic work of Elizabethan and Jacobean playwrights, these volumes make it possible, within the overall Revels enterprise, to examine the achievements of the major dramatists from a broader perspective. Other volumes provide a fuller context for the plays of the period by offering new collections of documentary evidence on Elizabethan theatrical conditions and on the performance of plays during that period and later. A third aim of the series is to offer modern critical interpretation, in the form of collections of essays or of monographs, of the dramatic achievement of the English Renaissance.

So wide a range of material necessarily precludes the standard format and uniform general editorial control which is possible in the original series of Revels Plays. To a considerable extent, therefore, treatment and approach are determined by the needs and intentions of individual volume editors. Within this rather ampler area, however, we hope that the Companion Library maintains the standards of scholarship that have for so long characterised The Revels Plays, and that it offers a useful enlargement of the work of the series in preserving, illuminating and celebrating the drama of Elizabethan and Jacobean England.

PETER CORBIN
J. R. MULRYNE
R. L. SMALLWOOD

ACKNOWLEDGEMENTS

I am indebted to the University of Newcastle, New South Wales, for the post-doctoral fellowship which allowed me to begin the research for and writing of this book.

An essay based on Chapter 6, 'Not "Shakespearean" but "Debatable": Rewriting the Narrative of Dramatic Character', won the 1996 Calvin and Rose G. Hoffman Prize for Distinguished Publication on Christopher Marlowe. A shorter version of this essay appears as 'Rewriting the Narrative of Dramatic Character, or, Not "Shakespearean" but "Debatable"' in *Medieval and Renaissance Drama in England* 14 (2001). I would like to thank the editor John Pitcher and publisher Fairleigh Dickinson University Press for permission to reprint this material.

Earlier versions of material now in Chapters 3, 6, and 7 have been published as 'Transforming the Emblematic: The Dramatic Emblem in the Plays of Marlowe', *Essays in Theatre* 9.2 (May 1991); 'Bridges "through the moving air": Christopher Marlowe and the "space between"', Essays in Theatre 11.1 (November 1992); 'Faustus and the Angels', *Sydney Studies in English* 16 (1990–91). My thanks to Harry Lane of *Essays in Theatre* and Margaret Harris of *Sydney Studies in English* for permission to reprint.

I am especially grateful to Hugh Craig, Sara Deats, David Frost, Mark Gauntlett, Peter Holbrook, and Nancy Wright, who have read and commented on the manuscript, and to the members of the Marlowe Society of America for their continuing encouragement.

This book would not have been possible without the love and support of my family. I appreciate this most of all.

CHAPTER 1

Ways of seeing

From jigging veins of rhyming mother-wits
And such conceits as clownage keeps in pay,
We'll lead you to the stately tent of War,
Where you shall hear the Scythian Tamburlaine
Threat'ning the world in high astounding terms
And scourging kingdoms with his conquering sword.
View but his picture in this tragic glass
And then applaud his fortunes as you please.

(*1 Tamburlaine*, Prologue 1–8)[1]

We have taken too much notice of the Prologue to Part One of *Tamburlaine the Great* – and too little. In reckoning what was 'new' about the plays of Christopher Marlowe, we have always been too ready to assume that they must fulfil the undertaking of the Prologue to discard old ways and old values. Such a premise is built into most commentaries on the plays, outlasting whole generations of change in critical fashions. Take three examples, all representative of their times. Harry Levin (in the earnest 1950s) describes Marlowe as the 'arrogant young scholar-poet' who 'sweeps aside the doggerel rhymes and clownish jigs of his predecessors' (47). Alvin Kernan (in the impatient, anti-Establishment 1970s) evokes a Marlowe who 'was proudly self-conscious of himself as the destroyer of the old and the creator of a new drama, a new style and new dramatic values', as opposed to 'the dreary scene and flat verse of the old drama' (251). Robert N. Watson (in the anxious, post-civilisation-as-we-knew-it 1990s) writes of 'overreaching heroes who conveyed the simultaneous grandeur and cynicism of this brave new Elizabethan world and its unbridled colonial appetites', finding a Marlowe who 'With astonishing energy ... liberated English drama from the complacencies of both its academic and its popular conventions' (312). Marlowe, 'our contemporary'.[2]

Sweeping aside, destroying, liberating: the terms aptly reflect these readjustments of viewpoint. At the same time, they are expressions that belong to a particular way of seeing the drama of the 1580s. They emphasise the discontinuity, the gap between earlier playhouse offerings ('clownish', 'dreary', complacent) and Marlowe's plays. Taking too much notice of *Tamburlaine*'s Prologue, accounts such as these – most commentaries, that is – turn aside from Marlowe's relationship with his past to focus upon defining his 'newness' along lines that have become quite predictable. They rehearse the standard list of 'new' dramatic practices inspired, many imply, by humanist learning: the 'mighty line', the astounding heroes, the 'revolutionary' ideas. At the same time, they position Marlowe in terms of one of the established critical stereotypes: the rebel, the subverter, the conduit of ambivalence – with occasional recourse to the orthodox moralist or Erasmian riddler. And so the treadmill of commonplaces keeps moving along.[3]

Too much notice, and too little. We have pursued Marlowe's 'newness' to the detriment of understanding either that newness or the changes in the London playhouse drama in the 1580s and 1590s. Because our attention has shifted away from Marlowe's dialogue with tradition, from his engagement with the conventional dramatic practices of the time, we have failed to appreciate the nature or extent of his achievement. Marlowe's 'newness' lies, as much as anything, in transforming the familiar, in the way he makes use of – rather than discards – old ways and old values. The spectacle, the verse, the heroes: all were undeniably important. And after *Tamburlaine* nothing was ever the same in the playhouse. But, as is indicated by the distance between Marlowe's plays and some of the less memorable ones of the time (*Alphonsus, King of Aragon*, perhaps, or *The Three Lords and Three Ladies of London*, both of which contain spectacle and verse and heroes inspired by the success of *Tamburlaine*), the new ways were not of themselves sufficient. The impact of the 'new' practices in Marlowe's plays is underpinned by new uses for the 'old'.

To understand these new uses of the old, we need to take notice of the changes that Marlowe's plays brought about at the level of theatrical experience – in the ways that people perceived, watched, felt, participated, and responded in the late sixteenth-century playhouse. The importance of these theatrical experiences to the processes of change is implicit in every line of the Prologue. For all its extravagant claims and promises (and, like most speeches of its kind, this is more sales pitch than affidavit), the Prologue is still anchored in the theatre. It has a strong sense of place and presence. The spectators will be 'led' by the players. They will 'hear'. They are enjoined to 'view' and given the choice to 'applaud'. Performance, suggests the Prologue, constructs experience, and this experience is the means by which spectators are to become aware of the different and the new.

This emphasis on the transforming power of experience may perhaps seem too obvious to require any comment; but in 1587 it is something new among the extant plays. The Prologue to *Tamburlaine* signals a realignment of perspectives. The prologues to earlier plays may speak of eyes and ears and what the players will present (that to *Clyomon and Clamydes*, written some ten years or so earlier but revived by the Queen's Men after 1583, calls upon the 'Glasse of glory' and 'gentle eares' before introducing the players: 'The actors come, who shall express the same to you at large').[4] But for all their promises of pleasant and superior mirth, earlier prologues insist conscientiously on the playing space as a place of proof and example rather than as a place of story and experience. Any 'seeing' by the audience is enlisted in the service of didacticism: for the spectators of *Clyomon and Clamydes* the 'just rewarde' for virtue or vice is to be 'manifestly showne'; for those of *An Interlude Entitled Like Will to Like Quoth the Devil to the Collier*:

> Herein as it were in a glass see you may
> The advancement of virtue, of vice the decay.
> To what ruin ruffians and roisters are brought.
> (*Like Will to Like* 17–19)

The promises are routine ones. Of the extant plays that may have been performed in the playhouses before *Tamburlaine*, Robert Wilson's *The Three Ladies of London* (written 1581, about six years earlier) is unusual, perhaps unique, in offering a prologue that omits reference to moral judgement. The Prologue in this case responds to the new commercialism of the London playhouses by using the analogy of a market stall: should the wares be 'good' and 'fine', the customers will return for more. The omission, however, is more than compensated for in the ensuing action of the *Three Ladies* with its repeated demonstrations of social wrongdoing. On the other hand, even as *Tamburlaine* preserves the old appeals it changes them. Eyes and ears are now enlisted to register the high points of the narrative; and the 'glass' retained from the old didacticism offers, not moral certainties, but an opportunity to 'applaud ... as you please'.

Marlowe's challenge is, in the first instance, located in the playhouse and dependent upon theatrical experience. Of this we have taken too little notice. Despite a number of calls since the 1960s for writers to consider the alternative Marlowe – the practising playwright – his plays are still treated very much as excavation sites for biography or ideology, with the excavators too often satisfied with fragments of text, scraps of dialogue.[5] And, whether the impulse has been historicist or polemical, the critical approach has been much the same. Studies of Marlowe, far more than for any other writer of his time, have been concerned primarily with finding ideas in the printed playtexts that echo other contemporary formulations or show the workings of contemporary society or suggest psychological pressures or exemplify some interpretative paradigm.[6] What we have, in consequence, is a great litter of critical commonplaces: from the feathers of the overreacher and the anxious jottings of Baines to the ashes of towns burnt by English merchants and the bootprints of the Elizabethan State.[7]

Many of these critical studies rely upon an essentially reflective model of the relationship between society and the theatre – and between the playwright and his plays. The shift of interest among the newer historicists from 'ideas' to 'social codes' or practices, and from reflective to negotiated or other models, has complicated but not essentially altered the basic approach. When Stephen Greenblatt, for example, proposes a 'poetics of culture', he argues that the text acquires its meaning from the 'cultural materials' it includes: 'cultural beliefs and experiences ... [are] shaped, moved from one medium to another, concentrated in manageable aesthetic form, offered for consumption' (*Shakespearean Negotiations* 5). In such studies, issues such as 'new' or 'old', subversion or conformity, are established by analogy, by reference to similarities between something in the plays and something elsewhere – then or since. While the initial stitching together of analogies is often quite tentative, the qualifications tend to be left behind as the argument develops. This can be seen in Greenblatt's own linking of *Tamburlaine* with the 'acquisitive energies of English merchants, entrepreneurs, and adventurers'. We 'might look', he suggests, for a hypothetical analogue: 'If, on returning to England in 1587, the merchant and his associates had gone to see the Lord Admiral's Men perform a new play, *Tamburlaine the Great*, they would have seen an extraordinary meditation on the roots of their own behavior' (*Renaissance Self-fashioning* 194). '*Might look ... If ... would have seen*': here as elsewhere, the rhetorical connections do not support the weight of the assertions that follow.[8]

Analogies may illuminate, may persuade, but all too often these accounts limit our view of moments of transition and cultural change. By privileging sameness, and especially by looking for similarities in ideas, they overlook the differences that arise as new discourses are constructed. We may, to adopt Greenblatt's terms (*Shakespearean Negotiations* 1–20), have realised that the past speaks not with a single voice (the single voice of the Elizabethan World Picture, let us say) but with many competing voices. Even so, we have not listened attentively enough to the voices – especially those on the other side of Shakespeare, such as that of *Tamburlaine*'s Prologue – which address their past and their contemporaries rather than our present. We forget too that this addressing is often far less a matter of 'ideas' than of ways of 'speaking'. And the effect of our selective listening, too often, is simply to re-invent the past in answer to the needs of the present.

In particular, the search for analogies has distracted us from attending to theatrical experience, although this is the place where the voices of difference, as the Prologue suggests, will impinge upon the spectator. This impinging entails more than the emotional satisfactions offered by the performance ('stately', 'astounding'), though, as Andrew Gurr suggests, such 'emotionalism' helped to secure the immediate success and the continued playing of *Tamburlaine* as well as *Doctor Faustus* and the *Spanish Tragedy*. Gurr identifies this increased 'emotionalism' of the drama of the late 1580s and the 1590s as a consequence of the 'mighty line', which had the power to sway the affections of the playhouse audience; and of powerful 'personation', which drew upon the 'deepest wells of emotion in the Elizabethan mind': preoccupations with power and justice and religious doubt (*Playgoing* 136–7). But, while blank verse and 'personation' may have extended the emotional range of performance, they did not necessarily involve any challenge to conventional ideas. This is so both of earlier blank-verse plays such as *Gorboduc* (1561; printed 1565, reprinted 1590), and of many playhouse offerings after *Tamburlaine*. What was more significant was the impact of performance on the audience's perspectives, a process that encompasses perception as well as interpretation. In the performance of Marlowe's plays the spectators were led to 'see' and 'hear' differently – to perceive, that is, in ways different from those of the past – and (at the same time) to change the ways that they 'saw' or made sense of the action and characters before them.[9]

These changes in 'seeing' provide the key to understanding both Marlowe's challenge to his past and the nature of his 'newness'. If,

in very general terms, we are to assess Marlowe's plays as revolutionary or liberating in his cultural context – if, that is, they
represent any more than a simple change in theatrical fashion – then
we should be able to discern this quality in the ways that the
perspectives of the audience are constructed during performance.[10]
The sixteenth and seventeenth centuries are identified generally as a
time of significant change in what people thought. In philosophy,
there was a turning from universe to self, with the spread of scepticism and relativism; in science, a new attention to 'natural' instead
of divine causes; in commerce and geography, an expansion of the
known world; in education, a revived emphasis on classical authors;
in law and language, a recognition of custom or convention.[11] But
what is often overlooked in discussions of this 'change of mind' (or
indeed of revolutionary ideas at any time) is a different dimension of
change. Cultural change – whatever model we use, whether we
describe it as philosophical or ideological, or as a matter of values or
attitudes or codes – happens not merely at the articulate and explicit
level of treatise or sermon or pamphlet where it is propounded and
debated, but at the level of 'ordinary' experience, where it can be
found in the moment-by-moment adjustments to what we notice
when we see (what is 'obvious', what simply not observed) and,
importantly, in the changes to the narratives we use to make sense
of what we see. This 'ordinary' experience deserves our attention. It
is, of course, decidedly ephemeral; but we can, even so, discover
something of its nature – of the expectations it involves, of its ways
of seeing and thinking – by looking at the experience that happens
in the theatre.

My project here is to explore changes of the 'ordinary' kind as
they occur in the London playhouses of the 1580s and 1590s. And
my interest lies less in what people might have thought than in how
their minds, by seeing differently, might have been changed. Because
of this emphasis, I shall be less concerned than most writers on
Marlowe and his contemporaries with any inherently 'subversive'
qualities in the ideas and stories they dramatised. The theatre is
always subversive, has always exploited notions that differ from the
received ones. Even in the most regimented or the most complacent
of societies, drama thrives on difference and contradiction and on
giving voice to social tensions; and its routine attractions include
displays of utter villainy. In late sixteenth-century London the
topical and sensational and controversial were the ordinary materials of popular drama – just as today they provide subject matter for
popular television – if only to entice patrons into the playhouses.

And the roles of those playhouses were various and variable: reflecting their society, to be sure, but also reinforcing received values, educating, observing, commenting upon, entertaining (not least) – and, if we listen to some contemporary voices, corrupting.[12]

Yet if 'subversion' is not simply a matter of 'ideas', neither is it chiefly a question of place or context. It has more to do with 'how' minds are changed than with 'what' or 'where'. Bringing Machiavelli on stage is certainly sensational but – for all the apprehensive comments of Robert Greene about 'pestilent Machivilian pollicy' (*Groatsworth of Wit* 43) – it is not necessarily subversive or revolutionary unless by the end of the play the processes of performance have led the spectators to view their world differently. 'Till experience', as Mephistopheles admonishes Faustus, 'change thy mind' (*Faustus* 2.1.131). Nor is this new viewpoint just a matter of spectators sallying forth from the playhouse to find Machiavels everywhere – or no more so than the occasions when they went forth to find Ambidexters or Dissimulations or Sensual Suggestions.[13] It was, after all, a commonplace that the world was a fallen and imperfect one; and one more fashion in sinfulness could readily be accommodated.

'An audience', as Raymond Williams reminds us in *Drama in Performance*, 'is always the most decisive inheritance, in any art. It is the way in which people have learned to see and respond that creates the first essential condition for drama' (178). Any theatre, that is, has its own expectations, its own customs, its own experiences. What is more, its conventions of representation are not just accepted ways of telling stories but are also implicated in particular ways of seeing, particular habits of perception and interpretation. As Williams also comments, 'a convention is not just a method: an arbitrary and voluntary technical choice. It embodies in itself those emphases, omissions, valuations, interests, indifferences, which compose a way of seeing life, and drama as part of life' (180). In reckoning the 'newness' of Marlowe's plays I propose to look at their engagement with – and challenge to – the theatrical inheritance of their first audiences: the popular dramatic tradition in the late sixteenth century.[14] In effect, I measure the experiences they construct for their spectators against those afforded by other 'popular' plays written between (about) 1565 and 1595. By 'popular' I mean the kind of play that was likely to have been performed before a general audience (very much David Bevington's sense in *From Mankind to Marlowe*), and hence to have been part of a London playgoer's experience in the new commercial playhouses, or for that matter in other intermittent or temporary venues – the innyards and marketplaces, the halls of towns and great houses.

There were of course other dramatic traditions – academic, court, and classical – accessible to the 1580s playwrights and to many in their playhouse audience. There were other ways of telling stories, other sets of expectations about genre, let us say, or character or dramatic construction, many of which are significant for what happens in Marlowe's plays.[15] And yet the popular tradition offered more than is generally recognised. In particular, as Alan Dessen suggests in *Shakespeare and the Late Moral Plays*, the late moralities should be taken more seriously as offering the playwrights who followed 'a variety of dramatic options or theatrical strategies' (9) found in earlier plays, but 'geared to the practical assets and liabilities of Elizabethan stages and staging' (160). The expectations of the playhouse audience were shaped, not only by seeing particular kinds of stories but also by seeing stories constructed and presented in particular ways:

> Unlike Roman drama or *Everyman*, these late moral plays had an on-stage life for several decades that made them well known as a form during the boyhoods of the major Elizabethan dramatists. Indeed, along with romances like *Common Conditions* and *Clyomon and Clamydes* (both of which contain a Vice), for roughly thirty years these late moral plays *were* English popular drama. We may *read* Marlowe, Shakespeare, and Jonson, but they *saw* plays like *The Trial of Treasure*, *The Tide Tarrieth No Man*, and *Apius and Virginia*.
>
> (*Late Moral Plays* 163)

'We may *read* ... but they *saw*.' Playwrights, and spectators too.

My aim in the chapters that follow is to explore the process by which 'old' became 'new' in the late sixteenth-century drama, to consider how the theatrical tradition represented by *The Tide Tarrieth No Man* metamorphosed so suddenly into *Doctor Faustus* and *Hamlet* and *Volpone*. What will be offered here is a new account of that transition, viewed from the perspective of pre-1595 playtexts and theatrical experience, in which the role of Shakespeare is neither central nor defining and Marlowe is the catalyst of change. My ambitions as historian or historicist are modest: I make no claims to any startlingly new 'readings', nor am I engaged in applying the theories of others. As indicated above, my analysis assumes that there was a 'change of mind' in sixteenth-century England, which was accompanied by changes in the drama. My concern, however, is less with any grand narrative than with observing the voices on the other side of Shakespeare, in dialogue with each other in the playhouse. These are voices – heard especially in the moralities and non-Shakespearean plays – that we have for the most part neglected.

The attention here to the specifics of the popular tradition (playtexts, playhouses, audiences) has certain advantages. There are different questions to be asked, lost connections to be explored between familiar and little-known texts, new insights to be gained. Indeed, as Scott McMillin and Sally-Beth MacLean suggest in introducing their study of the Queen's Men, 'things nearly forgotten' are important for historical understanding. If, they remark, we are properly to 'historicize' Shakespeare – rather than simply considering him 'our contemporary' – we need to recognise the differences between past and present, to 'study the things which he had to deal with and which our age is free to ignore' (xvi). Another advantage of looking afresh at pre-1595 playtexts is the opportunity it provides to redefine terms and reconsider criteria, to challenge (in effect) the weary commonplaces on which many writers rely. There is a chance, besides, to clarify the nature and timing of change in the theatre, to redraw the boundaries between 'traditional' and 'Shakespearean', between 'medieval' and 'modern' drama; and these are issues that continue to be under contention. Nor are the benefits of fresh looking limited to the theatrical. What happens in the theatre may reflect society, but audiences do not simply watch reflections. The way they experience has implications for 'historical' issues such as the impact of iconoclasm or the advent of 'subjectivity', and indeed for broader narratives of cultural change.

Chapter 2 ('Approaches and contexts') treats questions of critical method and theatrical context. It suggests that a rhetorical model provides the key to understanding not only what happens in the theatre during performance but also changes in theatrical experience, such as those that occurred in the late 1580s and early 1590s. 'Rhetoric' is used here in the sense of the active shaping of language to influence others; in this context it is 'dramatic' rather than verbal or literary. Under this model the task becomes one of identifying those structures in playtext and performance that organise perception and interpretation. This chapter also surveys the drama before *Tamburlaine*, defining the ways that Marlowe's audiences had 'learned to see and respond'. Robert Wilson's *The Three Ladies of London* (1581) is discussed as an example of the ways that traditional plays organised theatrical experience and constructed audience perspectives.

Each of the five chapters that follow treats an aspect – cultural, theatrical or spatial – of how the 'popular' drama told stories and constructed theatrical experience. Each is structured similarly, beginning with a survey of the critical issues and an account of traditional theatrical practice, then proceeding through a series of comparisons that locate Marlowe's practice against earlier and contemporary plays. These establish and define the differences between Marlowe and earlier plays and between Marlowe and his contemporaries, including early Shakespeare. These chapters explore the timing of particular changes. When, for example, does any new thinking about visual signs have an impact in the theatre? When does the Vice disappear from the popular drama? When does dramatic character change? When does the architecture of the new playhouses begin to affect the management of theatrical space? The common theme is how Marlowe's plays utilise traditional materials, but thereby change the ways that early audiences might see and interpret the action on stage.

The discussion begins with two chapters that position Marlowe's plays in relation to conventional ways of perceiving and making sense that were fundamental not only to the popular drama but to sixteenth-century cultural practices generally: the emblem and the exemplum. Chapter 3 ('Viewing the sign') discusses the 'emblematic' in sixteenth-century drama, with examples from the moralities including Wilson's 'London' plays. It suggests that – despite any influence elsewhere of iconoclasts – there is little change in the way visual signs could be interpreted in the theatre before the late 1580s. The 'emblematic' in sixteenth-century drama is sometimes identified with conservative, even 'medieval' values. Traditionally, the visual sign had drawn attention not to itself but to some underlying 'reality' or 'truth'. Traditionally, the spectator had been led to recognise and apply conventional meanings. Marlowe's plays, on the other hand, offer notable examples that challenge conventional ways of seeing and permit a new way of processing visual signs. This change emerges in the *Tamburlaine* plays through their imposition of more directly persuasive and narrative functions upon the older choric and allegorical uses of the emblematic. The challenges to tradition become more radical in other instances, especially in *Faustus*, where individual spectators are enabled to make their own sense of visual signs.

Chapter 4 ('Lessons of history') looks at how Marlowe modifies audience response to the cautionary tale, by breaking the connection between what the audience sees and conventional ways of making sense. *Edward II* is compared with other sixteenth-century plays on historical subjects, from Thomas Preston's *Cambises* in the 1560s to Shakespeare's early histories in the 1590s. The exemplum is a rhetorical technique common to all forms of discourse in the sixteenth century and earlier. It was indispensable to traditional ways of thinking and persuading, serving educational, religious, and political purposes. Its impact was commonly augmented by calling upon the appropriate emotional response, an approach that intensifies in late sixteenth-century drama. *Edward II* exploits this traditional exemplary rhetoric only to fracture it in the play's final scenes, where an attempt (it would seem) to exploit emotional extremes leads to the breaking of the connection between the particular instance and its moralising commentary, between the action the audience sees on stage and the expected, conventional ways of making sense.

The next two chapters shift attention to features more specifically associated with the popular tradition, to show how Marlowe's plays transform some of its theatrical clichés. They measure Marlowe's practice against the kind of play scorned in the Prologue to *Tamburlaine* by considering the devices that had been used in the late morality to construct audience perspectives. Chapter 5 ('Framing the action') considers aspects of framing rhetoric derived from the late morality, including the introductory monologue of the Vice, in tracing how *The Jew of Malta* unsettles conventional expectations and points of view. The period 1585 to 1595 generally saw a complication of framing rhetoric, with spectators frequently offered more than one perspective on the action. The *Jew*'s experimental rhetoric went further, however, in enabling the spectators to disengage from accustomed ways of seeing and feeling and responding. Where older, and indeed most contemporary plays provided an 'authorised version' to guide the spectators in making sense of the action, the *Jew* liberated competing voices. The audience is offered alternative ways of making sense without recourse to 'morality' perspectives. The Vice, for many years an essential part of theatrical experience, is cast adrift from the stage, making way for the new villains of the 1590s.

Chapter 6 ('Looking at Angels') deals with changes in the rhetoric of dramatic character, especially the arrival of the 'debatable' character. It explores Marlowe's transformation of the psychomachia as a key to understanding these changes. Most accounts of the angelic psychomachia in *Faustus* content themselves with pointing to its traditional and conventional functions. A more productive approach, I suggest, is to consider the convention in performance:

what it means, that is, for the spectators to see and hear the Angels physically present on stage before them. From this perspective, the Angels of *Faustus* do not simply reflect spiritual or psychological conflict but – by stressing Faustus's imperfect and separate seeing – also make it possible for the spectators to interpret his actions in new, non-traditional ways. Late sixteenth-century change in dramatic character is often described in terms of the advent of the 'Shakespearean' character; this chapter suggests that the rhetoric of character moved in two directions, towards complication and towards 'debatability', and that the latter shift is best explained in terms of a new relationship between spectator and character. Faustus represents the new 'debatable' character, about whom the audience asks psychological questions ('why?') rather than ethical ones ('should?'). The discussion here ranges from morality examples to Kyd's *Spanish Tragedy* and Shakespeare's *Titus Andronicus* and *Richard II*.

Chapter 7 ('Managing the space') also considers the conventional expectations of the playhouse audience, but turns to contemporary theatrical conditions, in particular the physical resources of the play-house. It is thus concerned with the more literal kind of 'seeing'. The chapter suggests that the 'newness' of Marlowe's plays in perfor-mance was not restricted to their more obviously spectacular effects; rather, that they also transformed the language of theatrical space. The chapter looks at the staging of ceremonies, comparing Marlowe's practice with that of earlier and contemporary plays. In the *Tamburlaine* plays the experience and expectations of early spec-tators are challenged by the organising of space rhetorically rather than conventionally. In later plays the theatrical space within the 'landscape of persons' on the platform stage becomes refractive rather than simply reflective. By refashioning the conventions of theatrical space, Marlowe's plays reshape the relationship of the audience with the action on stage, in a way that depends more upon what was inherited – the figure of the player – than upon any scenic or iconographic effects derived from playhouse architecture.

The concluding chapter, Chapter 8 ('Till experience change') surveys the main strands of the argument and their implications: the need, in particular, to revise both the reputation of Marlowe and our narratives of playhouse drama. By paying more attention to the rhetoric of plays and, in particular, the ways that spectators make sense of the action, this book is able to identify significant continu-ities in the popular tradition, and to locate change and innovation. In rewriting the narrative of late sixteenth-century drama, it challenges some of the more enduring critical commonplaces, including what is perhaps the oldest: the depth of the chasm between Marlowe's *Tamburlaine* and the 'jigging veins' and 'clownage' of its predecessors. Marlowe's challenge to traditional perspectives and values was achieved less by substituting new ideas for old than by the processes of performance. His plays offered early audiences new theatrical experiences that changed relationships with the action on stage, making change possible to older ways of seeing.[16]

CHAPTER 2

Approaches and contexts

＝＝

Dramatic rhetoric

What was different, then, in how the spectators 'saw' the dramatic action at an early performance of one of Marlowe's plays? In one sense, the question can never be answered. Any changes that might have occurred in theatrical experience were registered in the fleeting moments of performance four hundred years ago. Of these moments themselves only fragments of traces survive: scattered comments, brief anecdotes. These do of course have some value. The contemporary references to Marlowe's plays testify that they engaged both imagination and emotion; at times too, they suggest something of the flavour of performance, something of its visual impact. On the other hand, they rarely have any application in detail. Most of the memorable remarks occur only incidentally, in the process not of describing a performance but of making some other point. The 'one devil too many' appearing at a performance of *Doctor Faustus* belongs to a series of anecdotes directed against players and playing (Chambers 423–4); the devils and firecrackers John Melton mentions at the '*Fortune* in *Golding-Lane*' are used to point to the foolishness of those who would consult astrologers or 'astrologasters' (*Astrologaster* 31); the portrait of Tamburlaine, complete with 'the stalking steps of his great personage', adds colour to the clever young Joseph Hall's satire on contemporary tragedians, who are also much given, he claims, to drink and tobacco (*Virgidemiarum* 1.3.9–28).

Nor is this lack of specific evidence confined to the performance of Marlowe's plays. We know even less about most other plays written before 1595. Indeed, there are few accounts of any dramatic performances in the sixteenth or seventeenth centuries, even of Shakespeare's plays, and these too offer a minimum of information.

Hence, it is not surprising that some would argue that sixteenth-century performance can neither be recovered nor studied, or that only modern performances should be considered. The latter approach, of course, would exclude from discussion nearly everything not written by Shakespeare, as few non-Shakespearean plays are ever performed. These difficulties have had two notable consequences for the study of pre-Shakespearean plays: first, the insights of performance criticism have been applied only fitfully; second, our perceptions of the area have been dominated by the selective excavators of the printed playtext. Yet, while printed playtexts must remain important sources of evidence, we need at the same time to consider them in a different way.

In seeking to define change, we need to look beyond what may have happened at a performance four hundred years ago, with its multitude of variables and possibilities, to something more accessible: the nature of theatrical experience, as registered in what I shall term 'dramatic rhetoric'. The key to that experience, I would suggest, lies in how it is constructed in performance, in how the 'languages' or sign-systems of the play are organised to position the action in time and space. In this constructing too lies the key to locating changes in theatrical experience, and hence possible changes in audience perspectives. In using the terms 'rhetoric' and 'languages', I am not referring just to words, nor am I intending to suggest that the written playtext 'describes' what happens in performance; rather, that the text encodes many of the structures that operate in performance.

The term 'rhetoric' perhaps needs some comment. I am using it here to mean the active shaping of language to influence others.[1] This is a basic sense always present in writings about rhetoric from the time of the ancient Greeks and certainly one that sixteenth-century writers would have recognised. As schoolchild or scholar, Marlowe's contemporaries devoted much time to noting and imitating trope and figure. The purpose of all this activity was not, in theory at least, merely decorative – even if in the pursuit of *copia* many overloaded their writing with what to later tastes would be considered excessive ornamentation. The patterns of rhetoric received so much attention because they were believed to offer the most effective means of influencing an audience. For the sixteenth-century writer, the 'figures' inhered in – and gave their user the power to change – the very patterns of thought.[2]

A faith in figures, however, can take us only part of the way to understanding how theatrical experience is constructed. It would be

difficult to account for what happens in drama in terms of the traditional rhetoric of the sixteenth century, or that of the present day. In
modern discussions of sixteenth-century drama, 'rhetoric' is usually
limited to 'verbal' or 'literary' instances. Most accounts – whether
they focus upon the explication of rhetorical devices, or upon the
educational background ('small *Latine*, and lesse *Greeke*', or
Cambridge controversies about Ramus) – have dealt with the words
of the playtexts.[3] But words function differently in performance, even
the words of a rhetorical device, and performance is more than
words. As Alessandro Serpieri comments in 'Reading the Signs',
dramatic language 'acts' as well as 'refers': the performance context
of a verbal trope or figure may well alter its functioning (122–4).
Anthologised on the page, the hyperboles of Faustus's address to
Helen are glamorous; performed on stage they are, according to most
accounts, inescapably ironic. If we are to explore 'dramatic rhetoric',
our first step must be to recognise the limitations of mere words.

   In moving and persuading an audience in a theatre, a play uses
'languages' or sign systems of considerable complexity, such that the
terminology of traditional rhetoric is of only limited use in describing the structures and effects of performance. Theatrical language
presents problems for description, as it may include anything that is
seen and heard during performance. Or, for that matter, not seen
and not heard: in the theatre even gaps in language – silence and
empty space – can be eloquent and moving (McGuire, *Speechless
Dialect*; Brook). When we consider the impact of the shows of Helen
in *Faustus*, for example, we need to take note of the silent figures
that stand witness to them: Faustus to the first; the Old Man (in the
A-text) to the second. The elements of theatrical language can be
listed, but to list the aspects that may be important is of course much
easier than to provide an overall account of its operations.
Semioticians such as Patrice Pavis, Anne Ubersfeld, and especially
Keir Elam provide valuable inventories of the sign-systems of performance but, in charting the many factors involved, these accounts
either become very general or offer detailed schemes of analysis suitable only for highly specialised purposes.[4] In any case, as Bernard
Beckerman comments in 'Theatrical Perception', we need to look
beyond the processes of signification to the processes of 'perception'
(158). What is needed, I would suggest, in investigating theatrical
language is a scheme flexible enough to encompass both signification and perception; and that is to be found not in traditional
rhetoric itself nor in semiotics, but in a rhetorical model that incor-
porates features of both.[5]

A rhetorical model is useful for exploring theatrical experience for two significant reasons. The first is that it points to the elements involved in dramatic production: a social use of language in a specific context, with particular roles assigned to playwright, player, and playgoer. Traditional rhetoric taught an awareness of the social context of communication. Towards the end of the sixteenth century this was, if anything, strengthened by the new Ramist rhetoric and, more generally, by an increasing apprehension of language as the product of custom or 'convention' rather than of Nature.[6] The concept of distinctive roles is flexible enough to accommodate changes in cultural expectations and practices, thus helping us to understand different theatrical traditions, including the modern 'director's theatre'. The role of playwright may be taken by an individual or by several collaborators – or even the players in rehearsal. It has particular, socially defined purposes: storyteller, artificer with words, and transmitter of communal hopes and fears. The role of the player may be defined similarly in cultural terms, as both signifier and interpreter. The role of the playgoer is, as Marco de Marinis comments, active as well as passive, a matter of demands and expectations and 'making sense' as well as a matter of manipulation by performance (101).[7]

The second advantage of the rhetorical model is that it stresses pattern as the means of influencing an audience; but where the sixteenth century went searching for trope and figure we need to investigate those structures that organise theatrical perception and experience and response, that provide the spectators, in effect, with the means of making sense of what they see. These patterns may draw upon received ways of interpreting experience (theatrical or 'real-life'), or diverge from them. They may confirm or they may challenge patterns in 'the way in which people have learned to see and respond' (Williams 178). They operate, in any case, in conjunction with the spectator's urge to construct narratives and impose meaning.[8] As Thomas Postlewait comments of historical discourse, 'Narrativity is not merely a technique, borrowed from literature, but instead a condition of our temporal understanding of individual and social experience' (177). And these spectator narratives will in turn use, in Postlewait's terms, their own 'devices and designs'.

In seeking to identify the shaping patterns of 'dramatic rhetoric', we need to recognise first that it is the product of two distinct but interconnected rhetorics: the rhetoric of the playtext and the rhetoric of performance. Its operations in consequence are far from tidy or predictable. Perhaps because of this, studies of dramatic rhetoric have too often been sidetracked into defining the nature of the two elements of playtext and performance, with a minimum of application to actual plays. Thus the playtext has been described as script for or record of performance; it has been seen as prescribing certain effects, or alternatively as presenting multiple possibilities for performance. Performance has been described as supplement to, or as realisation or fulfilment of, the playtext (Carlson, 'Theatrical Performance'; Worthen), or even as something quite different in kind (Dawson).[9]

What is more pertinent, however, in exploring dramatic rhetoric is to recognise that the relationship between playtext and performance is variable – even from one moment to the next – hence confounding any attempt to categorise it simply. What is even more important is to accept that the differences between playtext and performance are not as significant as the connections. It does not matter, in effect, which of the two elements has priority, whether, in one sense, the performance is also a text, or, in another, any reading of the playtext is also a performance, if only in the 'theatre of the mind'. For those involved – playwright, player, playgoer – the relationship is always (potentially at least) a complementary or reciprocal one. It continues to be this way, even hundreds of years after the first performance, for the critic as well. The structures we identify as significant in the playtext are coloured by our experience of performance (and not just of the play we are discussing). Those we find in performance are conditioned by our 'reading' of the playtext. And not just theatrical performance: film versions from Olivier's *Hamlet* to Jarman's *Edward II* have also been influential in constructing – as much as recording or reinforcing – particular critical perspectives.

In considering changes in theatrical experience we need to be aware of both kinds of rhetoric, and the particular problems for analysis each entails. The rhetoric of the playtext provides a useful means of comparing plays and identifying changes in theatrical experience. The playtext offers not just a collection of possibilities for performance, but a structured one. This is so, whatever view we take of the 'authenticity' or origins or condition of the text. Sixteenth-century playtexts vary in nature, and scholarship since the 1980s has challenged the comfortable notion of an authoritative text in several ways: by re-examining the work of earlier editors; by calling attention to the practices of printers and compositors; by questioning labels such as 'bad quarto' or 'foul copy'; by raising issues of collaboration and 'social' authorship and materiality; by arguing for the separate printing and interpretation of texts that exist in more than one version (the two texts of *Doctor Faustus*, for example, or those of *King Lear*).[10] When, as in the last instances, a change in text changes the story and changes theatrical experience, then we need to be even more aware of the attendant changes in rhetoric.

The playtext constructs narratives that encode social values and serve stated or unstated purposes. Keir Elam tabulates cultural factors, ranging from aspects of discourse such as genre and narrative coherence to issues such as social hierarchy and notions of history (57–62). Because the playwright acts out a social role, the rhetoric of the playtext is shaped by an awareness of place and presence: of playing spaces and acting styles and audience preoccupations and expectations. Plays written within a particular theatrical tradition tend to share purposes and narrative strategies. Those typifying the old ways and old values in the 1580s are intrinsically didactic: whether they offer an audience pathos or farce or sensation, they also attempt to inculcate a certain viewpoint (an 'authorised version', in effect) by regular resort to explicit commentary on the action. They make their points simply, by multiplying examples, rather than developing a cause-and-effect narrative.

The rhetoric of performance is also variable, also a matter of possibilities and structures and cultural contexts. What is possible in performance – as well as what is possible in changes of performance rhetoric – will depend upon factors that range from the cultural and conventional to the architectural and technological. Though we may recover no more than glimpses of early performances, we can still, by consulting pictorial and archaeological records, and by utilising the approaches of performance criticism, reconstruct something of the rhetoric of performance in sixteenth-century plays. Aspects of cultural and theatrical practice constitute one important source of information about what might have been seen or done in the playhouse: elements of ceremony and ritual, visual conventions (costume, lighting, face-painting), acting styles and production practices (rehearsal, blocking), and – not least – the physical conditions of the playhouse with its censure and applause 'by contagion' (*Bartholomew Fair*, Induction 99).[11] At the same time, we need to remain aware that the imitation of social practices on stage, even the use of 'real' objects, does not of necessity involve the importation there of particular meanings or values. The rhetoric of performance will establish the range of possible meanings: how, that is, the ceremony (let us say) is to be seen, as confirming received values perhaps, or as subverting or parodying them.

Another source of information about performance rhetoric is the playtext, which provides supplementary information about how performance may have been organised, including details of staging. Whether this information derives from explicit stage directions or from the 'oblique imperatives' of the dialogue (the term is Ann Pasternak Slater's), it needs of course to be interpreted with some caution. Many scenes have no directions, but rely on the shared conventional understandings of player and spectator. The stage directions themselves in early playtexts are, in Alan Dessen's words, 'scattered, elusive, murky, but still potentially revealing' (*Elizabethan Stage Conventions* 52). They may, as Warren D. Smith suggests, compensate for faulty sightlines or stimulate imaginative making sense, by offering 'descriptions for those spectators who could not be expected at the moment to see clearly the action on the stage of the Elizabethan public playhouse' (311). Directions found in the playtext may not always record actual business, or be hopeful rather than performable. The kind of representation they call upon may vary. Thus when his brutal jailers 'shave' King Edward, the property knives may be real enough, but the beard is likely to be false and the puddle water imaginary. At the same time, this incident demonstrates something of the way that visual patterns may be used to shape theatrical experience. Within the play, the scene acts as an ironic visual echo of Edward's humiliation of the Bishop; more generally, it is emblematic, signifying initiation into suffering, as well as the humiliation of someone once-powerful. But such patterning does not necessarily add up to a coherent picture. As G. F. Reynolds pointed out many years ago in *The Staging of Plays at the Red Bull Theatre*, there was no necessary consistency in the way a play was staged, either from one moment to the next or from one performance or production to the next. The Henslowe accounts offer glimpses of some such changes in their payments for refurbishing costumes and for 'adiciones' to playtexts. The 1616 version of *Faustus*, for example, which probably records much of the new production in 1602, suggests a different emphasis in performance from the 1604 text, with what T. W. Craik once described as effects intended 'to give the spectators more devils and shows for their money' ('Reconstruction of Stage Action' 82 n. 7).[12]

Modern productions of early plays provide a third, and sometimes illuminating, source of suggestions about performance rhetoric and its possibilities in the late sixteenth-century playhouse.[13] There have been numerous small experiments which may be relevant: the effects obtained, for example, by doubling

Gaveston and Lightborn in *Edward II*, or Lechery and Helen in *Faustus* – even though sixteenth-century practice seems usually to have meant the doubling of unlike characters (Bevington, *Mankind to Marlowe* 108–12). In the 'division of the partes' suggested on the title-page of *Cambises*, for example, each player is allocated a mix of 'good' and 'bad' characters, with the player of the wicked king Cambises doubling as the moralising Epilogue. More generally, a number of attempts have been made to approximate early theatrical conditions, beginning late in the nineteenth century with the productions of, among others, William Poel.[14] In his study of the modern staging of Shakespeare, Dennis Kennedy suggests that the most lasting impact of these endeavours derives not from any antiquarian efforts to reproduce 'authentic' Shakespeare but rather from the development of alternatives to proscenium-arch staging, alternatives which alter the relationship between audience and action (41–2). Since the 1950s especially, the various new or remodelled theatres employing some sort of thrust or arena staging have offered audiences the chance to experience some of the elements of sixteenth-century spectating – and perhaps to speculate on sixteenth-century performance rhetoric. As Kennedy comments, 'The sight of others engaged in the same act of watching, replicating the viewers' contemporary manners and clothes, thoroughly conditions the visual experience' (164).

Dramatic rhetoric is complex and variable, a matter of contexts and possibilities and even contingencies. At the same time, it is also a matter of structure and pattern. Any analysis – whether our focus is upon an individual play at a particular moment in theatrical history, or upon the nature of change in London playhouses in the years before 1595 – needs to identify the patterns and processes that influence theatrical experience. The approach to be adopted here considers some of the important means by which the interconnected rhetorics of playtext and performance actively shape the perception of the audience and influence the narratives they employ to make sense of the action. These means, I would suggest, can profitably be explored in three areas: securing the spectators' attention; setting boundaries and contexts for their theatrical experience; and organising that experience into distinctive patterns.

One set of these rhetorical processes could be termed the 'deictic'. I am using the term in the general sense of 'pointing to' or 'demonstrative', but adding to this the recognition that such 'pointing to' entails an organising of perception.[15] Instances of the deictic secure audience attention, setting up priorities of perception amidst the multiplicity of signals that engage eye and ear. They may employ simple 'gestic terms like *this*, *there*, *here*, *yon*, and *thus*' (Dessen, *Elizabethan Stage Conventions* 53), but often make use of more striking means, verbal and visual. Whatever the method, an audience's making sense can be influenced by the ways that attention is secured, and how perception is sequenced and ranked. A simple but instructive instance is to be found in *1 Tamburlaine*. When Tamburlaine threatens the hapless Virgins of Damascus, their gaze (and that of the watching spectators) is directed from sword to point to 'slicing edge' and away to 'horsemen's spears' – even as the meaning of death shifts from 'fearful' to Death as instrument of Justice (the judge 'keeping his circuit') to Death as the servant of the conqueror:

> *Tamburlaine.*   Behold my sword, what see you at the point?
> *Virgins.*   Nothing but fear and fatal steel, my lord.
> *Tamburlaine.*   Your fearful minds are thick and misty, then,
>   For there sits Death, there sits imperious Death,
>   Keeping his circuit by the slicing edge.
>   But I am pleased you shall not see him there:
>   He now is seated on my horsemen's spears,
>   And on their points his fleshless body feeds.
>   Techelles, straight go charge a few of them
>   To charge these dames, and show my servant Death,
>   Sitting in scarlet on their armèd spears.
>   (*1 Tamburlaine* 5.1.108–18)

The second set of rhetorical structures, the 'framing', is involved in setting boundaries and contexts for theatrical experience. What the spectators 'notice' in the action before them, and how they make sense of what they see, will depend upon the perspectives established by the framing rhetoric – and how these relate to the experience and expectations they bring into the theatre (Carlson, 'Theatre Audiences'). One element of framing rhetoric is the 'playworld', which provides a context of expectations within which the action is observed. Also associated with the setting up of expectations is the use of conventional devices – a prologue, for example, or a visual signal such as a stage property or item of costume.[16]

Framing rhetoric is not necessarily restrictive or confining – nor even, for that matter, consistent. The possibilities suggested by the playtext are often too heterogenous for any one performance to contain: they may overlap, even conflict with each other (McGuire, *Speechless Dialect* 138); they may permit ambiguous, even opposed, interpretations (as in Norman Rabkin's reading of *Henry V* as 'rabbit/duck', 33–5). And yet the possibilities are not infinite, even if the boundaries are established only negatively: as 'what cannot happen' (McGuire). The degree of prescription or 'openness' varies not only between plays (*Faustus* offers a much wider range of performance options than a play such as *The Conflict of Conscience*) but from moment to moment within a single play (the second show of Helen in *Faustus* is more 'open' than the adjoining action with the Old Man and Mephistopheles). Performance contexts may similarly be more or less prescriptive, so that they sometimes restrict, sometimes multiply effects. Some contexts are particularly deterministic, as when the modern director emphasises a particular reading of the play. Two instances of this with *Faustus* are the Grotowski production, which inverted the moral values of the play, and John Barton's version with puppets (Grotowski; Tydeman).

A third set of rhetorical patterns is involved in 'shaping' performance and response. They include the distinctive structures of action and feeling inherent in the playtext, as well as narrative strategies such as the suppression and alternation identified by David Bevington in *Mankind to Marlowe*. In *Tamburlaine*, as the Prologue suggests, a key emphasis is upon largeness of scale ('threat'ning the world') and heightened emotions ('high astounding terms'). Another pattern, seen in the series of coronations and processional entries, involves an escalation in impressiveness and complexity. Though dramatic rhetoric cannot be contained within tropes and figures, some of the traditional terms are still relevant to an account of dramatic rhetoric, especially in defining how sign-systems may be structured: 'climax' for example, or 'anticlimax', or 'antithesis'. It is, moreover, sometimes the accumulation of a particular rhetorical device that exercises a marked influence upon theatrical experience. The insistent hyperboles of *Tamburlaine* (that once perhaps, as Hall suggests, 'ravishe[d] the gazing Scaffolders') establish a quite different structure of feeling from the one developed by the obsessive antitheses of the *Jew*, where little is said or done without calling attention to its opposite. Indeed Marlowe's plays are each quite distinctive in their shaping rhetoric.

The shaping power of dramatic rhetoric helps us to understand the impact upon the audience of contradictions and incongruities – of competing ideas, values, and energies – without the need to resort to one of the binary paradigms (thematic, cultural, psychological) or even to the deconstructive energies of language. The conflicts within a play may reflect wider issues, but they may also be used playfully or tangentially. They may always be presented in a particular way or resolved according to some particular pattern; but they may also be

presented and resolved variously. The ironies that sometimes preoccupied an earlier generation of critics may of course be subversive,
undermining a dominant or conventional positioning; but they may
also be complementary, defining that positioning more clearly. If we
contemplate the rhetorical strategies of drama, we soon realise their
potential for diversity. There is not one rhetorical strategy available
to the playwright (to challenge all signs of authority, let us say, or
deconstruct other signs), but many.

Using a rhetorical model to explore theatrical experience has
significant advantages. In brief, it accounts for more of what
happens in the theatre than do the critical approaches based on
author, or text, or society, or even on performance. It allows us to
redress their inadequacies, even as it is also able to exploit some of
their advantages. The first of these critical approaches concentrates
on the author, tracing the life and opinions as revealed in the works,
or seeking the effects of unconscious psychological processes. From
this biographical or psychoanalytical approach the rhetorical model
retains the idea of 'purpose'. In mentioning 'purpose', however, I am
referring less to the older notion of 'authorial intention' than to the
purposes associated with a particular, socially defined role, that of
playwright. This book will consider Marlowe and his contemporaries in this role.

A second approach, associated particularly with New Criticism,
is centred on the playtext, but essentially the text on the printed page
rather than that as performed. The text is seen as self-contained and
thematically unified, with the consequence that criticism endeavours
to produce ever-more-convincing 'readings' of the play (R. Levin,
New Readings). From this textual approach, the rhetorical retains a
close attention to the detail of the playtext. Words still matter, but
these are words as spoken in the playhouse before an audience, not
words as disembodied on the printed page. There is an emphasis too
upon the time and space dimensions of performance, upon, in particular, the sequential, moment-by-moment nature of experience in the
theatre.

A third approach, currently the established orthodoxy in the criticism of early modern drama, emphasises the social and historical
context, with the playtext becoming one more culturally produced
text among many. From this approach the rhetorical model retains
a recognition of the text as a social construct, but considers how it
functions – on stage, and in the presence of an audience – rather than
how it evidences social processes or contemporary ideas. The playtext is thus, in potential at least, an active making-sense of its

context, and not merely reflection or illustration or (for that matter) economic transaction.

The fourth common approach is that of performance criticism. Much commentary of this kind, developing from drama theorists and modern productions of Shakespeare, stresses the potential of the playtext for variable performances and multiple interpretations.[17] From the performance approach, the rhetorical retains an awareness of particular place and particular time, of theatrical expectations and experiences, but insists upon the importance of pattern and structure. The degree of 'openness' may vary, but any performed play – for playwright, player, and playgoer – is more of a structured collection of possibilities than an open one. The task of the rhetorical approach is to identify these structures and to explore what they mean for theatrical experience.

Theatrical contexts

This book uses a rhetorical model to explore a brief but intense moment of transition and cultural change. It offers the chance to look afresh at the commonplaces of 'development' in sixteenth-century drama, and at a period which, falling between the 'medieval' and the 'Shakespearean', has been relatively neglected. Much of the popular tradition has been well documented; indeed I am considerably in debt to the classic studies of Muriel Bradbrook, Glynne Wickham, Wolfgang Clemen, Bernard Spivack, David Bevington, and Robert Weimann. At the same time, I am troubled by their inadequacies, especially as they apply to plays between 1580 and 1595. In part, this is simply a matter of time passing and critical perspectives changing. The studies mentioned above were for the most part published in the 1960s and 1970s; and some of the critical notions they employ to explain how Marlowe treats particular aspects – the set-speech, let us say, or the Vice figure – are no longer tenable. Bernard Spivack's description of Barabas as occupying a half-way stage between the Vice of the moralities and Iago (half conventional device, half 'realistic' character) begins from and depends upon the once-fashionable view that the *Jew* is broken-backed, switching at about the end of Act 2 from tragedy (where Barabas is 'real' individual) to farce (where Barabas is conventional device). If we now generally see the play as more coherent and 'realism' as having its own conventions, then we need to reconsider both our description of Barabas and our account of the Vice tradition.

Developmental studies have become less fashionable since the notion of evolution towards 'realism' dropped out of critical favour. Despite this, however, the weary commonplaces persist. Most commentators, if they concern themselves with change at all, still tell the same stories about what happened in the drama, and many still attribute late sixteenth-century change to the humanist learning of the 'University Wits' and/or the genius of Shakespeare. There have of course been revisionist challenges to the conventional narratives. Some of this endeavour has been directed towards postponing the date of significant change from the late sixteenth century and Shakespeare, to the seventeenth century (Belsey) or eighteenth (Barker; Burns; Sinfield, for example). Other writers emphasise the continuities between medieval and modern culture; the 'new medievalists' (Aers; Patterson, for example) discover 'modern' features in earlier texts, challenging the notion of the 'medieval' as 'primitive', 'uncomplicated', or 'non-transgressive'. The present book takes into account these revisionist arguments about the boundaries between 'medieval' and 'modern', 'traditional' and 'Shakespearean'; but it redraws the lines in a different way: by iden- tifying changes in playhouse experience, where spectators were enabled to see and make sense differently.

This book offers a new narrative of change, by stepping aside from the usual perspectives – including those that stress the influence of traditional ideas and practices – to consider what happens when Marlowe retains the old ways, but uses them differently. Marlowe's plays register moments of change in theatrical experience, when perceptions were altered and past experiences reinterpreted. In looking at these moments, I have attempted to approach them from the less-travelled direction, looking forward from the 1580s play- house offerings and across to the plays in the London repertory before 1595, rather than backward from the mature Shakespeare. In doing this, I am discarding the usual teleology of developmental studies: the assumption, stated or unstated, that the goal of all this 'development' was the drama of Shakespeare, to whom Marlowe played Bajazeth the convenient footstool. Too many studies look backward from Shakespeare (and post-1595 Shakespeare at that) to find relevant-to-Shakespeare aspects of the tradition.[18] But the popular tradition afforded other, and sometimes equally forceful, possibilities to the 1580s and 1590s playwright. Some of these were later taken up and transformed by Shakespeare, but not all. Marlowe's transformations of the popular tradition were not only earlier and more radical, but at times quite different from those of Shakespeare, who was at first more likely to preserve and elaborate upon old ways and old values. Before 1595 – and indeed until the late 1590s – Marlowe was the first and most significant innovator in the playhouse drama; Kyd possibly the second, but on a more limited scale; Shakespeare the third, and belated.[19]

Playwrights may innovate but an audience 'is always the most decisive inheritance, in any art' (Williams 178). This book looks accordingly at Marlowe's plays in their own theatrical context – and especially in terms of the ways that their spectators had 'learned to see and respond': those expectations and experiences brought into the London playhouses in (about) 1587, when 1 Tamburlaine was first presented, and before 1595.[20] These audiences were most probably diverse, more likely (as Andrew Gurr suggests in Playgoing in Shakespeare's London) than later audiences to encompass a wide range of social levels. They may also, as Thomas Cartelli argues from contemporary accounts, have possessed a 'psychic disposition' towards arrogance, impulsiveness, volatility, violence, irreverence, scepticism, disorder, and seeking novelty (Economy of Theatrical Experience 44–56). But such characteristics, even if widely shared, influence only part of an audience's seeing and responding. Sixteenth-century playgoers may have brought to the performance of a play a capacity for aggressive and transgressive fantasising (Cartelli's view), but they arrived also with a headful of expectations – based on their general cultural experiences as well as their viewing of plays – that stories incorporating such fantasies would be told in particular ways and call upon particular patterns of response. Such expectations are always important in theatrical experience. If what Cartelli terms 'theatrical pleasure' arises, to whatever extent, from the experience of feeling intensely, then we also should take into account, along with any pleasant fantasising, the acutely felt reactions that derive from an audience's learning to expect and see and make sense in particular ways: the keenness of anticipation, let us say, or recognition, of frustration or disappointment, of satisfaction or surprise.[21]

The expectations of Marlowe's audience were shaped by their experience of 'popular' plays. Those to be considered here include some known to be connected with the London playhouses and others whose 'popularity' is suggested by contemporary allusions or by reprintings. An example of the latter group is Thomas Preston's Cambises. This was written in the 1560s and may first have been performed at court (the Epilogue calls for prayers for the Queen and 'her honorable Councel');[22] but it was read more widely (there are three early editions recorded, two of them in the 1580s) and possibly continued to be performed for some time. Indeed 'Cambyses vein' was familiar enough to a playhouse audience to be alluded to in Shakespeare's *1 Henry IV* in the late 1590s.

Our knowledge of the plays written between 1565 and 1595 is defective. Most of them have not survived, except as fragmentary references to title or subject in the Revels Office accounts or Henslowe's diary or the Stationers' Register – or even in anti-play pamphlets. This is especially so for the earlier years, even the early 1580s.[23] After 1587 brought a rush of new playwrights and printings, more plays survived, though these are still only a fraction of what was performed. The surviving playtexts include, of those earlier than Marlowe, plays such as *Cambises* (stories of famous personages), *Like Will to Like* (moralities), and *Clyomon and Clamydes* (romances). Of plays contemporary with Marlowe's, there are those of Greene, Nashe, Lodge, Peele, Kyd; the later plays of the actor-dramatist Robert Wilson (*The Three Lords and the Three Ladies of London*, *The Cobbler's Prophecy*); and the early plays of Shakespeare – from *The Comedy of Errors* to *The Taming of the Shrew* and *Titus Andronicus*, from *1 Henry VI* to *Richard III* and (no later than) *King John*.[24]

What, in general, were these plays like? Andrew Gurr suggests that the typical fare of the playhouses in the years immediately before *Tamburlaine* consisted of plays recycled from the 1560s and 1570s: romantic narratives with moralising commentary, of the kind ridiculed by Sidney and Gosson as 'tragicomic gallimaufrey' with brown-paper monsters; as well as plays featuring the figure of the 'cunning rustic clown' made famous by Tarlton. After *Tamburlaine*, popular taste shifted to militaristic and heroic adventures, to versions of English history, and to romantic comedy (*Playgoing* 135–53). On the other hand, and despite the constant pressure for novelty in entertainment, there was a deal of continuity. The older taste for fantasy and fooling was not entirely supplanted by the new plays of the late 1580s and early 1590s. *Tamburlaine* itself draws upon much the same escapist impulses as an earlier play such as *Clyomon and Clamydes*: indeed the prologues to both plays promise elevated subject matter for those of superior tastes.[25] At the same time, the early performances of *Tamburlaine* included 'fond and frivolous gestures'; and there are abundant instances thereafter of mixing comic with serious action in the tradition of the 'gallimaufrey': in *A Looking Glass for London and England* or *Friar Bacon and Friar Bungay*, for instance, both written about 1590 (or in *Doctor Faustus* or, even later, *1 Henry IV*).[26]

For all their medley of ingredients, however, the texts that survive from before 1587 show a remarkable uniformity in what they expect of their audiences and how they organise theatrical experience. This can perhaps best be demonstrated by looking at one of the more complex examples of the late morality, Robert Wilson's *A Right Excellent and Famous Comedy Called the Three Ladies of London* (1584 title-page). In this, Lady Love and Lady Conscience attempt to survive in a city dominated by 'Lady Lucar' (Lucre). They fail: Love becomes Lust and marries Dissimulation, and Conscience is bought by Lucre. The *Three Ladies* provides important evidence of the kinds of experience available in the playhouses before Marlowe. The play itself may well have been familiar to many in Marlowe's first audiences. It was written and probably first performed in 1581, commented upon by Stephen Gosson in 1582, and printed in a modified version in 1584.[27] It was even considered worth reviving in the late 1580s – after the staging of the *Spanish Tragedy* and the two Parts of *Tamburlaine* – before being reprinted in 1592. Like *Tamburlaine*, it was accorded a sequel, *The Three Lords and the Three Ladies of London* (1588), although this is noticeably more up-to-date with its blank verse and post-Armada patriotism.

At first glance the *Three Ladies* could easily be dismissed as one of those plays held up to scorn in the prologue to *Tamburlaine*, with their 'jigging veins of rhyming mother-wits, / And such conceits as clownage keeps in pay'. The verse in particular seems awkward, of little merit. But this impression is misleading. As Scott McMillin suggests, the irregular fourteeners with their not-quite-predictable rhymes permitted actors experienced in the interlude tradition to display their skill and versatility: the fourteener's 'reality is the enactment of a long line which exists to be answered by an echoing line, equally long, dancing its way to a rhyme. It is a speaker's ballet, and its exhilaration comes from its continually successful closure, against long odds' ('Queen's Men' 16). What the *Three Ladies* does show, moreover, is that the late moralities could have considerable theatrical vitality. It is a play which sets out consciously to entertain its paying audience. There is plenty of effectively farcical business, such as Simplicity's request to be whipped naked to save his clothes. There are songs, humorous and appealing, and witty playing on words. Simplicity, H. S. D. Mithal claims, is the first character in English drama to be always stumbling into malapropisms. The confrontations between characters are lively, evoking the ordinary language of the city: 'If no body cared for Conscience more than I', says Dissimulation, 'They would hang her up like Bacon in a chimney to drie' (1004–5). And the play is topical as well as entertaining: Margot

Heinemann stresses its outspoken 'political' nature, noting the rehearsal of grievances against the Church in particular.[28]

Although the *Three Ladies* has didactic intent, it does not decline into interminable moralising or dreary allegorical action. This is a considerable achievement, and especially notable when the play is compared with some of the more earnest efforts of the period such as *The Conflict of Conscience* or some of the school plays – or *Gorboduc* for that matter. It is neither turgid (as is *Clyomon and Clamydes*) nor simple-minded (as is *Like Will to Like*). In the *Three Ladies* the illustrations to the moral lessons are direct, down-to-earth, and topical: lists of the commodities England must export, for example, to provide foolish English ladies with imported trinkets and trifles. At the same time, the messages are not simplistic: the attractive characters are not rescued at the end in typical morality fashion by a character such as Heavenly Justice. Instead, they are punished – Simplicity is whipped, Lady Conscience imprisoned, Lady Love (who has become Lust) sentenced to join Lady Lucre in the torments of hell – while the Vices (Dissimulation, Fraud, Simony, and Usury) survive unscathed to continue their depredations on society.[29]

The *Three Ladies* is very much a professional and stageable play, giving the impression of being confidently in touch with its audience. This may be so because its author was one of the leading actors in London in the years before Edward Alleyn and Richard Burbage. Like Tarlton, also prominent in the 1580s, Robert Wilson achieved fame for his skills as a comic actor. The part of Simplicity in this play and its sequel is a display piece for the Clown – with its elements of naive wit, sound heart, and demanding stomach – and could well be one that he wrote for himself.[30] In its own way too, *The Three Ladies of London* is quite innovative. It challenges contemporary practice, setting up its own dialogue with tradition. The Prologue to the play addresses the new urban audience of the London playhouses; it rests its appeal on presenting everyday life rather than some escapist romance, claiming that it will have nothing to do with 'honors seate' and 'loves delights' or even, for that matter, with 'countery toile'.

For all this theatrical effectiveness *The Three Ladies of London* is a very different play from those of Marlowe or indeed most plays after 1587. Yet the most important differences are not the obvious ones connected with 'jigging' and 'clownage', as claimed by *Tamburlaine*'s Prologue, but lie instead in different ways of constructing theatrical experience. The *Three Ladies* is typical of the drama before Marlowe in the way that it draws upon old habits of perception and interpretation. To begin at a very general level, traditional (or what might be termed 'medieval') culture saw and interpreted the evidence of its eyes in characteristic ways. To traditional ways of thinking and perceiving, 'reality' lay behind all the appearances of the visible world. The visual sign, for instance, was important not of itself but for the concept it illustrated: it was definable by its place in the vast network of correspondences and analogies of which the universe was constructed. 'Medieval' drama – and this applies to most plays written before the late 1580s – depended upon this way of seeing: first in the treatment of visual details but also in the utilising of characters that represent moral qualities or social types, and of incidents that translate readily as allegory. None of this meant that such plays were simple-minded, or out of touch with ordinary experience; indeed, they are often observant of behaviour, and acutely aware of the ironies and ambiguities of existence. The rhetoric of their Vices in particular was based on dissembling, on disparities between being and seeming.

The 'seeing' of their audiences was, nevertheless, structured in quite distinctive ways. In these plays the action that occurs on stage is essentially transparent, to be seen through by the spectators to the underlying concepts. In the *Three Ladies*, two of the ladies, Lady Love and Lady Conscience, move to London, where they succumb to poverty and take up immorality. The third, Lady Lucre, is already in residence there and responsible for the city's fraud, corruption, and vice, with accomplices ranging from avaricious merchants to unprincipled clergymen to thieves and murderers. On her own, neither Love nor Conscience can prevail against society's desire for Lucre. In addition to such narrative structuring, few of the moralities are without one or more passages of elaborately allegorical action. One memorable instance in the *Three Ladies* occurs when Lady Love becomes Lust upon marrying Dissimulation: to signify the change she enters with two faces, her own and '*a visard behind*' (1766–7). Even more notable is the occasion when Lady Conscience, defeated by poverty, agrees to keep the house where Lady Lucre will commit adultery. Lucre sends for 'the boxe of all abhomination that stands in the window', and the spectators watch her '*open the boxe and dip her finger in it, and spotte Conscience face, saying as followeth*':

> This face is of favor, these cheekes are reddy and white,
> These lips are cherry red, and full of deepe delight.
> Quick rowling eyes, her temples hygh, and forhead white as snowe,
> Her eye-browes seemely set in frame, with dimpled chinne below.
>
> (1407–9, 1412–15)

As Lucre 'spots' each feature with ink, Conscience sits calmly counting the money Lucre has given her. The message to be read from the
spotting is quite plain, and it is later formulated explicitly in the
closing speech of the play: even the most virtuous, suggests Judge
Nemo, is liable to be 'corrupted with the unsatiate desire of vanish-
ing earthly treasure' (1958–9).

The transparency extends beyond these especially memorable
instances. What the spectators are directed to notice – repeatedly –
are messages of supposedly universal validity. That such messages
changed significantly in detail during the sixteenth century, as
drama was employed by Protestant or Catholic or Puritan or
humanist educator or youthful lawyer or professional entertainer,
does not alter the point. The way of seeing called upon was intrinsically the same: the notion of 'truth' was always absolute, never
relative. In the *Three Ladies* the perspectives are Puritan (though not
anti-theatrical), nationalist, and (most importantly perhaps) anti-
materialist: the play attacks 'covetousnesse' in general, and foreign
imports (including Usury, Simony, and a caricatured Italian
merchant) in particular.

Wilson exhibits considerable ingenuity in constructing action that
will both entertain the audience and lead them to share these
perspectives. Like several other plays of the period, the play is an
'estates morality', one in which the psychomachia of the individual
soul is extended to the whole of society, with society separated out
into its component parts (Dessen, *Late Moral Plays* 143).[31] Indeed,
the title-page of the early editions announces the play in this way, as
'A PERFECT PATTERNE FOR ALL Estates to looke into, and a
worke right worthie to be marked' (Mithal xcix). In performance the
impression of social diversity was sustained by 'a system of acting by
brilliant stereotype', a traditional acting style able 'to encompass the
unmistakable characteristics for all the social and moral types the
age could recognize' (McMillin and MacLean 127). The characters
include representatives of all the 'estates': rich and poor, criminal
and law-abiding: judges and beggars, merchants and clergymen, city
folk and country 'clown'. The action illustrates social and, in particular, economic behaviour: Usury killing Hospitality (Charity) in an
outburst of farcical aggression; a charitable Jew giving up all claim
to the debt of a Christian rogue; Simony providing a benefice for the
uneducated and unprincipled 'Sir Peter Pleaseman', who is 'of all
religions' though 'for the most part a Protestant' (936–7) while the
honest Sincerity is fobbed off with 'the parsonage of S. Nihil' (in
effect, nothing).

At the same time, the play includes features of the more traditional psychomachia. As well as illustrating social roles, many characters embody spiritual or psychological values, with the relationships between characters being predicated upon definitions of words and concepts, and devised to support conventional moral messages.[32] Thus Simplicity is able to become the servant of Love but not of Conscience. Without the influence of Conscience, however, he is encumbered by his appetites: his chief interest in life becomes eating large quantities of food (indeed he claims to have 'a gift for eating'). By morality convention names also establish the limits of roles. Simplicity because of his 'simple' commonsense can recognise Fraud when he sees him, but he is too 'simple' (obtuse, narrow) to realise that Hospitality is virtuous (he sees only that Hospitality is old and does not provide him with enough food), and too 'simple' (uneducated, naive) to understand that a parish known as 'S. Nihil's' will provide no living for the virtuous clergyman Sincerity.

The Three Ladies of London is constructed according to expectations that its audience will observe the action in the traditional way, as offering visible signs of underlying concepts. At the same time, the play provides structures for interpretation, specific and once again traditional ways for the spectators to make sense of what they see. In making them aware of its theses Wilson's play does not shrink from either commentary or outright sermonising. It exposes the hypocrisy and self-seeking of those in authority. It offers lengthy descriptions of social ills and the fraudulent practices in various trades. It gives plenty of ironic advice on the methods to use in exploiting poor tenants or circumventing the law or even influencing debate in Parliament. At times too the audience is addressed as if from the pulpit, with Conscience urging Usury's lack of charity by referring to St Paul and the will of God, and Judge Nemo concluding the play with an exhortation to remember the relevance of Conscience to the afterlife.

Like most plays before *Tamburlaine*, the shaping rhetoric of the *Three Ladies* is essentially demonstrative, proceeding from general notions about experience to particular illustrations: the structure, in effect, of thesis and demonstration.[33] Much of the action proceeds quite methodically, by multiplying exempla. The early scenes show a series of characters suing for patronage or employment: Love and Lucre hire appropriate servants, and the Vices line their pockets in recruiting like-minded followers. The action then progresses to displays of violence and deception, and later to alternating scenes

showing contrasts in fortune. In the sixteenth century, this exemplary method was intrinsic to traditional ways of thinking and
persuading. The action of *Cambises*, for example, is preceded by the
promise that 'His crueltie we wil dilate, and make the matter plain'
(Prologue 34). *Enough Is as Good as a Feast* (1560s), like a number
of other plays, signals its thesis in its title:

> Our title is *Inough is as good as a feast*,
> Which Rhethorically we shall amplyfye:
> So that it shall appeer bothe to moste and least
> That our meaning is but honestie.

> (Prologue 79–82)

In a play such as the *Three Ladies* perhaps the most significant
aspect in the construction of theatrical experience is the degree to
which it is predetermined. In narrative framing and commentary
and sermonising, in the remorseless progression of exempla, the
audience is provided with an 'authorised version' of the play's
meaning, a particular way of making sense of the action. This does
not mean that opposing versions are suppressed in performance.
Every rogue has his or her say. As with other moralities the
controlling perspective may be subverted, for a time, by the anarchic energies of the Vice (or in this case the Vices). But the Vice's
role is essentially one of licensed play, with its own conventional
limits – and in the end the Vice always knows his place. Thus the
Vice may invite the audience's complicity, but the effect is always
ultimately to engage them in judgement on the action.[34] A similar
process of containment operates with the play's didactic ironies.
The uneducated and lazy Sir Peter Pleaseman may gain a 'living'
instead of the deserving Sincerity, but the irony at such times
defines the problem without subverting the principle. In all, the
one controlling view is persistently reinforced, and not subject to
reinterpretation.

Marlowe inherited an audience that had 'learned to see and
respond' in a particular way, whatever their opinions might have
been. His exploiting of the traditional rhetoric of the popular play
enabled that audience to disagree – and critics four hundred years
later to quarrel – about what the 'authorised version' of a play might
be. If we turn to Marlowe's plays, from the theatre of proof and
example to the theatre of story and experience, our first impressions
may well be defined by the gulf between 'jigging veins' and 'high
astounding terms'. But our impressions are coloured by the sales talk
of the *Tamburlaine* Prologue and by our own conventional narratives of Renaissance drama in England. It is time to recognise the

importance of Marlowe's dialogue with the popular tradition. That, more than the use of what is obviously 'new', is the key to Marlowe's difference. And identifying that difference is the key to understanding innovation in the rhetoric of drama before 1595.

CHAPTER 3

Viewing the sign

Visual signs

By leading audiences to see differently, Marlowe's plays changed the ways that they perceived and interpreted visual signs in the late sixteenth-century playhouses. This is a transformation of some note, not least because of the degree to which dramatic rhetoric in the period depended upon visual symbolism, but also for its wider cultural implications. Every culture is illuminated by its icons. Grasping their import, however, is not just a case of taking into account which icons or emblems or visual signs are meaningful in or characteristic of a particular time and place. What matter too are the roles that visual symbols play in a culture, their connections, that is, with its 'ways of seeing': those customary ways of viewing and interpreting that are intrinsic to its perception of how things 'are'.

Sixteenth-century cultural practices drew upon traditional ways of looking at visual signs and using them to make sense of experience.[1] In drama as in civic pageantry or religious ceremony, the sign drew attention not to itself but to an underlying 'reality'; it was to be 'read' quite straightforwardly as illustrating a 'true' concept. When Elizabeth in her coronation 'triumph' improved upon the pageant by asking for the English Bible and then embracing it ('how reverently did she with both her handes take it, kiss it, & lay it upon her breast to the great comfort of the lookers on'), she assumed an audience that would regard the scene as the outward sign of eternal verities, and would read its significance accordingly.[2] When, in the playhouse a generation later, the beauty of Lady Conscience was 'spotted' by the inky finger of Lady Lucre (see above, Chapter 2), the audience was expected to recognise an obvious lesson in the way things 'are': that money may corrupt even the most virtuous.

The traditional way of 'reading through' visual signs was of course not always the simple or universal process such descriptions might suggest. The point is made in both new medievalist (Rubin; Beckwith) and iconographic studies. As well as the more obvious readings there had always been complex or expert or elite or even personal ones. Medieval exegesis had encouraged a search for several levels of meaning (the Bible could be interpreted at four) that persisted in sixteenth-century education and all kinds of commentary. Court interludes or masques featured abstractions or moral qualities but regularly invested them with additional topical or political reference. And the 'studious Artisan' could read through signs that to the uninitiated were only 'Lines, circles, signs, letters, and characters' (*Faustus* 1.1.53).

In the second place, there were ironic or alternative readings. A number of commonplace signs invoked conventional ironies: the various representations of Fortune in terms of wheel or chariot-driver, for instance, could draw attention to the fallen as much as to the exalted, could warn of hubris as much as celebrate triumph. Other signs had multiple, sometimes conflicting, meanings: the snake could signify cleverness, poisonous slander, or (with tail in mouth) eternity (Daly 43, citing Harsdoffer); the lion could 'denote Christ, the devil, the just Christian, or the heretic' (Daly 84). These contradictions did not derive so much from the arbitrary imposition of meanings as from the recognition of 'essential qualities'. As Daly comments: 'Nature can be interpreted in this way because the observer recognizes good and evil qualities in the objects of nature' (43). This potential for objects to bear alternative meanings extended to dramatic properties; it is illustrated quite literally in the morality *The Tide Tarrieth No Man* (printed 1576). When Christianity enters, he carries '*a sword, with a title of pollicy; but on the other side of the tytle must be written Gods word: also a shield whereon must be written Riches; but on the other side of the shield must be Fayth*' (p. 63). At first because of the behaviour of the 'greater part', Christianity presents himself as 'in thrall' and 'deformed', and the titles 'Pollicy' and 'Riches' are displayed (p. 63). He is then restored to his 'former estate' – once hopefully (p. 65) but at last permanently (p. 82) – by the character Faithful Few who (the stage directions note) simply '*turneth the titles*'.

The visual sign might be regarded as transparent, but it was also, like all the appearances of this visible world, potentially deceptive. The gap between appearance and reality was not a late sixteenth-century discovery (as some studies of Shakespeare would suggest) but a cultural commonplace, applications of which had generated much of the action in traditional plays. From Mankind in the late fifteenth century to Simplicity in the late sixteenth the drama is full of 'Everyman' characters who mistake what they see, or of those whose costume disguises their 'real' nature. Indeed many of the liveliest Vices are persistent manipulators of visual signs, from Titivillus in *Mankind* to Haphazard in *Apius and Virginia* or Ambidexter in *Cambises*.[3] And yet, while perception might be portrayed as relative, the truth was always regarded as absolute. The spectators, it was assumed, were always able to see through the deceptive sign to the one true way of making sense of the action – even if they needed some guidance to do so.

These older habits of seeing endured even as notions of the truth diversified. They survived, especially, in ordinary theatrical experience, despite any new ways of thinking – and despite the onslaughts of iconoclasts and reformers.[4] Iconoclasm itself was not new: there had been sporadic outbreaks within the Church for hundreds of years. Reformist thought in the sixteenth century had defined itself in opposition to the images and ceremonies of the late medieval Church, privileging the 'Word' of Scripture above the seductions or distractions of the visual image. The movement was inclined in varying degrees to iconoclasm; and, as Michael O'Connell shows, the iconoclasts were influential in England from the 1520s. They helped to shape government policy and insisted on modifying religious observance. Their anxiety about visual signs lay behind the destruction of religious images, the suppression of the mystery cycles, the ban on theatrical representation of the sacred, and the writing of anti-theatrical pamphlets to attack the dangers and idolatry of playing (O'Connell 282–7; 297–9). But to focus upon the iconoclasts is to oversimplify. Many reformist thinkers did not repudiate visual signs: instead they distinguished between 'proper' signs (which made possible a spiritual 'remembrance' of religious truths) and 'improper' ones (which induced us to idolatrous, 'physical' worship); in any case, the reformers were prepared to control the meaning of signs by vigorous explication.[5] In practice, as Elizabeth's triumph indicates, the visual was too effective an element of rhetoric to discard: as Mark Breitenberg comments, the Protestant establishment 'appropriated rather than dismissed visual sources of representation' (199).[6] In a century marked by religious and political controversy, potent signs like the defeated leader as footstool were recycled to endorse changing versions of the 'truth' (King 35–61). Whatever new 'thinking' was abroad, visual signs continued

to be used in the old way as indices to the 'reality' beyond, a reality
that the perceiver was to recognise as 'true'.

This was especially so in the playhouse, where traditional habits
of seeing persisted, indeed flourished, in plays contemporary with
Marlowe's. Robert Wilson's *The Pleasant and Stately Moral, of the
Three Lords and Three Ladies of London* was first performed by the
Queen's Men in late 1588 or 1589: that is, after *Tamburlaine* and
no more than four years before *Doctor Faustus*. This sequel to *The
Three Ladies of London* was a resolutely up-to-date play, utilising
the newly fashionable blank verse and exploiting popular taste for
the spectacular.[7] It is lively, topical (decidedly anti-Spanish post-
Armada), and entertaining. At the same time it calls upon quite
familiar ways of seeing. The play is populated by characters with
names such as Policy, Conscience, Dissimulation, Simplicity, and
'painefull Penurie' – thirty-four of them, plus the City of London,
who is ushered on stage by four Angels, two of them holding 'bright
Rapiers'. Much of the play's energy is directed towards calling attention to the correspondences between what the audience sees and
what the action means. Thus Lord Policy of London is attended by
the page Wit, and opposed by the Spanish lord Majesty (who is
really, we are carefully informed, Pride), who is attended by his page
Modesty (who is really Shame). And so on. They – and another two
lords of London, another two lords of Spain, and (proving the superiority of the metropolis by their lack of success with the Ladies)
three lords of Lincoln – act up to their names.

In interpreting the play the spectators simply 'read' the visual
signs in a quite straightforward manner. Where the 'real' meaning is
not immediately obvious (and in many cases where it is) the signs are
accompanied by a commentary that offers an authorised version of
the action. Other readings are certainly not envisaged. The play
devotes considerable time to explicating properties: these range from
ones appropriate to an old-fashioned morality (three stones labelled
Remorse, Charity, and Care, on which the penitent ladies are seen
sitting) to a collection of elaborately emblematic shields, which
derive from contemporary interest in tournament and show. One
small but typical example of how the play organises experience for
an audience can be seen in the explication of Policy's shield. The
page Wit is clarifying the device for the Clown Simplicity (and for
any simple souls in the audience):

> A Tortoys my boy, whose shell is so hard, that a loaden cart may goe
> over and not break it, and so she is safe within, and wheresoever shee
> goes, she beares it on her backe, needing neither other succour or shilter

but her shell: the woord underneath her is *Providens securus*, the provident is safe, like to the Tortoys, armed with his owne defence, and
defended with his owne armour: in shape somewhat rounde, signifying
compasse, wherein alwaies the provident forsee to keepe themselves
within their owne compasse, my boy. (139–47)

And there are five more shields remaining for Wit and others to
explicate. The six shields become the centrepiece properties in an
elaborate symbolic battle between the London and Spanish lords,
which provides the spectacular climax of the play. In this passage of
action, the challenge, contest, and victory are all signified by the
hanging up and taking down of shields.[8] Good triumphs over evil,
of course: London Policy, Pomp, and Pleasure, with Wit, Wealth,
and Will in their service, prevail over Spanish Majesty, Honour, and
Government (who the audience know are really Pride, Ambition,
and Tyranny) and their servants Shame, Treachery, and Terror.

The *Three Lords* arrived on the playhouse stage in late 1588, or
soon thereafter.[9] The date merits some attention. It is quite possible
that both Parts of *Tamburlaine* were still in the repertory at this
time; but, even if they were not, they are likely to have been fresh in
the memory of a regular playgoer who came to see the new play
performed by the Queen's Men and their revival the same year of
The Three Ladies of London. Considered together, and that may
have been possible for at least some of the early playgoers, the four
plays have important similarities. All of them make use of striking
emblematic moments or passages of action. Against the 'spotting' of
Lady Conscience or the entry of double-visaged Lady Love or the
contest with shields, the *Tamburlaine* plays offered such memorable
scenes as the conqueror's 'sights of power' near the end of Part One
(his victorious pose above the bodies of king and emperor), and his
triumphant entry in the chariot drawn by kings. At moments like
these all four plays draw upon the experience of their spectators in
recognising and applying conventional visual meanings.

But the *Tamburlaine* plays demanded more of their early spectators. The 'sights of power' and the chariot are different from the
'spotting' and the shield-battle because they induce in their spectators a different way of seeing the action. This difference was not
essentially one of time and place, nor – remembering the intricate
iconography and elaborate shows of the *Three Lords* – was it simply
a matter of complexity and spectacle. One way perhaps of approaching the difference is to think in terms of sufficiency. For the spectator
to grasp the point of the 'spotting' or the shield-battle, it is sufficient
to read through the visual signs. With the *Tamburlaine* instances,

however – though not, it should be stressed, with every instance of the emblematic in the *Tamburlaine* plays – reading through is not sufficient. The point of the 'sights of power' or the chariot is not primarily some general observation about, for example, Pride or Ambition, nor about Tamburlaine as an exemplar of such abstract concepts. Neither emblem makes adequate sense as the sum of its iconography, even if each one draws upon a range of conventional visual meanings. The chariot alone has prompted a deal of critical endeavour. Modern writers, in estimating the meaning of the chariot for its late sixteenth-century audience, have ransacked history and mythology for an impressive array of antecedents and analogues. Among these are the chariots of Pride and Covetousness; of Ambition and Fortune; of Apollo and Phaethon and Hippolytus; of Lucifera and Sesostres; and any number of triumphal chariots from history and civic pageantry, especially Roman ones but including recent English examples.[10] Each of the suggested chariots entails a different way of making sense of the action, a different attitude to the conqueror.[11] But even if we were to agree on how to interpret the chariot, it is only one detail of the stage-image. If we turn to other details – Tamburlaine's scourge, or the king-horses – we encounter further sets of possibilities.

In too many of our discussions we have continued to 'read' Tamburlaine's entry with chariot as if only the old ways of seeing applied – as if, that is, its rhetoric were the same as that of the 'spotting' of Conscience or the shield of Policy. We pin down the 'best' analogue, and any loose ends are labelled as the product of irony or inconsistency or incoherence or worse. Chariot, we suggest, equals 'spotting' plus ambiguity. Add, and stir well. The problem is not so much that this way of reading leads to multiple or complex inter-pretations – in this respect it is simply an extension of traditional practice and the recognition in the sign of essential but contradictory qualities – but that it cannot explain how meanings are able to multiply, how Marlowe's use of the traditional rhetoric of visual signs made it possible for audiences to make sense in ways that are not confined to the meanings conventionally assigned by iconogra-phy. Our readings, in effect, do not recognise the new ways of seeing made possible by Marlowe's plays, especially their changes to the use of visual signs on the late sixteenth-century stage. Before explor-ing these changes, however, we need to clarify the terms found generally in studies of the visual sign and to survey some of the issues involved.

Defining the emblematic

The 'emblematic' character of Renaissance drama has become one of the commonplaces of criticism, in performance and iconographic studies especially.[12] Playwrights of the 1580s and 1590s inherited a dramatic tradition in which visual signs offered a conspicuous means of organising theatrical experience. That inheritance was a complex one; and, as the various uses of the term 'emblematic' suggest, the continuity with the past operated in a number of ways. In performance studies, 'emblematic' has been applied to all aspects of dramatic presentation: to properties and costumes, gestures and stage grouping, ritual and pageantry, character type and narrative structure.[13] In iconographic studies, 'emblematic' has sometimes become little more than a synonym for 'symbolic', with 'emblem' serving to denote any visual image which signifies more than the literal, as well as any verbal image or allusion with some visual implication. In perhaps its most widespread use, 'emblematic' has been equated with 'allegorical'. And, since what was obvious or unremarkable to the sixteenth-century spectator might well be alien or obscure to the modern reader, there has been a proliferation of studies seeking to interpret emblems by referring to other, though mainly non-dramatic, materials and sources.[14]

We may recognise the continuity between medieval and later plays in their use of the emblematic, but the nature of that continuity deserves more attention. It is not only that later plays continue to employ a set of traditional theatrical practices or draw upon a vast heap of conventional visual meanings. We will understand neither continuity nor change if we view the emblematic simply as a medieval survival, or identify it as endorsing 'medieval' or conservative values. Such viewpoints are nevertheless commonplace in both performance and iconographic studies. David Bevington for instance speaks of the 'medieval thrust' of conventional visual symbolism and 'the inertia of emblematic statement' (*Action Is Eloquence* 11, 12). Catherine Belsey in *The Subject of Tragedy* assumes that the emblematic or medieval is diametrically opposed to the illusionist or modern.[15] Nor is it sufficient to describe late sixteenth-century change primarily in terms of the impact of Reformation theology – whether (with C. L. Barber) we see playhouse spectacle as compensating for a lost world of Catholic ritual (125); or (with Huston Diehl) we identify a new 'Protestant' approach to the presentation of visual signs, with a play such as *Hamlet* fostering a new 'mode of sight that is skeptical, mediated, self-reflexive, analogical and ... distinctly Protestant' ('Observing the Lord's Supper' 168).

In fact, the emblematic, in the drama as in cultural practices generally, is not opposed in any simple way to the 'modern' or 'realistic' or even 'Protestant'. In defining what happens to visual signs on the popular stage late in the sixteenth century, we need a different model of cultural change: to think in terms of dialogue with tradition rather than dialectic, of adjustments rather than antagonisms. In particular, we need to recognise that this time of transition had its own distinctive attributes. Renaissance culture – and I am thinking particularly of England from the mid sixteenth to the mid seventeenth century – invested even more heavily in visual signs than had the medieval. This entailed not merely an abundance of signs, with the new learning and new discoveries offering a surfeit of classical images and contemporary examples, but also – despite the strictures of iconoclasts – an increasing emphasis on the visual as the key to making sense of reality. It was a time of cultural convergence, of 'the typological thinking of the Middle Ages, and the Neoplatonism of the Renaissance' (Daly 83), but also a time when, as Philip McGuire suggests, 'long-established, deeply engrained modes of perceiving, thinking and expressing which were predominantly oral and aural came to be crossed with and increasingly subordinated to intensely visual modes fostered by the development and proliferation of printed books' (Introduction xviii). A realignment of perception – in effect a different way of processing what was seen – happened concurrently with more articulate kinds of cultural change. There were in particular new ways of representing, or responding to, space: in maps of the world and the heavens, in the typography of books and the designing of tableaux, in the use of 'perspective' in theatre design and the visual arts.[16]

The late sixteenth century was, especially, the age of the emblem, an age which collected emblem-books, which had an eye for – and government regulations about – distinctive costume, which entertained itself at the court with elaborate masques, and which marked public occasions with lavish allegorical pageantry. For the maker of plays there were opportunities to be exploited: new signs, new strategies, and new possibilities for spectacle and display in playhouse and court theatre alike. One consequence of this visual excitement was a sudden increase in the number and complexity of visual signs in most plays of the late 1580s, with the associated expectation, it seems, that audiences had suddenly become more proficient in reading them – much as modern audiences have become

more proficient in 'reading' the language of film. Another consequence was a last, late, prodigal flowering of the 'medieval' way of
seeing. Until well into the seventeenth century, plays generally –
those of Shakespeare included – continued to call upon their audiences to read through visual signs to some statement of general
truth, continued to offer careful explanations of emblematic properties and scenes and situations. The plays of the period 1585 to 1595,
those that provided the ordinary experience of Marlowe's first audiences, were particularly rich in these visual signs that directed
attention to conventional understandings, and exploited conventional ironies: the mutilation of Lavinia in *Titus Andronicus*, for
example, or the deformity of Richard III, or the penitential robes of
the Duchess of Gloucester (*2 Henry VI*). More generally, in play
after play, there were crowns and swords, beds and thrones, daggers
and halters, kneelings and embracings, processions of triumph and
the bodies of the once-powerful littering the stage. Marlowe's plays
themselves include a great many instances of signs that can be read
straightforwardly: the white, red, and black of Tamburlaine's
rituals; the poisoned flowers of Barabas; the Mower who appears in
the scene of Edward's capture; the giving of crowns and rich apparel
in *Faustus*.[17]

There was a flowering and there was abundant harvest.
Increasingly, however, visual signs became less transparent, more
arbitrary, with meanings less dependent on essential nature than (in
effect) designated or assigned – more, that is, recognisably 'modern'.
They did not so much obviously 'mean' but became available for
purposes other than inculcating the 'truth' or affirming a shared
view of the world. They were appropriated for rhetorical purposes;
they were adopted by coteries and insiders. Gradually the traditional
sense of an integrated universe to which visual signs gave access
faded. The emblematic impulse dwindled into the decorative and
domestic (interior design, needlework) and the merely platitudinous.
The purposes of the emblem-book declined from persuading the
powerful (Whitney's notable collection, as John Manning argues,
offered propaganda and support for Leicester's campaign in the
Netherlands) to edifying little children in nineteenth-century Sunday
schools (Höltgen). Long before this happened, however, the plays of
Marlowe offered an insight into and -- for the popular stage – early
indications of the processes of cultural change.

The late sixteenth-century fascination with the emblematic led to
experiments with new or modified forms. These included the
'dramatic emblem', a term which has been applied in a particular

sense to the play in performance, to refer to those instances of the emblematic where a significant stage image is combined with verbal commentary.[18] When we describe Renaissance drama as 'emblematic' we draw attention not only to its medieval heritage but also to the similarities between contemporary visual and dramatic arts: between, in particular, the emblem-book (and related visual forms including device and *impresa*) and the several kinds of 'dramatic' presentation: stage play and masque, dumb show and pageant.[19] An analogy is sometimes cited between the page of a sixteenth-century emblem-book and the 'dramatic emblem' (Mehl, 'English Renaissance Drama' 51; Zucker 6–7; Fleischer 2–3). Three parts of the emblem on the page have specific relevance to such moments in the drama: the allegorical picture, often built up of separate but significant items; the verse or prose explanation and amplification; and the motto which encapsulates the emblem's significance.[20]

The emblem-book analogy is especially useful in pointing to an aspect of the dramatic emblem that is frequently ignored: its distinctive rhetoric. When an image is combined with commentary, the words organise perception and response, leading to the construction of a narrative to make sense of what is seen. On the emblem-book page, the words draw the reader's attention to specific details in the allegorical picture, ensuring first that they are noticed, and then that they are perceived in a certain order and in relation to the emblem's message or theme. In the theatre, the words select and relate visual details within a complex stage image, organising the perception of the spectator. At the same time, on both page and stage, and to an extent that varies with the individual instance and the particular play, the visual imagery exerts its own influence upon the reception and signification of the words.

The dramatic emblem became an important technique of dramatic rhetoric in plays of the late 1580s, though it can be found in rudimentary form in earlier plays, where it serves as exemplary reinforcement. In Ulpian Fulwell's *Like Will to Like* (written in the 1560s, reprinted in 1587), Virtuous Living is presented with the sword of victory and crowned by Honour (in token of a 'greater crown' after death), whereupon God's Promises and Good Fame expound upon the rewards of virtue. In contrast, two of the rogues are presented with halters, placed about their necks by the Vice (assisted by the Judge, Severity): 'here is the snare / That shall lead you to the Land called the Two-legged Mare' (1111–12). In Thomas Preston's *Cambises* (written in the late 1560s but reprinted twice in the 1580s) the astoundingly wicked king makes his final entrance '*without a gown, a swoord thrust up into his side bleeding*' (1152.1–2); the sight is explained and commented upon as an emblem of divine punishment: 'A just reward for my misdeeds, my death dooth plain declare' (1166). The audience is not permitted to misunderstand, to diverge in their making sense, as both explanation and message are repeated by the Lords who find the body – 'A just reward for his misdeeds, the God aboove hath wrought' (1187).

Later, more developed examples of the dramatic emblem are plentiful in plays contemporary with those of Marlowe. Thomas Kyd's *Spanish Tragedy*, as Michael Hattaway suggests, uses dramatic emblems to underline key moments in the action, providing such memorable examples as Hieronymo's lament by the fatal arbour (110–11). Shakespeare's early play *3 Henry VI* (1590–91) has an elaborate triple emblem that expounds on the cares of kingship and the tragic consequences of civil war, with the king seated on a molehill, and entries of '*a Son that hath killed his father, at one door* [*bearing the body in his arms*]' and '*at another door*' of '*a Father that hath killed his son, bearing of his son*' (2.5.1–124).[21] *Richard III* offers an emblem of hypocrisy in the tableau of Richard, seeming-godly, posed between two divines, and set above the citizens of London (3.7).

For the late sixteenth-century playwright, the dramatic emblem afforded a useful means of making the audience aware of the issues involved in the action. In most instances, the function of dramatic emblems is choric. They use traditional iconography to reinforce their messages; they extend and supplement the action, clarifying details, amplifying and explaining; they exploit conventional ironies and (as in Richard's 'show' of 'devotion and right Christian zeal') illustrate the deceptiveness of signs.[22] In functioning like this, dramatic emblems accorded with the expectations and the theatrical experience of their first audiences. They drew, that is, upon traditional ways of seeing, traditional expectations that such visual signs were transparent and that an audience, with more or less assistance, would interpret by recognising the 'truth' beyond the sign.

Many dramatic emblems in Marlowe's plays function in this traditional, choric way. When Mephistopheles offers the dagger of Despair to Faustus; when Edward lies on the stage floor with his weary, defeated head in the lap of the Abbot; when Dido addresses the 'tackling, oars, and sails' of Aeneas; even when Tamburlaine removes his shepherd's 'weeds' in order to assume the role of the heroic warrior: all require little or no more than the familiar 'seeing through' and the recognition of quite conventional ideas and values.

At the same time, other dramatic emblems in Marlowe's plays challenge traditional ways of seeing. Their impact on an audience cannot be accounted for simply in terms of allegorical meaning or choric function, or even (as Hattaway suggests of Kyd) of underlining key moments in the action. And they include the plays' most spectacular and memorable moments: Tamburlaine's entry in his chariot, Barabas's plunge into the cauldron, the funeral scene at the end of *Edward II* with its hearse and severed head. All of these have been subject to extensive, and often conflicting, iconographic explication. In all of them, however, the conventional message becomes less important as Marlowe adapts the device of dramatic emblem for complex rhetorical and narrative purposes. They may, or may not, appear to give access to new versions of the 'truth'; more importantly, however, they make it possible for spectators to view and make sense in non-traditional ways.

'All sights of power'

An insight into the differences between old and new can be gained if we consider the last scene of *1 Tamburlaine*, and two dramatic emblems in particular: the lament of Zenocrate for Bajazeth and Zabina (5.1.340–77), and Tamburlaine's tableau of conquest (469–79). Each of these important images is typical of late sixteenth-century playhouse practice in exploiting visual spectacle and, more particularly, typical of the late 1580s in recalling the emblem-book page. Each instance begins with an appeal for attention, shifting the direction of gaze of the spectators, whether offstage or on ('But see another bloody spectacle!', 340; 'And see, my lord, a sight of strange import', 469).[23] Each proceeds to a formal amplification and elaboration of what is seen: Zenocrate marvels at the disparity between the 'honour of their birth' and their 'death so barbarous', developing from this a conventional warning for 'Those that are proud of fickle empery / And place their chiefest good in earthly pomp' (353–4); Tamburlaine contrasts his own 'honour' in victory with the lowly remains of those who 'have desperately despatched their slavish lives' (473). Each ends with the equivalent of the emblem-book's motto, a summation of its significance, involving once more an appeal to the visual. Zenocrate applies the lesson to herself and her own lack of pity; Tamburlaine speaks of the 'mirror' in which may be seen 'His honour, that consists in shedding blood / When men presume to manage arms with him' (478–9).[24]

Considered individually, each of these dramatic emblems can be interpreted in the traditional way, as an index to the reality beyond. The audience is expected to recognise the commonplaces:

> Earth, cast up fountains from thy entrails,
> And wet thy cheeks for their untimely deaths;
> Shake with their weight in sign of fear and grief.
> Blush, heaven, that gave them honour at their birth
> And let them die a death so barbarous.
> Those that are proud of fickle empery
> And place their chiefest good in earthly pomp –
> Behold the Turk and his great emperess!
> Ah Tamburlaine my love, sweet Tamburlaine,
> That fightest for sceptres and for slippery crowns,
> Behold the Turk and his great emperess!
>
> (*1 Tamburlaine* 5.1.348–58)

Zenocrate's lament may reflect her anxieties and provoke her maid to disagree, but it is essentially choric, an emblem commenting on the insecurity of 'earthly pomp', like many others in earlier and contemporary plays. It anticipates, for example, Marlowe's King Edward, lying on the stage floor and reflecting, quite conventionally, on the fortunes of the powerful:

> Stately and proud, in riches and in train,
> Whilom I was, powerful and full of pomp;
> But what is he whom rule and empery
> Have not in life or death made miserable?
>
> (*Edward II* 4.7.12–15)

Or Shakespeare's Earl of Warwick, directing the attention of the audience to specific visual signs (eyes, brows) that recall his career as king-maker but which lead more importantly to a familiar *de casibus* message:[25]

> These eyes, that now are dimm'd with death's black veil,
> Have been as piercing as the mid-day sun
> To search the secret treasons of the world;
> The wrinkles in my brows, now fill'd with blood,
> Were liken'd oft to kingly sepulchres;
> For who liv'd King but I could dig his grave?
> And who durst smile when Warwick bent his brow?
> Lo now my glory smear'd in dust and blood!
> My parks, my walks, my manors that I had,
> Even now forsake me; and of all my lands
> Is nothing left me but my body's length.
> Why, what is pomp, rule, reign, but earth and dust?
> And live we how we can, yet die we must.
>
> (*3 Henry VI* 5.2.16–28)

Like these instances, Tamburlaine's tableau of conquest can be read through quite traditionally. The conqueror elevated above his enemies can be seen as a figure representing Power or Ambition or the favoured of Fortune. The bodies suggest the complementary *de casibus* ironies: they are reminders of common mortality, of the inconstancy of fortune, of the vanity of trusting to 'earthly pomp' or the 'honour of birth'.[26] And these conventional messages have multiple illustrations on stage. Early spectators saw before them a platform crowded with as many actors and hirelings as the company could afford. Objects and personages jostled for their attention: treasure chests, perhaps, taken at Damascus; a throne, waiting for the coronation of Zenocrate; the iron cage, sombre, with Bajazeth lying brained within and Zabina alongside; nearby, the bloodied corpse of the King of Arabia; the three lieutenants, crowned the day before as 'contributory kings'; the 'divine' Zenocrate, reunited with her father, tremulous now with joy as well as grief; the Soldan, sumptuously attired even in defeat; and the conqueror himself, magnificent in black and arrogant in victory. Dominating this multiplicity of visual detail is a single voice as the words of Tamburlaine direct attention to his 'breathless' opponents:

> And see, my lord, a sight of strange import –
> Emperors and kings lie breathless at my feet:
> The Turk and his great empress, as it seems,
> Left to themselves while we were at the fight,
> Have desperately despatched their slavish lives;
> With them Arabia too hath left his life –
> All sights of power to grace my victory;
> And such are objects fit for Tamburlaine,
> Wherein as in a mirror may be seen
> His honour, that consists in shedding blood
> When men presume to manage arms with him.
>
> (*1 Tamburlaine* 5.1.469–79)

And yet, despite this balancing of signs of earthly glory against signs of earthly loss, Tamburlaine's 'sights of power' do not lead simply to conventional messages or ways of seeing. Unlike Zenocrate's lament or Edward's abasement or Warwick's eyes and brows, the tableau of victory supports a quite different kind of perceiving and interpreting. This depends, importantly, upon the cumulative effect of the dramatic emblems in both Parts of *Tamburlaine*, which is quite different from that in other contemporary plays – Kyd's *Spanish Tragedy*, for example, or Shakespeare's *Henry VI* plays, or even the first four acts of *Edward II* – where a series of dramatic emblems asks the audience to view what happens

on stage in terms of a vast backdrop of moral and political commonplaces, with the effect of reinforcing a shared sense of how actions
should be judged.

The *Tamburlaine* emblems do seem at first to follow this
expected, conventional path. They structure the narrative, marking
(in Part One) the stages of Tamburlaine's acquisition of power and
exemplifying (in Part Two) more aspects of his 'bloody Conquests':
his 'impassionate fury', his 'form of exhortation and discipline', and
'the manner of his own death' (title-page, Part Two), as well as
demonstrating power and destructiveness, and the impotence of his
enemies. They comment on the important events of the play, thus
establishing, it would appear, a general narrative for the spectator to
make sense of the action.

But this impression deceives, and therein lies one significant
difference in the way that dramatic emblems such as the 'sights' or
footstool or chariot construct theatrical experience. As in other
plays, there is a controlling viewpoint – the speaking voice heard
offering a commentary on the emblem – but the interpretation it
offers is not fixed. The speaking voice is not choric in the traditional
sense, guiding the audience to read through the signs to certain
'truths', or providing unambiguous reference points for the explica-
tors of iconography. There are no 'terminally authoritative
judgements' in G. K. Hunter's phrase (*English Drama* 34), as there
are in earlier plays like *The Three Ladies of London*, or for that
matter in most contemporary plays. Rather, the authorised version
of *Tamburlaine* continues to change, with each major dramatic
emblem superimposing a new meaning on the action rather than
locating its significance in terms of some eternal scale of values.

Emblems such as the 'sights of power' operate not simply as
commentaries on the narrative, but also as elements in a new kind of
dramatic structure. Especially in Part One but in Part Two as well
with instances such as the chariot, the emblems are used to redefine
the action, and to establish points of transition from one phase to
the next. Their perspectives are thus not always consistent with each
other; and their impact on the audience's making sense is sequential,
with the latest in the series becoming the most persuasive and super-
seding earlier versions. As Cosroe lies dying, Tamburlaine justifies
his rebellion with talk of 'aspiring minds' and of 'souls' restless in
their search for 'the sweet fruition of an earthly crown' (*1
Tamburlaine* 2.7.12–29); later, enthroned above his 'footstool', the
visual imagery suggesting the legitimisation of his power and his
language appropriating the feudal terminology of his opponents

('base villain, vassal, slave to Tamburlaine'), he claims that he is the 'scourge and terror' of heaven and that his actions have astral and meteorological consequences. The emblem of 'sights of power', of Tamburlaine triumphant, denotes yet another stage in the process, one in which power may include force and bloodshed as well as majesty and elevation: gore, we discover, can be redefined as glory. In its dramatic context the emblem effects the transformation of Tamburlaine from tormentor of emperors and butcher of Damascus to the astounding conqueror endorsed by the Soldan:

> Mighty hath God and Mahomet made thy hand,
> Renownèd Tamburlaine, to whom all kings
> Of force must yield their crowns and emperies.
>
> (*1 Tamburlaine* 5.1.480–2)

Similarly, in the closing scenes of Part Two, the successive appearances of the chariot mark abrupt switches in the presentation of Tamburlaine to the audience, from brutality to aspiration to destructiveness to impiety to physical suffering to, at last, apotheosis. The cumulative impact of the major dramatic emblems in the *Tamburlaine* plays is thus quite unlike that of similar series of emblems elsewhere. In terms of the expectations and experience of early playgoers, the *Tamburlaine* plays offer ways of making sense of experience that are neither reassuring nor, it must be admitted, particularly coherent.

This insistent process of redefining, central to the shaping rhetoric of the *Tamburlaine* plays, has important consequences for the theatrical experience of the playgoers. How spectators might view Tamburlaine's tableau depends upon their experiencing of the dramatic emblem in sequence and as part of a sequence, as a reworking of particular visual and verbal details. The effects are not limited to redefining the power of Tamburlaine. The emblem of 'sights of power' also reinterprets in detail the action it follows, in particular Zenocrate's lament over Bajazeth and Zabina, with its commonplace sentiments and its conventional warning for 'Those that are proud of fickle empery'. In directly challenging these familiar responses, the 'sights of power' calls into question powerful habits of viewing and interpreting. Instead of being directed towards recognising the 'truth' beyond visual signs, the focus of the spectators' interest becomes the opportunism of Tamburlaine as he progressively reinterprets his motives and role, making and remaking his own interpretive narrative.

Tamburlaine is shown throughout as actively shaping experience

for his own ends, as seizing upon and interpreting visual signs: treasure chests and crowns, robes and swords, hearse and map; the
white, red, and black of sieges; the faces of friend and foe; the 'town
burning' and the bonfire of books. Heaven (in various guises)
becomes a convenient sanction for deeds and ambitions. Even
Zenocrate's death cannot be attributed merely to natural causes;
something as cogent as the desires of the gods must needs be postu-
lated as overriding those of Tamburlaine. Stephen Greenblatt notes
this pattern of 'appropriation' and assertion as intrinsic to
Tamburlaine's 'self-fashioning' (*Renaissance Self-fashioning* 213).
The spectators' attention, however, is drawn less to the elusiveness
of 'the objects of desire' (which Greenblatt emphasises) than to the
processes of obtaining and validating power. The emblem of 'sights
of power' at the end of Part One is not, as Greenblatt suggests, 'a
mirror reflecting yet another goal' (218), but an eloquent redefinition of goals achieved.

The rhetoric of redefining utilises a distinctive method of containing discordant elements, however they might be labelled: as ironies,
perhaps, or ambiguities, alterities, subversions, fissures. In this
instance, the conventional ironies suggested by Zenocrate's lament are
again exploited – but only initially, and only in order to supersede
them. Tamburlaine's words, 'The Turk and his great empress', echo
Zenocrate's refrain, 'Behold the Turk and his great emperess'. They
direct attention to similarities and call upon related emotional
responses. Zenocrate has marvelled at the disparity between the
'honour of their birth' and their 'death so barbarous'; now
Tamburlaine calls upon his audience to respond with wonder to this
'sight of strange import'. But the 'sight' to be admired is the complex
tableau of victory. The echoes call attention to a shift in interpretation.
The spectators are offered a new and more persuasive way of making
sense of the action. The redefinition is supported by the conspicuous
change in the stage picture: where Zenocrate has been seen grieving
with only her maid beside her, Tamburlaine's stage is processional
and crowded, including and containing the earlier tableau.

The pattern of first exploiting discordant elements, then super-
seding them, is typical of the dramatic emblems in the *Tamburlaine*
plays; but it is also a pattern that operates more generally in their
dramatic rhetoric, both visual and verbal. It is to be found, for
example, in the way that comparisons are shaped:

But ere I march to wealthy Persia
Or leave Damascus and th'Egyptian fields,
As was the fame of Clymen's brain-sick son

That almost brent the axletree of heaven,
So shall our swords, our lances and our shot
Fill all the air with fiery meteors.

(*1 Tamburlaine* 4.1.47–52)

Enthroned above his 'footstool', Bajazeth, Tamburlaine plays with rhetorical fire: the allusion to Phaethon is one that conventionally drew attention to the dangers of presumption. But then its significance is immediately redefined. The point of the comparison becomes the 'fame' of the event and its prodigious consequences, rather than disaster or failure; and the lines describing future deeds acquire more emphasis by a syntactical inversion, by being placed in the later, climactic position.

That the ironies are effectively contained in this and in instances such as the 'sights of power' is perhaps not the generally accepted view. Most discussions of the final scene of Part One, for example, argue that its ironies subvert its rhetoric.[27] Visual details in particular – the cage and corpses, the silent figure of Zenocrate – are held to challenge the dominance of Tamburlaine's values and viewpoint. On the other hand, I would suggest, we need to distinguish between what might be termed subversive and complementary ironies. The subversive is a voice that competes with the dominant interpretation, the complementary a voice that defines it more clearly. The latter was familiar from earlier plays and *Tamburlaine* exploits the conventional expectations of early audiences. The figure of Tamburlaine is perceived more distinctly because he is set against minor figures such as Mycetes or Almeda or the king-horses, or more substantial opponents such as Bajazeth and Callapine, or even Agydas and Zenocrate – just as Sincerity is set against the other representatives of the clergy (Sir Peter Pleaseman and Simony) in *The Three Ladies of London*. The same process of achieving definition can be observed with visual signs. The narrative offered by the 'sights of power' may be new, but it takes advantage of a traditional grouping of visual signs and traditional ways of seeing. When Tamburlaine strikes a pose near the corpses of his enemies, the visual ironies are no more than might be expected in some conventional representation of Fortune: these typically included some image of the unfortunate, humbled by the turning of the Wheel. The visual ironies are thus essentially complementary – as in earlier plays – rather than subversive; and the commentary supports a familiar redirecting of audience attention away from the individual significance of the victims towards their place in the new tableau.

But even as old habits of making sense are drawn upon, they are exploited and superseded. Tamburlaine's commentary intervenes and the conventional understandings are redirected, a different set of possibilities contained: the bodies, redefined and reduced to 'sights' and 'objects', provide visual proof of Tamburlaine's elevation above the ordinary rules of history and the operations of Fortune. The ceremonies that follow – homage, enthronement, and coronation – confirm the lesson. The fates of others do not predict Tamburlaine's, as Zenocrate had feared. The stage image may include the usual visual and narrative ironies; yet, as elsewhere in the *Tamburlaine* plays, they are contained within a larger, superimposed pattern of shaping rhetoric. The emblem of 'sights of power' compels admiration for Tamburlaine, supporting his claims to glory rather than denying their validity.[28]

The rhetoric of redefining exposed the emblematic to different ways of making sense. At the same time, when associated with other features of the shaping rhetoric of the *Tamburlaine* plays – the insistent hyperboles, the equally insistent escalation to rhetorical climax in every speech, every passage of action, every set of visual signs (more crowns, increasingly elaborate processions) – redefining seems ultimately to have proved too inflexible, to have opened up possibilities for competing narratives only to foreclose on them. For one thing, ironies were suppressed even when ironies were intended: Part Two, despite its emphasis on the problems that Tamburlaine must encounter, is ultimately imprisoned by its rhetoric. After *Tamburlaine*, the distinctive *Tamburlaine* verbal rhetoric became the distinguishing mark first of heroes (briefly, with characters such as Greene's Alphonsus) and then of sundry ranters and presumers. Ferneze speaks of drinking the ocean dry (*Jew* 5.5.120), while the Guise aspires to honour and glory and crowns (*Massacre* 2.34–56). And our admiration is elicited by neither.[29]

It is not, however, the obvious flaws in these imitations, with their old-fashioned messages about deceptive appearances, that epitomise the impact of the *Tamburlaine* plays on early audiences. What the memorable moments of *Tamburlaine* reveal is a new and different alignment for the emblematic in the popular drama. In this, the traditional allegorical uses are included in, but now appropriated by and subordinated to, narrative and rhetorical ones. The visual sign loses some of its transparency and becomes increasingly arbitrary in nature, although this change is by no means complete or even consistent. Traditionally the visual sign had drawn attention not to itself but to an underlying reality. When the sign draws attention to itself first, as in the case of the footstool or 'sights' or chariot, the familiar method of making sense by simply reading through is no longer sufficient. The spectators may still recognise 'truths', but their making sense becomes a less straightforward process, increasingly influenced by the shaping patterns of dramatic rhetoric, including the plays' extravagance and spectacle. In redirecting audience attention from the concepts that visual signs embody to the processes they illustrate, the conqueror's reinterpretative narratives included, the *Tamburlaine* emblems call upon spectators to change their old habits of seeing and interpreting.

These changed emphases in the rhetoric of visual signs help to explain the contemporary impact of the plays and elements of the response they generated. The redefinitions, with their elaborate eloquence, unsettle old habits. The audience may remain aware of the horror that attends Tamburlaine's search for glory, but they are unlikely to read the signs merely as illustrating moral or political commonplaces. This response would have been especially so for the first spectators: physically closer to the action than most members of a modern audience, they were confronted by extravagant sights and sounds, seeing 'the stalking steps of his great personage' (Joseph Hall) and hearing 'everie worde filling the mouth like the faburden of Bo-Bell' (Greene, *Perimedes* 8). Richard Levin argues that modern ironic interpretations are not supported by the contemporary references to *Tamburlaine*: 'whether they approve of Tamburlaine or not (and most of them ... do not, for moral or esthetic reasons), they all agree that he was not condemned by the play but rather was intended to evoke the audience's wonder or admiration' ('Contemporary Perception' 55). This impression is confirmed by the nature of the early dramatic imitations of *Tamburlaine*, with their accent on 'splendid rhetoric and glamorous stage effects' rather than 'the discomfort of unconventional ideas' (Berek 59).[30] That a modern production can still effect a response with some element of admiration is shown by the comments of J. S. Cunningham and Roger Warren on the 1976 National Theatre version: 'We were spared none of the consequences of our impulse to admire the conqueror ... we applauded Tamburlaine – not just the play, but, embarrassingly, the hero – as he left this obscene stage in triumph at the end of Part One' (160–1).

'View here this blood': a new reading of signs

Marlowe's experiments with the rhetoric of visual signs did not end with *Tamburlaine*. The important dramatic emblems of the later plays (*The Jew of Malta, Edward II, The Massacre at Paris, Doctor Faustus*) continue to redirect the emblematic away from its traditional didacticism. Images such as the cauldron in the *Jew*, for example, have a theatrical impact that can only partly be explained by their iconography. At the same time, each play has its own particular way of shaping theatrical experience, which complicates and influences the making sense of its spectators. In brief, *The Jew of Malta* is characterised by a rhetoric of contradiction; *Edward II*, by a rhetoric of anticlimax; *Doctor Faustus*, by a rhetoric of deflation; *The Massacre at Paris*, by a rhetoric of contrast. The form of dramatic emblems also changes, with few later examples approaching the formality and elaboration of the significant *Tamburlaine* emblems. Indeed, the 'emblem-book' rhetoric with its call to attention, detailed explication, and closing motto reaches a peak of development in the relatively static, ceremonial world of *Tamburlaine*. Thereafter, action pauses less frequently to create a tableau, and the verbal structure of the set-speech becomes less rigid. In *Tamburlaine* perception is organised by the speaking voice; in the later plays, commentary is briefer and sometimes shared between speakers. The motto, when used, is less likely to be choric, more likely to be limited to the perspective of the individual character.

The experimentation, however, extends further than variations in structure or shaping rhetoric. Several dramatic emblems in *Doctor Faustus* and *Edward II* begin to organise theatrical experience in an even more radical way. These instances shift the focus of audience attention from messages of general validity to individual moments of non-representative experience. The effect is, in part, to invert the processes of viewing the emblem, with conventional visual signs giving access to new perspectives on the action while also serving, in the traditional manner, as indices to truth. Edward's death scene provides one instance of this, with others afforded by the early appearances of the Angels in *Faustus* and the second 'show' of Helen. Still another is the 'bond-signing' (2.1), the passage where Faustus cuts his arm to sign in blood his formal agreement with hell – with its congealing and streaming blood, its saucer of coals, its inscription on the arm. Here the audience sees Faustus swinging between desperation and resolution, between seeing and not-seeing, until Mephistopheles distracts him at last with a show of dancing and gift-giving devils:

> Faustus.   [*Cutting his arm.*]
>   Lo, Mephistopheles, for love of thee
>   I cut mine arm, and with my proper blood

Assure my soul to be great Lucifer's,
Chief lord and regent of perpetual night.
View here the blood that trickles from mine arm,
And let it be propitious for my wish.
Mephistopheles.   But Faustus, thou must write it in manner of a
     deed of gift.
Faustus.   Ay, so I will. [*He writes.*] But Mephistopheles,
     My blood congeals, and I can write no more.
     Mephistopheles. I'll fetch thee fire to dissolve it straight.   *Exit.*
Faustus.   What might the staying of my blood portend?
     Is it unwilling I should write this bill?
     Why streams it not, that I may write afresh?
     'Faustus gives to thee his soul' – ah, there it stayed!
     Why shouldst thou not? Is not thy soul thine own?
     Then write again: 'Faustus gives to thee his soul.'

          Enter MEPHISTOPHELES *with a chafer of coals.*

Mephistopheles.   Here's fire. Come Faustus, set it on.
Faustus.   So; now the blood begins to clear again,
     Now will I make an end immediately.   [*He writes.*]
Mephistopheles.   [*Aside.*]
     O, what will not I do to obtain his soul?
Faustus.   *Consummatum est.* This bill is ended,
     And Faustus hath bequeathed his soul to Lucifer.
     But what is this inscription on mine arm?
     '*Homo, fuge!*' Whither should I fly?
     If unto God, he'll throw thee down to hell. –
     My senses are deceived; here's nothing writ. –
     I see it plain. Here in this place is writ
     '*Homo fuge!*' Yet shall not Faustus fly.
Mephistopheles.   [*Aside.*]
     I'll fetch him somewhat to delight his mind.   *Exit.*

          Enter [MEPHISTOPHELES] *with* Devils, *giving crowns and*
          rich apparel to Faustus, and dance and then depart.

Faustus.   Speak, Mephistopheles, what means this show?
Mephistopheles.   Nothing, Faustus, but to delight thy mind withal
     And to show thee what magic can perform.

                                   (2.1.53–85)[31]

The passage calls, in the first instance, upon quite traditional
ways of seeing, with visual signs that can be read through easily in
terms of conventional iconography. The early spectators were
presented, in effect, with signs that were culturally 'obvious'. They
will recognise the issues at stake without difficulty: these are no less
than spiritual life or death. The knife (or is it a dagger?) that Faustus
uses to cut his arm is the implement of Despair, and the action
reveals his spiritual state: despair of salvation, which results in a
turning to hell. The 'chafer of coals' that Mephistopheles carries on

to the stage – seen and probably also smelt by the audience – signifies the fearful presence of hell. The blood – trickling, congealing,
streaming – is the sign of both redemption and life. When Faustus's
blood refuses to move, when his senses deceive (or do not deceive)
him, the signs are quite transparent. The pact is unnatural, opposed
not merely by the body but by God and Nature. The assumption of
'crowns and rich apparel', which follows, denotes initiation into a
new life of power and wealth.[32] Considered thus, the bond-signing
is a potent appeal to old habits of viewing and interpreting. It offers
transparent visual signs, translating directly into abstract meaning,
providing the spectators with an easily formulated narrative to make
sense of the agreement with hell. That the signing is against both
heaven and Nature is seen in the recalcitrant blood. That hell is ruth-
less and relentless ('What will I not do to obtain his soul') is evident
in the magic fire and the dance of devils by which Mephistopheles
manipulates Faustus.

But audience experience is also influenced by the play's distinctive
rhetoric of deflation. In *Faustus*, the aspirations are unrealised, the
magic ultimately disappoints. In both versions of the play, in stage
image and verbal language, the spectators are called upon repeatedly
to notice other, undermining perspectives. The A-text version of the
second show of Helen ('Was this the face ... ?') has a silent witness
in the Old Man; the B-text incident of the Papal 'footstool' is framed
by the mischief-making of Faustus and Mephistopheles. Even the
early speeches of aspiration are modified by their structure: instead
of building confidently to a rhetorical climax like the speeches of
Tamburlaine, there is a progressive contraction in the scale and
importance of the verbal imagery. In the soliloquy that ends the
third scene, after he has 'proven' his magic powers by summoning
Mephistopheles, Faustus is exultant: 'Had I as many souls as there
be stars' (1.3.104–16). Yet the images of his day-dream descend
from stars to vast geography to German politics; and the audience
has already been made aware that Mephistopheles is far from the
'pliant' servant Faustus believes him to be. In the bond-signing the
claim of Faustus to be in control of events is subverted by the images
of stage action: the display of the 'scroll', the interrupted attempts to
write, the staring at imagined inscriptions, the sudden and spectacular entry of the devils.

What happens during the bond-signing, however, cannot be sufficiently explained in terms of conventional signs or deflationary
rhetoric. The radical nature of the bond-signing lies in the way that
it calls upon its spectators to take notice and make sense of what

they see before them. This difference from the traditional is perhaps first suggested by the nature of the emblem's commentary. The visual signs are clearly emblematic and receive some amplification in the dialogue; and yet the words are inadequate. Faustus has been presented as able to articulate his dreams but he cannot now explain the images of his experience. The speaking voice reacts rather than interprets: there is little sense of shaping or control. As well, the dramatic emblem has no motto, no explicit summation of its significance. Faustus may perceive his blood's congealing as an emblem in need of a commentary ('What might the staying of my blood portend?' 64), but he can give no sufficient answer. Mephistopheles may be able to explain, but does not. When he returns with the chafer, both Faustus and the audience must accept without question, it seems, the magic of fire that can make blood 'stream' again.

What is more significant, however, is the way that the attention of the audience is focused during the signing of the bond. The difference becomes apparent if we set the attempt to sign against the action that precedes and follows it. In the arm-cutting and devil show, the visual signs function in the older, straightforward manner, making the spectators aware of the traditional implications of the action. In the intervening section – the bond-signing – something else happens, side-by-side with the traditional iconography. The attention of the audience is drawn most forcibly to the separate and individual moments of Faustus's experience, with an accumulating series of appeals to the visual: 'View here the blood that trickles from mine arm' (2.1.57); 'My blood congeals, and I can write no more' (62); 'Is it unwilling I should write this bill' (65); 'Why streams it not' (62); 'ah, there it stayed' (67); 'Then write again: "Faustus gives to thee his soul"' (69); 'Here's fire. Come Faustus, set it on' (70); or the B-text's 'See Faustus, here is fire'; 'So; now the blood begins to clear again' (71); 'But what is this inscription on mine arm?' (76); 'Homo fuge' (77, 81); 'My senses are deceived; here's nothing writ' (79); 'I see it plain. Here in this place is writ' (80).

Traditional dramatic emblems, even the emblems of *Tamburlaine*, invited the spectators to read through particular items in a complex stage picture, like Warwick's eyes and brows or Tamburlaine's 'kings and emperors' or the biting off of Hieronymo's tongue. Here, however, they are enjoined to watch particular moments in the experience of an individual figure on the stage, a figure whose reactions are presented as fragmentary and confused, and whose perceptions, it would seem, are distorted by the intensity of an inner conflict. The

apparent immersion of Faustus in his own sensations is epitomised
by the incident of the inscription on his arm; this is seen, or not seen,
by Faustus alone, as his words imply: 'My senses are deceived; here's
nothing writ. – / I see it plain' (79–80). He is aware of some pressing danger, but despairs. He believes for a moment that the words
have disappeared. He takes refuge in calling upon the 'manly fortitude' he has commended to Mephistopheles when the devil has
shown himself 'so passionate / For being deprivèd of the joys of
heaven' (1.3.85–6). The emphasis upon the moment-by-moment
experience of the senses is reinforced by other elements in the verbal
language that suggest incoherence and confusion: the rapid changes
in syntax, for example, or the switching of viewpoint between first,
second, and third persons. Faustus is seen by the audience as
attempting to impose an order on his experience. He hails the blood
as it 'trickles' from his arm as 'propitious'; he resorts to repeating
'Faustus gives to thee his soul' when the blood congeals; he appropriates the last words of Christ, '*Consummatum est*', in announcing
that 'this Bill is ended'. But all these efforts to construct a narrative
that makes sense of his experience are also seen, promptly, to be
contradicted. Like the blood that is 'unwilling' and 'streaming' in
turn, like the inscription that appears and vanishes, the meanings of
words shift and slide.

The bond-signing restructures the traditional rhetoric of visual
signs. In recording experience-as-it-happens, this passage – and a
few other similar moments in *Doctor Faustus* and *Edward II* –
opened up new areas of theatrical experience and made possible new
ways of making sense. Though the conventional message of the
action remains clear, these moments do not merely illustrate such
concepts as despair and damnation or signify the contest between
heaven and hell, but they acquire as well their own impact, their
own interest and importance. The 'bond-signing' may exploit the
culturally obvious signs of dagger and blood and fire, may make a
potent appeal to traditional ways of seeing, but it also provides
something that (in effect) resists familiar habits. The emblem draws
upon what appears to be a 'readiness' in the spectators to change,
less at the level of 'thinking' than at the level of 'experience'. What
they are called upon to view – and to make sense of – is not simply
the visible sign of an idea, but (it would seem) individual, and non-
representative, experience: that of Faustus, the particular person.

When, shortly after the bond-signing, Faustus asserts that hell is
a 'fable', Mephistopheles responds: 'Ay, think so still, till experience
change thy mind' (2.1.130). One sixteenth-century meaning of the

'experience' that changes minds is 'experiment' or testing.[33] Something of such a process is exhibited before the spectators, in what presents as Faustus's disordered thinking, faulty perception, foolish distractability. In making sense of what they see, the spectators are not provided with the explicit commentary they would traditionally expect – there is only Faustus's desperate questioning or the devil's evading – and they may well resort in their reading of signs to what they know from their own experience with others, to, in effect, their own notions of psychology. The rhetoric of the bond-signing thus permits both (for instance) the view that Faustus chooses wilfully and the view that Faustus is not allowed to choose wisely; both that Faustus is a morality figure, bounded by a heavenly ordained universe, the embodiment of Despair, and the view that Faustus is 'predominantly a free-standing, literal figure in a geographically- and chronologically-specific world' (Belsey, *Subject of Tragedy* 43). By challenging the spectators to interpret as particular individuals, the dramatic rhetoric of this passage offers a radical new way for them to relate to the action on stage.

This theatrical experience could well, in Mephistopheles's terms, 'change ... [the] mind'. The way of perceiving called upon in the bond-signing, and the way of thinking about what is seen, amount to something quite different from the traditional way of seeing. In the traditional rhetoric of visual signs, even in the *Tamburlaine* rhetoric, the individual details – the most striking ones included – are always essentially 'representative'. They acquire their importance from illustrating some general rule. This can readily be illustrated in other plays of the 1580s and 1590s. In 'spotting' Lady Conscience, the wicked Lady Lucre draws the spectators' attention, feature by feature, to her (typically sixteenth-century) beauty: 'cherry red' lips, 'forhead white as snow', 'dimpled chin', and so on. But these details only matter in reinforcing the moral lesson. Until this scene, Conscience (though always in 'character') has been one of the play's few sympathetic figures: beautiful, virtuous, even if somewhat naive. When her beauty is 'spotted', however, the attention of the spectators is drawn neither to the distress of her situation (she has been reduced by poverty to caretaking a house of adultery) nor to her feelings – in any case she submits without protest and sits counting her money. What matters in making sense of the scene is not her individual experience but the message to be read from the spots – and that is quite plain: even the most virtuous can be corrupted.

The early plays of Shakespeare are more eloquent than this in drawing attention to, and elaborating upon, the details of a scene, but – as in the death of Warwick or the penance of the Duchess of Gloucester – they still use these details as indices to abstract understanding rather than as keys to non-representative experience. It is not until later Shakespearean plays that the rhetoric of visual signs changes: when Macbeth sees a dagger before him, the details (the handle pointed toward him, the 'gouts of blood') may indicate some lesson about conscience or temptation, but they also, as in *Faustus*, call upon the audience to observe something important for Macbeth's individual, moment-by-moment experience.

Doctor Faustus, unlike its contemporaries, asked of its early audiences two quite different ways of 'seeing' or processing visual signs, sometimes simultaneously. This double asking was, of course, only intermittent. In *Faustus* some passages depend little upon specific visual signs, including the major soliloquies and speeches of aspiration. Others still function in the traditional way, even crucial moments of decision: only hours before his twenty-four years must expire, Faustus must choose between the Old Man and Mephistopheles, between the (unseen) 'vial full of precious grace' and the (fully visible) dagger of Despair (5.1.52–5).[34] These signs – as well as the second signing in blood which follows ('And with my blood again I will confirm / My former vow I made to Lucifer', 5.1.72–3) – are quite transparent, able to be read through conventionally and unambiguously.

Yet although the new way of seeing was called upon directly only at scattered moments and in response to particular visual signs, it exerts a more general influence upon the audience's experience of the play. In making sense of what they saw, the early spectators were led to take notice of two different but intersecting worlds which frame the action: one where the signs (both visual and verbal) can be 'read' easily and where the traditional universe is both recognised and affirmed; the other where signs are confused and arbitrary. For much of the play their attention is held by the latter. Faustus is not alone in a deceptive and unstable world. The spectators are repeatedly made aware of the consequences of his actions, but they are also invited to share in his perspectives and are distracted by a stage busy with clowning and magic, with parody and spectacle. They join with the Students and Faustus in admiring Helen; they watch, enjoined to 'dumb silence', as the elaborate dumb show of Alexander unfolds to the accompaniment of music and trumpets; they stare, in some trepidation perhaps, as 'shagge-hayr'd Devills runne roaring over the Stage with Squibs in their mouthes, while Drummers make Thunder in the Tyring-house, and the twelve-penny Hirelings make artificiall Lightning in their Heavens' (Melton 31). The action of the play encourages the audience to set aside explication for experience, to share in the theatrical excitement, to be distracted by shows that, they are told, 'delight the mind'.[35]

How spectators will eventually make sense of their experience is far less straightforward than in earlier plays such as *The Three Ladies of London* or even in many other contemporary plays. They will be swayed to a greater or lesser degree by the play's shaping rhetoric of deflation, constantly directing their attention to the inevitability of failure, loss, and damnation. They may linger in the world of arbitrary signs and 'enjoy the show'; or they may return to the world of traditional signs with the second bond-signing and (in the B-text version) the throne let down from the 'heavens' and the hell-mouth pushed on to the platform. They may – or they may not – discover in these signs and spectacles an educative purpose, whether this involves some conventional moral lesson (as the apologists for playing would maintain) or leads – by 'watching characters watch the magician's and the devil's theatrical shows' – to an interrogation of the spectacle (Diehl, *Staging Reform* 77).

Rethinking the emblematic

None of the usual critical approaches to the emblematic in late sixteenth-century drama accounts sufficiently for what happens in the popular drama before 1595 and, more particularly, in Marlowe's plays. The explanation in terms of traditional survivals helps us to understand the conventional functions of visual signs and the expectations of early audiences; its emphasis on continuities, however, often means a failure to recognise the special nature of the emblematic in late sixteenth-century cultural practice, including the popular play. The explanation in terms of iconography recovers unfamiliar meanings for modern readers; yet it often does not distinguish between potential meanings and those activated in performance, nor does it come to terms with change. The explanation in terms of reformed religion does identify some change in ways of seeing; its perspectives, even so, are restrictive, and it does not take into account other kinds of change, nor the proliferation of secular signs at the same time that the iconoclasts were endeavouring to exclude the visual from worship.

Some of the difficulty with these three approaches arises from their definitions of the emblematic, and the inadequacies that result when they attempt to describe audience response. In his comprehensive review of emblem studies in both dramatic and non-dramatic literature James S. Dees (415–16) remarks that they have generally avoided thinking too precisely about the nature of emblem or the emblematic. He notes that many discussions simply follow Rosemary Freeman's classic study of English emblem-books and assume a disjunction between word and picture. In drama this notion is often extended to require a breach between verbal and visual elements, or between emblem and narrative action. Most comments on theatrical response to the emblematic have in consequence been too reductive, arguing from the assumed 'nature' of emblem to a response that is typically ambivalent or detached – rather than allowing for the processes of viewing and interpreting.[36] Arguing a disjunction between speech and spectacle ignores the intense emotional impact of many straightforward, traditional uses of the emblematic, whether we look to instances in earlier plays or consider ones from Marlowe and Shakespeare.[37] It also offers too simple a view of how more complex emblems of the kind found in Marlowe's plays construct theatrical experience. When Tamburlaine speaks above the dying Cosroe (the instance is discussed by Belsey, *Subject of Tragedy* 29–30), the disparities are to be found not merely between speech and spectacle but also within the spectacle (the familiar complementary ironies of Fortune), and within the set-speech itself. It is the shaping of all these disparities by the play's distinctive rhetoric, however, that establishes the way spectators will view and make sense of the scene.

The bond-signing in *Faustus* perhaps elicits a response closer to the ambivalence suggested by Belsey and others, but that too over-simplifies. In 'seeing double' and processing the visual signs in two different ways, the spectators become aware of two levels or kinds of experience, without necessarily being conscious of or articulating any conflict between them, and without necessarily adopting a double perspective on the action. Their response need not be characterised as the 'radical uncertainty' suggested by Belsey, which is generated 'precisely by withholding from the spectator the single position from which a single and unified meaning is produced' (*Subject of Tragedy* 29). What the rhetoric of the bond-signing provides for a spectator is the possibility of choosing one's own individual viewing point. The role of interpreter is, in effect, handed from text to spectator, who may then make sense of the action in terms of the traditional psychomachia perhaps, or in terms of the 'liberal humanist' subject, or in terms of something else entirely.

Whatever the spectator may choose, the response is not necessarily detached or, for that matter, engaged.

Whether these new ways of processing visual signs are also distinctively 'Protestant' may well be a matter of definition. Siemon suggests that in approaching the Eucharist the Reformers 'insisted upon the active role of human consciousness in determining the significance of object or event' (59); and this 'active role' has affinities with that suggested above for the audience watching *Faustus*. Others have looked to Reformist suspicion of visual signs. Huston Diehl suggests that both Protestant ritual and Renaissance play foster 'a distrust of externals': the new 'mode of seeing' is 'skeptical' and 'self-reflexive' but also 'receptive to the capacity of signs, in conjunction with spoken words, to move, persuade, and transform' ('Observing the Lord's Supper' 151). This recognition of the rhetorical power of signs accords with the new uses of signs in *Tamburlaine* and *Faustus*; and instances abound of late sixteenth-century spectators being expected to distrust spectacle and become aware of their own spectating.

And yet, this defining of change in terms of Reformist notions offers too limited an account of the rhetoric of visual signs on the playhouse stage. Traditional signs and seeing had always accommodated the ambiguous and illusory. Traditional drama had expected its audiences to be 'aware', expected them also to be suspicious of worldly display – as appropriate, and certainly in the case of tyrannical figures like Cambises or Judge Apius. Indeed iconoclasm itself is a more complex movement than often realised. In one sense it is the fulfilment of a long tradition of scepticism about – and at times vehement opposition towards – visual signs. In another, it reflects a general epistemological change: a realignment in processing the visual, in the ways that the sixteenth century saw and made sense of signs. Hence iconoclasm may not be so much the catalyst of change, but a development that parallels changes in the rhetoric of visual signs. And it is of course the simply visual, the 'unmediated' element in Faustus's experience rather than any intervention by words, which offers the early audiences something least traditional, which provides the 'newest' challenge for the spectators of these plays. In the rhetoric of visual signs it is not new theology that matters, but new ways of viewing the sign.

The major dramatic emblems of Marlowe's plays called upon their early audiences to set aside old habits and 'see' differently. They remind us that we too need to look afresh, especially in our narratives of visual signs in Renaissance drama. My concern here has been less with the conventional meanings of signs than with changes to ordinary experience – in particular, to the ways that spectators in the playhouse might perceive and interpret visual signs. What sixteenth-century playtexts indicate is that – despite all the new 'thinking' in the sixteenth century, despite any new attitudes to visual signs – traditional habits of perceiving and making sense persisted. And despite any new ways of seeing visual signs that may have emerged in, or been encouraged by, devotional writings or lyric poetry or even the sophisticated drama of the court, it is not until about 1590 that the rhetoric of the popular drama begins to draw upon a cultural readiness to process visual signs in a radical, 'modern' way, as arbitrary rather than transparent.

Of the changes this involves in the drama, the plays of Marlowe offer notable – and early – examples. Their challenges to the old ways of making sense developed out of their exploitation of the traditional rhetoric of visual signs. The complex dramatic emblems of *Tamburlaine* and later plays call upon the audience to do more than read through and recognise conventional meanings. They make possible new uses for the emblematic in the popular drama, expanding the dramatic functions of the emblematic beyond the choric and allegorical, and shifting its emphasis from the didactic and informative to the persuasive and affective. A few emblems in *Doctor Faustus* and *Edward II* achieve an even more radical change in the ways that spectators might process visual signs, marking an important point of cultural transition. These instances may retain conventional iconography and still appeal to a truth beyond signs, but they also refocus audience attention on those signs as images of individual, non-representative experience. Their appeal to a double processing of signs, to a double vision of the action, opened up possibilities for the emblematic which were to be exploited in later Shakespearean plays. Their visual rhetoric is the key to the difference – especially for audience experience – between Hieronymo's bloody handkerchief and Macbeth's bloody dagger; between the penitent Duchess of Gloucester, barefoot on the flinty road, and the penitent Lady Macbeth, washing her hands; between the sight of his Lords kneeling to Marlowe's Edward and that of Lear, clad in new garments, kneeling to Cordelia. By exploiting the allegorical potential of visual signs for other, non-allegorical purposes, the dramatic emblems of Marlowe's plays broke the link for spectators between the visual sign and traditional perspectives and values.

CHAPTER 4

Lessons of history

———

'A manifest signe'

When Marlowe died, the manner of his death was seized upon by sundry moralisers as an exemplum of poetic justice. They included Thomas Beard, whose version of the event is recorded in *The Theatre of God's Judgements*, first printed 1597.[1] Beard's account is of interest not merely for its errors and distortions and aggressive self-righteousness but also for the way it uses the exemplum. This manner of use brings into focus a distinctive, conventional rhetoric which is called upon, and then challenged, in Edward's death by poker. How that challenge works provides an insight into Marlowe's refashioning of response to the cautionary tale. Like the emblematic the exemplum was enmeshed, in the theatre as else-where, in traditional habits of viewing and interpreting. And as happens with the emblematic, the changes that matter are those that occur at the level of theatrical experience, where spectators see and feel and make sense.

Beard includes Marlowe among his exemplars of 'Epicures and Atheists'; he is allotted a place alongside such 'continental mirrors of iniquity' as Pope Julius II and Rabelais (Maclure 4). Beard sketches Marlowe's career (scholar, playmaker, and 'a Poet of scurrilitie'), before indicating the causes of his downfall ('giving too large a swinge to his owne wit, and suffering his lust to have the full raines'), and the nature of his 'outrage and extremitie': blasphemy both spoken and written. Beard lingers on the sensational details: the denial of God; the books 'affirming our Saviour to be but a deceiver, and *Moses* to be but a conjurer and seducer of the people, and the holy Bible to be but vaine and idle stories, and all religion but a device of pollicie'. Retribution is at hand:

But see what a hooke the Lord put in the nosthrils of this barking dogge:
It so fell out, that in London streets as he purposed to stab one whome
hee ought a grudge unto with his dagger, the other party perceiving so
avoided the stroke, that withall catching hold of his wrest, he stabbed his
owne dagger into his owne head, in such sort, that notwithstanding all
the meanes of surgerie that could be wrought, hee shortly after died
thereof. The manner of his death being so terrible (for hee even cursed
and blasphemed to his last gaspe, and togither with his breath an oth
flew out of his mouth) that it was not only a manifest signe of Gods
judgement, but also an horrible and fearefull terrour to all that beheld
him. But herein did the justice of God most notably appeare, in that hee
compelled his owne hand which had written those blasphemies to be the
instrument to punish him, and that in his braine, which had devised the
same. I would to God (and I pray it from my heart) that all Atheists in
this realme, and in all the world beside, would by the remembrance and
consideration of this example, either forsake their horrible impietie, or
that they might in like manner come to destruction: and so that abom-
inable sinne which so flourisheth amongst men of greatest name, might
either be quite extinquished and rooted out, or at least smothered and
kept under, that it durst not shew it head any more in the worlds eye.
(Beard 147–8)

Beard's account belongs to a tradition of popular writing that has
its antecedents in the preaching of medieval friars (Wimsatt 141)
and, in the playhouse itself, contemporary parallels in such plays as
A Looking Glass for London and England. Sixteenth-century audiences were familiar with cautionary tales, familiar too with the
rhetorical strategies their tellers employed. Beard's exemplum illustrates a number of these. For all his suspicion of the theatre, his
account is none the less incorrigibly dramatic. In inviting his readers
to respond piously, he also calls upon them to feel intensely, to
participate in this 'theatre of God's judgements'. The language is
vigorously emotional, the commentary marked by statement and
restatement – 'I would to God (and I pray it from my heart)'. The
details of the incident can readily be visualised, the readers called
upon to share the viewpoint of 'all that beheld him'. Their attention
is drawn to the details of the attack in the street, the catching hold
of the wrist, the hand wielding the dagger, the last-gasp cursing, the
whole 'horrible and fearefull terrour' of this 'manifest signe of Gods
judgement'.

But Beard stresses more than the theatrical and sensational
aspects of the event. The readers are also provided with a particular
interpretive narrative. The death is presented as exemplifying an
entirely appropriate justice: the hand 'which had written those blasphemies' is the instrument of punishment; the brain 'which had
devised the same' the site of mortal injury. In these connections,

Beard asserts, 'did the justice of God most notably appear'. What is more, the very horror this 'justice' evokes is seen not just as adding to the emotional impact of the incident but as, in some way, validating the lesson: 'The manner of his death being so terrible ... that it was not only a manifest signe of Gods judgement'. The closing comments apply the lesson: all atheists should learn from 'the remembrance and consideration of this example' – and if they do not, they should 'in like manner come to destruction'. Blasphemy, especially 'amongst men of greatest name', should be 'quite extinguished and rooted out, or at least smothered and kept under, that it durst not shew it head any more in the worlds eye'.

If we move from this version of a death to Marlowe's presentation of Edward's, we find elements that seem, initially at least, to echo the ways of perceiving and interpreting that are called upon by Beard:

> *Edward.*   But that grief keeps me waking, I should sleep;
>   For not these ten days have these eyes' lids closed.
>   Now as I speak they fall, and yet with fear
>   Open again. O wherefore sits thou here?
> *Lightborn.*   If you mistrust me, I'll be gone, my lord.
> *Edward.*   No, no, for if thou mean'st to murder me,
>   Thou wilt return again, and therefore stay.
> *Lightborn.*   He sleeps.
> *Edward.*   O let me not die! Yet stay, O stay a while.
> *Lightborn.*   How now, my lord?
> *Edward.*   Something still buzzeth in mine ears
>   And tells me if I sleep I never wake.
>   This fear is that which makes me tremble thus;
>   And therefore tell me, wherefore art thou come?
> *Lightborn.*   To rid thee of thy life. Matrevis, come!
> *Edward.*   I am too weak and feeble to resist.
>   Assist me, sweet God, and receive my soul.
> *Lightborn.*   Run for the table.
> *Edward.*   O spare me! Or dispatch me in a trice!
> *Lightborn.*   So, lay the table down, and stamp on it,
>   But not too hard, lest that you bruise his body.
> *Matrevis.*   I fear me that this cry will raise the town,
>   And therefore let us take horse and away.
> *Lightborn.*   Tell me, sirs, was it not bravely done?
> *Gurney.*   Excellent well. Take this for thy reward.
>
> *Then* GURNEY *stabs* LIGHTBORN.
>
> Come, let us cast the body in the moat,
> And bear the king's to Mortimer, our lord.
> Away!
>
>   (5.5.92–119)[2]

The death by poker could well have inspired in its spectators 'an horrible and fearefull terrour'. As in Beard's account, they are enjoined to see: here before them on stage are figures sitting, sleeping and waking, trembling, laying the table down, stamping and stabbing. They are enjoined to feel: here are 'grief' and 'fear' and 'murther', desperate pleas and prayers, and a 'cry' that may 'rouse the town'. The dramatic rhetoric of the death scene focuses their attention on its visual horror. The details of the killing are not, as some earlier commentators maintained, 'decently obscured, both in the dialogue and in the business' (H. Levin, *Overreacher* 124), but quite apparent to the spectators.[3] Edward is assassinated as he lies on a bed; and he has been lying there in view of the audience for the previous eighteen lines, alternating between sleep and waking, between fear and acceptance. The dialogue during the murder may be brief, but it is also generally consistent with the contemporary versions, such as Holinshed's (1587):

> they came suddenlie one night into the chamber where hee laie in bed fast asleepe, and with heavie feather beddes or a table (as some write) being cast upon him, they kept him down and withall put into his fundament an horne, and through the same they thrust up into his bodie a hote spitte, or (as other have) through the pipe of a trumpet a plumbers instrument of iron made verie hot, the which passing up into his intrailes, and being rolled to and fro, burnt the same, but so as no appearance of any wound or hurt outwardlie might be once perceived. (587)

In performance the terrible 'manner of his death' gains in impact from contrasts between sound and silence. During the murder itself, the dialogue is minimal. There is a pause while the table is being brought on stage and positioned on Edward, another to allow Matrevis and Gurney to climb on to the table; and (to maximise its theatrical effect) there may well be an extended silence after Edward's cry. The effect of these silences is to direct the spectators' attention to the visual. Indeed the most powerful images in the whole scene are of the stage rather than the words: the beating drum; the conversation in aside of Matrevis and Gurney on the fate of Lightborn; the light carried to the dungeon; the tattered robes of the King; the false tears of Lightborn and Edward's anxious searching of his face; the giving of the last token; Edward's involuntary trembling; Lightborn's sitting watch on the drowsy King; the business of table, featherbed, and poker; and then, after the two murders, the carrying off of the bodies, one perhaps unceremoniously ('let us cast the body in the moat'), the other, unmarked, carefully ('And bear the king's to Mortimer, our lord').

At the same time, there is also a sense of something staged, of a show organised by some supernatural agency – for spectators as much as jailers. As Karen Cunningham notes (215), the assassin calls attention to his performance by asking for applause: 'Tell me, sirs, was it not bravely done?' Like the readers of Beard, the spectators in the midst of their daily lives are confronted, it would seem, with the awesome evidence of supernatural intervention. The fearfulness of Edward's death is augmented by suggestions that he is being perse-cuted by the forces of evil, old and new: the figure of Lightborn hints at Lucifer (H. Levin, *Overreacher* 124) and morality Vice as well as Machiavel. References to hell and torture increase in the final section of the play. Though many of these are stereotyped images of suffering, as conventional as the earlier use of hell imagery to repre-sent the separation of lovers, they culminate in the spectacle of Edward's torment. In his last moments his experience becomes convincingly hell-like: the persecution by Lightborn and subsidiary fiends is both constant and gratuitous ('Send for him out thence, and I will anger him', 5.5.13); and Lightborn's 'braver way' is reminis-cent of the torments of hell found in medieval pictures, or as described by the Ghost of Andrea at the beginning of the *Spanish Tragedy*.

Edward's death is often cited as an exemplum of poetic justice, and perhaps many of the early spectators accepted it as a 'manifest signe'.[4] For the homosexual King, there is a grim appropriateness in the 'manner of his death' and the site of punishment. Earlier commentators pointed to traditional notions of hell and the punish-ment of sinners: 'That suffering and death should bear an appropriate relation to sins committed is a commonplace of mediae-val thought, theological, literary or aesthetic' (Merchant xxi). More recently, writers have drawn attention to public displays of 'justice' in Renaissance England and Europe: Karen Cunningham finds parallels for the instruments of death in the red-hot iron used in trial by ordeal, and in the 'pressing' used in the Tower to obtain confes-sions (219). But, unlike Beard's story, the play provides no immediate, dogmatic moralising, and critical opinion differs on how the death scene will affect an audience and what its implications might be for the play. Is Edward a deserving, or a hapless, victim? Will the spectators ('those that beheld him') accept the scene as a 'manifest signe' or, as Greenblatt and others have suggested, recoil 'in disgust' (*Renaissance Self-fashioning* 203) since the lesson is too abhorrent to be contemplated?[5]

In what ways does the death by poker illustrate, deny, or challenge providential order or political orthodoxy? The answers to these questions, I would suggest, lie not in modern theorising but in sixteenth-century rhetorical practice and theatrical experience. We need to recognise, first, that the horror of Edward's death is not necessarily the point at issue, even though many accounts of this scene locate its challenge to orthodoxy in that horror. Huston Diehl, for example, suggests that 'Marlowe brings into creative interplay the conventional message of the violent icon and the excruciating pain of the dying man, forcing his audience to confront the difference between the harsh, unrelenting sentence of divine justice and the pitiable suffering of a human being' ('Iconography of Violence' 43). But 'excruciating pain' may be witnessed by an audience without much distress. Barabas's agony in the cauldron is only one of the many possible examples. And horror, even with the consequent emotional shock, does not of itself produce a questioning of conventional values. This is shown in other plays of the period, where horrifying moments act (as Diehl also suggests) to reinforce some moral lesson.

Those who saw Edward's death by poker in the playhouse may also have purchased a copy of *Cambises* when it was reprinted in the late 1580s, and read about the flaying of Sisamnes in the presence of his son:

> *Smite him in the neck with a swoord to signify his death.*

> *Praxapes.*   Beholde (O king) how he dooth bleed, beeing of life bereft.
> *King.*   In this wise, he shall not yet be left.
>   Pul his skin over his eares, to make his death more vile:
>   A wretch he was, a cruel theef my commons to begile.

> *Flea him with a false skin.*

> *Otian.* What childe is he of natures mould, could bide the same to see
>   His Father fleaed in this wise? Oh how it greeveth me.
> (Cambises 460.1–466)

They may well have seen (or were soon to see) the deserved punishment of the wicked brothers Chiron and Demetrius in *Titus Andronicus* (5.2), where Titus cuts their throats and Lavinia catches the blood in a basin held between her 'stumps' (the brothers have earlier cut off her hands). The regular playgoer would have seen any number of bloody murders and bloody dismemberments, complete with bladders of blood or vinegar ('*A little bladder of Vineger prikt*', *Cambises* 726.1), dripping swords, scaffolds, and appropriate sound effects.[6] As the rhetoric of Beard's 'manifest signe' suggests, reacting with horror is an appropriate and quite conventional response to such cautionary tales. What is more, the sense of horror has both aesthetic and didactic satisfactions. Beard calls upon his readers to indulge in the pleasures of participating in the sensational – as well as the pleasures of self-righteousness. In the death by poker Marlowe draws upon both of these expected, conventional responses. When, like Beard, he exaggerates the horror of the scene, this could be just another exercise in the sensational, providing the audience with the excitements of the playhouse they had paid to see. The audience, as in Beard's 'theatre' of judgements, expected to have its emotions strongly stirred. But, in such cautionary tales, the horror of the event is also its implicit authentication; and the stronger the emotional response, the more cogent the moral lesson.

And yet, even if we discount the violence and horror as routine accompaniments to the cautionary tale, the problem remains. Edward's death has an impact different from that of other deserved deaths in sixteenth-century plays. No one grieves for Cambises or Richard III or Barabas, and it is only a wicked, adulterous Queen who will lament for Suffolk (*2 Henry VI*) or Mortimer (*Edward II*) or the Guise (*Massacre at Paris*). The death by poker is more disturbing and challenging in performance than the deaths of any of these; and that is something which the rhetoric of Beard is insufficient to explain. Its impact is not primarily a matter of unconventional or novel or sensational ideas. What happens in Edward's death scene, and in the final scene of the play, is a radical change in the way that audiences are enabled to respond to a cautionary tale.

The exemplary tradition

We can appreciate the extent of that change in exemplary rhetoric by viewing the death by poker in the context of traditional practice. Though this is not a new approach, it is usually pursued too narrowly, and with reference more to the conventional values associated with the exemplary method than to its rhetorical possibilities. Stephen Greenblatt, for example, locates the cautionary tale at the heart of sixteenth-century cultural practices. He points to the 'culturally dominant' view that 'recurrent patterns exist in the history of individuals or nations in order to inculcate crucial moral values', with literature taking its place as 'part of a vast, interlocking system of repetitions, embracing homilies and hangings, royal progresses and rote learning' (*Renaissance Self-fashioning* 201). This comment is useful in pointing to the exemplary as a way of interpreting as well as a way of teaching; it adopts, however, too restrictive a view. The cautionary tale itself is but one form of the exemplum, and the exemplum is not limited to inculcating obedience to hierarchy or providence. To define what happens to the caution- ary tale in *Edward II*, we need to adopt a wider perspective, to look beyond cautionary tales to the exemplum generally. Marlowe by no means rejects the exemplary method (as many critics maintain); he does, nevertheless, redirect its rhetoric to serve different theatrical purposes. To understand this, we need to clarify what the use of exempla entailed for sixteenth-century writers and playgoers.

What was the 'exemplum'?[7] As with the 'emblematic', we should distinguish between different applications of the term. As a device of traditional rhetoric, the exemplum is a particular instance that illus- trates some general 'truth' (the truth will be relevant to the particular text, but not necessarily its overall 'message'). In literary and other discourse before Marlowe, the exemplum took a variety of forms. For the medieval preacher, the exemplum had been an anecdote used to give point and colour to the sermon (much of this sense survives in works such as Beard's). For the sixteenth-century student of rhetoric, it could be a fable, proverb, parable, or narra- tive used in the interests of *copia* to develop a theme (Donker and Muldrow 59).[8] Then, as Puttenham comments of 'historicall Poesie': 'no kinde of argument in all the Oratorie craft, doth better perswade and more universally satisfie then example ... to behold as it were in a glasse the lively image of our deare forefathers, their noble and vertuous maner of life' (39).[9] Translated into dramatic terms, the exemplum could take the form of an anecdote or description, a passage of action, a ceremony, even a dramatic emblem (from one perspective, the dramatic emblem is simply a kind of exemplum). The significance of the exempla in a play might be announced by a Prologue or Chorus, or developed by commentary and motto.

The exemplum was also the building block of thought. In perfor- mance, the exempla provided the spectators with structures of interpretation: specific ways for them to make sense of what they saw. The ways of seeing they called upon were essentially the same as those assumed in the traditional uses of the emblematic. Like the visual sign, the particular instance acquired value only in so far as it made manifest some concept or general rule. It could be 'read through' to reveal eternal 'truths' about the universe or, by exten- sion, about social experience or political behavour or human nature; and these truths were often referred to in authorised versions of the action or show. Like the visual sign, the exemplum drew upon a shared understanding of the 'obvious': what is 'good'; what is 'important'; or how someone 'ought' to behave. Like the visual sign, then, the exemplum was conventionally associated with traditional or received values; but, like the visual sign too, the exemplum might be interpreted variously.

When the 1580s playgoers entered the playhouse, they expected to make sense of the action by identifying the exempla, and then reading through them to some received wisdom. That had been their experience, and not only while attending plays. Many instances of the exemplum on stage were overtly exemplary in the tradition of 'mirror' literature: they established an image of the ideal, of 'what should be', or provided a warning or caution.[10] The early play *Cambises* is a collection of such cautionary tales. Using the skin of the corrupt Sisamnes for a seat-cover is not just an exercise in regal cruelty but also a salutary lesson to future judges. The incident exemplifies proper justice, and even Sisamnes's own son agrees: 'O King, to me this is a glasse, with greef in it I view: / Example that unto your grace, I doo not prove untrue' (469–70). When Cambises shoots the son of Praxapes through the heart, or has Murder and Crueltie kill his own brother, the incidents exemplify tyranny. The moralising comments are usually brief but on each occasion the spectators are left in no doubt of the lessons to be drawn.[11]

The exemplary element is still strong in the popular drama between 1585 and 1595, as seen in Lodge and Greene's *A Looking Glass for London and England*. In this version of the biblical story, the wickedness of Nineveh – demonstrated in plenty of sensational detail – and the repentance of its inhabitants are used to provide a warning for the sinful city of London, place of 'Corruption, whordome, drunkennesse, and pride'. The prophet Oseas watches the action from a place above. He is '*set down over the Stage in a Throne*' (p. 133), interrupting every few scenes to sum up the exempla of wickedness and draw parallels with life in London: 'London, take heed, these sinnes abound in thee' (p. 145); 'Pride hath his judgement, London looke about, / Tis not inough in show to be devout' (p. 153); and so on. The play ends with the prophet Jonas proclaiming its exemplary message:

London awake, for feare the Lord do frowne,
I set a looking Glasse before thine eyes.
O turne, O turne, with weeping to the Lord.

(p. 232)

Other instances were perhaps not so much 'mirrors' as simply choric, relating what happened on stage to some point of conventional wisdom or (as with many dramatic emblems) to eternal truths beyond the action. Certain themes were presented on stage repeatedly, challenging the inventiveness of playwright and player alike. Thus any of the various representations of Fortune could serve to demonstrate the frailty of earthly glory. In the years immediately before the humiliation of the king in *Edward II* – itself presented in a whole series of exempla – there were a number of spectacular exempla of great men suffering a reversal of fortune: the Viceroy of Portugal prostrate on the stage platform, grieving for his son (*Spanish Tragedy* 1.3); Richard Duke of York wearing a paper crown and enthroned on a molehill (*3 Henry VI* 1.4); and, not least, the emperor Bajazeth lamenting his confinement in the iron cage. Instances such as these accommodate new stories or dramatic materials to old habits of seeing. Their restating of moral and political commonplaces calls upon audiences to recognise – and reinforces a shared sense of – the way things 'are'.

In most sixteenth-century plays the exemplum was the key to organising theatrical experience, to shaping interpretation and response. In many moralities, for instance, the action is little more than a series of exempla illustrating the play's thesis (Dessen, *Late Moral Plays* 135). Elsewhere, the exemplum is used to provide an occasion for debate, and the play becomes a series of lengthy discussions. The rhetorical function of exempla as the building blocks of persuasion meant that interpretations might well differ, or that an exemplum might be detached from its context to 'prove' a different point. Many of the plays of the 1580s and early 1590s have an episodic narrative structure, with periodic pauses to debate the exempla that arise in the narrative. In the years just before *Edward II*, debates flourished on the interpretation of exempla, especially in plays dealing with historical and political subjects.[12] In *The Troublesome Reign of John, King of England* (staged late 1580s, printed 1591), '*five moons appear*' at the moment of John's crowning; they are interpreted by characters first as ominous, then as auspicious, but always with patent political bias (*2 Troublesome Reign* 1665–717). Other notable instances are found in Shakespeare's early plays about English history, with their disputes in gardens and council chambers and on battlefields. The second act of *2 Henry VI* presents in scene after scene an extended series of exempla showing the goodness and wisdom of Humphrey Duke of Gloucester, exempla which are debated – but finally interpreted awry by his enemies to serve their own ends. For all this, however, these disputes seldom offer any real challenge to conventional moral and political wisdom; as the fate of Humphrey demonstrates, different characters may interpret events in different ways, but the spectators are left in no doubt where the 'truth' lies.[13]

The exemplum not only suggested to spectators how to think but also notified them how to feel. Exemplary rhetoric was concerned with eliciting appropriate emotions as much as with guiding them to appropriate judgement. This is apparent in Beard's account of Marlowe's death or in the scenes that precede Edward's. The appeal to emotion was often quite explicit: 'My heart with pity earns to see this sight', comments the Abbot on the capture of Edward, 'A king to bear these words and proud commands' (*Edward* 4.7.70–1). When the English hero Talbot dies on a battlefield in France, holding his dead, heroic son in his arms, the spectators' attention is directed first to the humiliation and waste of death (Talbot, says the Pucelle, lies 'Stinking and fly-blown ... here at our feet'), then to the 'proud commanding spirit' Talbot has represented: 'from their ashes shall be rear'd / A phoenix that shall make all France afeard' (*1 Henry VI* 4.7.76, 88, 92–3). The contemporary response to the staging of Talbot's death is recorded by Thomas Nashe in *Pierce Penilesse*. Even allowing for some over-statement, the account testifies to a considerable – and appropriate – emotional impact:

> How would it have joyed brave *Talbot* (the terror of the French) to thinke that after he had lyne two hundred yeares in his Tombe, hee should triumphe againe on the Stage, and have his bones newe embalmed with the teares of ten thousand spectators at least, (at severall times) who in the Tragedian that represents his person, imagine they behold him fresh bleeding. (87)

To Nashe, the exemplary message of this and other incidents from the 'English Chronicles' was clear: 'what', he asks with feeling, 'can be a sharper reproofe to these degenerate effeminate dayes of ours'?

A 'troublesome reign'

Marlowe's refashioning of the cautionary tale begins with *Tamburlaine*. It develops from that reorientation of theatrical approach foreshadowed in the Prologue to Part One: from didactic to persuasive, from the lessons that confirm conventional wisdom to the sights and sounds of performance. In prologue and emblem the *Tamburlaine* plays challenge the mirror tradition. The major emblems or exempla displace conventional meanings by rhetorical ones. They exploit the tensions that develop between the 'expected' response and the 'rhetorical' one, between, for example, the anxieties called forth by the *de casibus* tradition and the appeal for admiration. At the same time, the plays employ an exemplary method of construction. They contain many exempla which, taken individually, fulfil the conventional expectations of the audience; and this is especially so of the subsidiary action with figures such as Cosroe or Theridamus or Callapine. In sequence, even so, the familiar messages tend to be overwhelmed by the conqueror's rhetoric of redefinition.[14]

What happens at the end of *Edward II* is, however, a far more radical change in the construction of theatrical experience. *Edward II* is 'new' in the context of the early 1590s rather than, as with *Tamburlaine* Part One, in the context of the playhouse of 1587. By the time *Edward II* was devised, about five years after *Tamburlaine*, much of what had been innovative in *Tamburlaine* had itself become quite conventional. *Edward II* is new in its own way, conducting its own dialogue on the one hand with the tradition of exemplary rhetoric and on the other with that significant group of contemporary plays usually labelled as 'histories', most of which were themselves conducting their own dialogue with *Tamburlaine*. In particular, it defines itself against two early plays of Shakespeare: *2 Henry VI* and *3 Henry VI*. Their influence can be seen in the play's glimpses of a providentialist framework and in its proliferation of ironic contrasts.[15] Of course, neither of these elements is essentially new. The providentialist frame informs all drama before 1587 and nearly all thereafter; its revitalised form in the early 1590s is in many ways a response to the humanist hero-king of plays such as *Tamburlaine* (Riggs 33; J. Shapiro 86). And though the early histories of Shakespeare effectively exploit the disparities between what 'is' and what 'should be', the sense of an imperfect world was always an important element in the popular tradition. The late moralities, in particular, cultivated ironic contrasts in their many demonstrations of social abuses.

In the action before the death by poker Marlowe draws upon the conventional uses of the exemplum. The effect is largely to establish a certain pattern of expectations, which is then exploited in the death scene. This, the exempla suggest, is an exemplary history, and the spectators are to make sense of the action in terms of some stable set of traditional values. As in other history plays of the time, the action is much concerned with issues that were the commonplaces of contemporary political discussion. Edward's kingdom is shown as suffering from the disruptive forces of lust, ambition, and pride (like the kingdom of Henry VI). Edward's failings as king are attributed to the standard causes, such as the influence of evil counsellors and flatterers (much the same is urged against Richard II). At various times, the characters rehearse the standard justifications for and arguments against rebellion – appealing to heaven, to justice, to tradition, to the good of the realm, and even to the successful use of armed force. As the 1598 title-page suggests, the careers of Edward, Gaveston, and Mortimer serve to illustrate different versions of *de casibus* tragedy, with its conventional warnings against setting too high a value upon earthly glory: 'The troublesome raigne and lamentable death of Edward the second, King of England: with the tragicall fall of proud Mortimer: And also the life and death of Peirs Gaveston, the great Earle of Cornewall, and mighty favorite of king Edward the second'. When Edward 'falls', there is a whole series of choric commentaries on the reversal of fortune: by Edward himself, Leicester, the Abbot, and Edward's friends (4.7). For all this lamenting, however, the suffering is representative, the sentiments routine.

As in other contemporary plays, the exempla of political order and disorder in *Edward II* can be read through as referring to a system of providential and hierarchical values; in particular, the play's visual language reinforces the sense of an underlying order. As Fleischer points out, early performances of the play drew upon the visual vocabulary of royal power common to plays of the period.[16] The play's 'image of perfectly functioning government' (Fleischer 33) is that moment in the fourth scene when Edward is reconciled with the nobles, and the reconciliation is sealed by their kneeling to the King, as one by one they are assigned a special place in the restored 'order' (1.4.336–66). Queen Isabella calls upon the audience to recognise the conventional message of the scene: 'Now is the king of England rich and strong, / Having the love of his renownèd peers' (1.4.365–6). Other instances invoke traditional values even as they exemplify political disorder: when Edward shares his throne with Gaveston (1.4.8–34), the barons respond with assorted allusions to other reversals of order ('*Quam male conveniunt*'; 'ignoble vassal, that like Phaethon'; 'Can kingly lions fawn on creeping ants?').[17] The confrontation is conducted in terms that call the audience's attention to the ideal hierarchical order that is being breached:

> *Edward.*   Were he a peasant, being my minion,
>   I'll make the proudest of you stoop to him.
> *Lancaster.*   My lord, you may not thus disparage us.
>
> (1.4.30–2)

Here the structures of the language ('I'll make', 'you may not') and its terms ('peasant', 'stoop', 'my lord', 'disparage') underline the issues of rank and hierarchy. King and barons may disagree, but the exemplum directs attention to traditional values as the standard by which their actions are to be judged.[18]

Several commentators have stressed the ironic contrast between these ceremonies and perspectives and most of the action. J. R. Mulryne and Stephen Fender suggest that Marlowe dramatises 'a gap between (on the one hand) all the official positions, the public motives, the apparent universal order, and (on the other hand) all the private prejudices, the selfish motives, the real universal chaos' (62). But this ironic contrast is quite consistent with the conventions of 'mirror' literature, which usually offered more patterns to avoid than to emulate. *Edward II* has brief moments of ceremony and whole scenes of disorder; but in this it differs little from a play such as *3 Henry VI* with its brawling between royal factions. Indeed, the conventional contrast – with its complementary rather than subversive ironies – is intensified by the way in which most of the ceremonial moments are set apart from the narrative, almost in a sense detachable like the exempla of a school text. Isabella's choric comment on the tableau of reconciliation, 'Now is the King of England rich and strong' (1.4.365–6), expresses entirely conventional sentiments. Her speech refers directly to what is seen on stage at that moment, and is only indirectly relevant to the preceding action with its dissembling and confrontations. The audience may forget, for the moment, her recent deceits and conspiracies. In a similar way, the various commentaries in the capture and abdication scenes refer more specifically to the immediate stage pictures and their exempla of abasement and humiliation than to the scenes they follow or precede: the specious political rhetoric of Isabella's victory (4.5) and the machinations of Mortimer (5.2).

Before the scene of Edward's death, then, the exempla of the play call upon quite conventional ways of seeing. And the death by poker itself appears at first to function as one of the series, fulfilling the pattern of expectation and response that earlier exempla have encouraged. Where they offered instances typifying various political commonplaces, this, in presenting an extreme version of the fall from high estate, also suggests another traditional notion for an audience to recognise: that sins are, or should be, punished appropriately. That lesson is supported by what a number of writers identify as symmetries of structure: inversions and parallels which link action near the end of the play with that earlier (Deats,

'Marlowe's Symmetry'). If we consider Edward's homosexual love, then physical sin is shown to be matched by physical punishment. The emphasis upon the sensual and physical in the love of Edward and Gaveston – Isabella complains that the King 'claps his cheeks and hangs about his neck, / Smiles in his face and whispers in his ears' (1.2.51–2) – is paralleled by the emphasis upon physical suffering and the assault on the senses in Edward's final scenes. The connection is sustained by visual reminders in the death scene of the gestures of love. Giving and embracing are hinted at in the handing over of the jewel and in Lightborn's nearness to the reclining King – 'O wherefore sits thou here?' (5.5.95) – and there is also Edward's gesture to prevent Lightborn from moving: 'Yet stay, O stay a while!' (100).[19]

Yet what the spectators are called upon to notice is something more than a story of homosexual love. Edward's love for Gaveston is shown to affect his behaviour as king; it typifies his wilfulness and irresponsibility even more than his sensuality. The audience is frequently reminded that Edward himself has brought about the disintegration of his kingdom. He suffers for his political sins; and the events of the final section demonstrate the appropriateness of that suffering by presenting a series of contrasts between past and present. The confirmation of Edward's kingly power in the scene of reconciliation with the nobles becomes visible loss of that power in the abdication; his arrogance in triumph becomes humiliation in defeat; his wilfulness with his court becomes submission to the whims of his sadistic jailers. The play's accumulated ironies ensure that Edward's present is continually haunted by his past: his final message to Isabel, with its fragmentary memory of being her champion at a tournament long ago, revives the picture of a king who once spared no expense to organise 'a general tilt and tournament', whose soldiers 'marched like players' while he appeared with 'spangled crest, / Where women's favours hung like labels down' (2.2.185–6) – and who has long since discarded the Queen. The deaths that follow Edward's – Lightborn's in response to the riddling message he carries ('Pereat iste'), Mortimer's from betrayal by his own instrument, 'false Gurney' – continue to hold out to the audience the prospect of poetic justice.

The weight of the play's action – its ironies of structure, the values implicit in its exempla – could well suggest that the audience should accept Edward's death as a 'manifest signe'. And probably many of its early spectators did so, making sense of the play in terms of poetic justice and accepting the horrific action as validating the message.

But this exemplum defies any simple reading through. To understand how it changes the way that spectators might see the action,
how, in effect, it makes it possible for them to cast their theatrical
experience adrift from moralising generalities, we need to consider
the dramatic rhetoric of the death and final scenes. In these Marlowe
challenges the tradition of exemplary rhetoric, first by presenting a
new kind of dramatic experience that suggests cautionary tales are
irrelevant, and then by subverting the young king's attempt to
impose an 'authorised version'.

Refashioning the cautionary tale

The particular impact of the death scene arises from an attempt to
present extremes of feeling. In this it follows, but transcends, its
contemporaries. The playhouse drama of the late 1580s and early
1590s was much concerned to exploit the emotions of its audience.
This was especially so in connection with cautionary tales. In the
three *Henry VI* plays, for example, there are few rational discussions
but plenty of harrowing death scenes complete with exemplary
messages. That of Talbot in Part One has been mentioned above,
with Nashe's description of its effect on 'ten thousand spectators, at
least'. One especially horrific death in a chain of killings is the ritual
stabbing on stage of the Prince, heir to Henry VI, by the three venge-
ful sons of York (King Edward, Richard of Gloucester, and George
of Clarence). Their actions mimic the killing of Caesar, but the
difference is brutal, as Queen Margaret laments:

> O Ned, sweet Ned, speak to thy mother, boy!
> Canst thou not speak? O traitors! murderers!
> They that stabb'd Caesar shed no blood at all,
> Did not offend, nor were not worthy blame,
> If this foul deed were by to equal it.
> He was a man; this, in respect, a child;
> And men ne'er spend their fury on a child.
>
> (*3 Henry VI* 5.5.49–55)

This is ironically (of course) the same Queen Margaret who has
incited the ritual murder of York, not long after he described her as
having a 'tiger's heart wrapp'd in a woman's hide' (1.4.137) when
she gives him a napkin stained with the blood of his other son, the
young Rutland – the victim of another piece of on-stage butchery. As
moments like these suggest, exemplary incidents in these plays – and
for that matter in other contemporary plays such as the anonymous
Arden of Faversham or *Troublesome Reign* – exhibit a notable lack

of restraint in either visual or verbal rhetoric. They exploit the Senecan rhetoric of Kyd and the 'mighty line' of *Tamburlaine* to persuade audiences to experience intensely, even as they see and feel appropriately.

The same stirring of conventional passions in the audience is evident in many scenes in *Edward II*, but especially in the sequence of action from capture to ritual shaving that precedes the death scene. The emphasis here is upon Edward's fall from high estate and the acute suffering that ensues – largely irrespective of any earlier exempla showing the king's foolish or wilful or even resolute behaviour. As in other contemporary plays there is little restraint in word or action. Edward's reactions to his reversal of fortune are conveyed in exaggerated gestures: 'Here, man, rip up this panting breast of mine' (4.7.66); '*The* King *rageth*' (5.1.85.1); 'Well may I rend his name that rends my heart!' (5.1.140); 'unbowel straight this breast' (5.3.10). These actions are accompanied by verbal language that is both highly emotional and frequently uninspired. It is a language that lacks precision, being concerned to evoke a response of unthinking and unfocused pity. There are repeated references to 'lamentation' and 'grief', to 'distress' and 'despair', to 'torment' and 'murder' and 'death'. Edward's soul is 'cloyed' by 'outrageous passions' (5.1.19); he is reluctant to yield the crown, since it is his one comfort when his mind is filled 'with strange despairing thoughts, / Which thoughts are martyrèd with endless torments' (79–80). The verbal imagery of his suffering is likewise extreme: his mind is preoccupied with bleeding and stony hearts; he speaks of prisons and caves and dungeons, of tigers and wolves, and of the lion that 'rends and tears' flesh when it is already 'gored' (5.1.11–12). And then even when Edward is seen to accept his suffering, his commentary could perhaps best be described as platitudinous. His mind – it would seem – is limited to the commonplace and clichéd: 'Well that shall be, shall be' (4.7.94); 'but of this I am assured, / That death ends all, and I can die but once' (5.1.152–3); 'For me, both thou [Gaveston] and both the Spencers died, / And for your sakes a thousand wrongs I'll take' (5.3.42–3). There is little indeed in the 'fall' sequence to challenge conventional sentiments or ways of thinking.[20]

After all this vigorous but conventional lamentation the death scene calls upon the audience to see differently: to focus upon Edward's individual, non-representative experience. The death by poker is different from exempla earlier in the play in its redirection of the spectators' attention from the moral lesson to the moments of experience. The effect is even more pronounced than it is in the bond-signing in *Faustus*. Instead of attending to the lesson, the spectators are first distracted, and then absorbed, by the spectacle of the King's suffering. In directing audience attention to these details, the death by poker sets up responses that run counter to the expectations aroused by the previous action of the play – and ultimately counter to any 'moral' lessons. The conventional pattern of responses is disrupted, the exemplary rhetoric fractured. No longer restrained by appeals to the wisdom of commonplaces, the sense of horror overflows.

The shift in focus begins not long before the actual death. From the moment the jailers Matrevis and Gurney enter, words and action confront the spectators with particular, rather than representative, experience. Their attention is compelled by a moment-by-moment account of sensations: the 'mire and puddle', the beating drum, the stifling 'savour' of the dungeon, the loss of coherence, the physical and emotional exhaustion. The verbal language changes to a profusion of concrete, sensuous imagery:

Matrevis.   Gurney, I wonder the king dies not,
             Being in a vault up to the knees in water,
             To which the channels of the castle run,
             From whence a damp continually ariseth ...

Gurney.   I opened but the door to throw him meat,
           And I was almost stifled with the savour ...

Edward.   And there in mire and puddle have I stood
           This ten days' space; and lest that I should sleep,
           One plays continually upon a drum.

                                          (5.5.1–4,8–9,58–60)

Edward's anticipations of death are presented in terms of immediate physical sensations: he can 'see' his death 'written in thy [Lightborn's] brows' (73). When he tries to forget his premonitions, involuntary fear makes him tremble; as he gives the jewel, 'Still fear I, and I know not what's the cause, / But every joint shakes as I give it thee' (84–5).

The spectators see the extent of Edward's physical torture as it is shown in his resulting disorientation; he comments upon this himself in a relatively lucid moment:

So that, for want to sleep and sustenance
My mind's distempered, and my body's numbed,
And whether I have limbs or no I know not.

                                          (62–4)

They see how distortions of perception dominate his final moments, when his awareness of his surroundings (and of the intentions of Lightborn) fluctuates as he drifts between sleep and waking:

> But that grief keeps me waking, I should sleep;
> For not these ten days have these eyes' lids clos'd.
> Now as I speak they fall, and yet with fear
> Open again. O wherefore sits thou here?
>
> (92–5)

In this state he hears a voice that 'buzzeth in mine ears' (102), like the half-apprehended Angel voices of *Faustus* (the Bad Angel also 'buzzeth'). His confusion is exacerbated by Lightborn's 'assailing' (12) of his mind. The assassin announces that the King will be 'finely handled' (39). He does this by a false show of sympathy ('And what eyes can refrain from shedding tears / To see a king in this most piteous state?' 49–50); by ambiguous promises ('These hands were never stained with innocent blood, / Nor shall they now be tainted with a king's', 80–1); and by a pretence of consideration ('You're overwatched, my lord. Lie down and rest', 91). His courtesy tempts the King to hope even as he knows Lightborn means to murder him. This feigned friendship is rewarded by Edward with the gift of his last jewel, a gift also serving as the traditional offering to one's executioner (Zucker 140).

The use of specific, striking detail in the death scene is both old and up-to-date, traditional as well as experimental. The persuasiveness of the cautionary tale had always depended upon the extent to which it engaged its audience. When Marlowe 'stabbed his owne dagger into his owne head' (Beard) or Talbot's corpse is 'stinking and fly-blown' or 'sweet Ned' (the phrase urges particular gesture) cannot speak or Edward is shaved with knives and 'channel water' – or when Hieronymo holds aloft 'this handkercher besmear'd with blood' and points to 'those wounds that yet are bleeding fresh' (*Spanish Tragedy* 2.5.51, 53) – all such examples were potent means of securing attention and inducing an audience to heed the lessons to be imparted. At the same time, the death scene also reflects contemporary experiments in exemplary rhetoric that sought greater emotional impact by drawing attention to more detail, especially the concrete, visible (or strongly imagined), and onstage.[21] These culminate by about 1595 in scenes such as that in Shakespeare's *King John* where the virtuous Prince Arthur dissuades his keeper, Hubert, from putting out his eyes. Each section of this lengthy dialogue elaborates upon things seen on stage: brows, eyes, tongue, fire, iron, cords. Near the end of the scene, the iron cools and Hubert vows to 'revive' it. Arthur replies:

> And if you do, you will but make it blush
> And glow with shame of your proceedings, Hubert:
> Nay, it perchance will sparkle in your eyes;
> And, like a dog that is compell'd to fight,
> Snatch at his master that doth tarre him on.
> All things that you should use to do me wrong
> Deny their office; only you do lack
> That mercy which fierce fire and iron extends –
> Creatures of note for mercy lacking uses!
>
> (*King John* 4.1.112–20)[22]

This passage derives its emotional impact from its specificity, from its calling attention – as in Edward's death scene – to what the audience can see, and anchoring this in ordinary experience. Like that scene, this lingers on the details of the visual signs which the spectators perceive before them. On the other hand, and unlike Edward's death scene, the scene in *King John* does not invite an audience to focus on moment-by-moment, non-representative experience, nor make sense of the action in any individual way. Instead, the spectators are called upon to perceive and make sense in a familiar, traditional way, to recognise the message behind the signs. The explication is orderly and predictable, and there is no sense of confused perception, no disorderly overflow of detail. The visual signs, for all their particularity, are none the less representative; and the lingering on them provides above all an emotional reinforcement to the lesson: 'fierce iron and fire' teach Hubert – and by extension, the audience – something about 'mercy'. The exemplary rhetoric is more complex than, but still essentially the same as, the speech of Hieronymo some years earlier – where the bloody handkerchief and wounds intensify the effects of first, Hieronymo's vow of certain vengeance and then, of Isabella's pious commonplaces:

> The heavens are just, murder cannot be hid,
> Time is the author both of truth and right,
> And time will bring this treachery to light.
>
> (*Spanish Tragedy* 2.5.57–9)

New lessons of history

While Edward's suffering challenges the conventional processes of viewing cautionary tales, the delayed and redefining commentary frustrates their conventional interpretation. The spectators, and this may be especially so for those who have retained a judgemental distance in the death scene and viewed the action as a 'manifest signe', are confronted with uncertainties about the exemplum's significance. Some of this uncertainty arises from the absence of commentary during and after the murder, with the immediate comments limited to Matrevis's 'fear' about Edward's cry and Lightborn's 'bravely done'. This is a cautionary tale without the caution, and the considerable emotional reinforcement generated by the scene's horrifying details is not explicitly applied to any exemplary lesson. The almost dumb show is unusual in Marlowe's plays, especially at such an important moment. Death elsewhere is matter for amplification and explication, with other death scenes full of characters busily commenting on the action. Even in *Edward II* the other losses of the King inspire protracted lamentations. Here, language itself disintegrates. Words ultimately are inadequate to define Edward's experience; and only the tortured cry suggests its horror.

After this, the only 'authorised version' of events offered to the spectators is that of the young King, but it is a version that runs counter to the earlier symmetries and expectations. When Edward's son assumes power and avenges his father's death, the audience is called upon to view his actions as a victory for legitimacy and order over usurpation and disorder. In consequence, Edward's death must be reinterpreted as undeserved, as the result of treachery rather than providential justice. The closing scene is sometimes described as showing the restoration of traditional order (Bevington and Shapiro 274), and there are certainly elements of this in the behaviour of the young King. He seems an exemplar of royal virtues: he is conscious of his inheritance ('Traitor, in me my loving father speaks', 5.6.40), and resolute in his royal duty when he deals with Mortimer and his mother. But the young King also offers the audience a redefinition of events and a realignment of perspectives: the son grieves for a 'loving father', is angry that 'his kingly body was too soon interred' (32), and is concerned to exact vengeance: 'Sweet father, here unto thy murdered ghost, / I offer up this wicked traitor's head' (98–9). His tears bear witness to his 'grief and innocency' (100). His redefinition of events is accorded visual confirmation in the play's final ceremony, the funeral ritual, and made emphatic, once again, by the counterpointing of sound and silence. The stage image of new King and attendant lords, contrasted with the hearse and head, suggests both renewal, in the youth of the King, and the royal authority, in his crown and supporting nobles (Zucker 141–2). It stresses the ultimate victory of Edward's kingly power over Mortimer's usurping, emphasising the sincerity and innocence of the young King and adding emotional conviction to his loss. That loss is great, and the only guilt that of Mortimer and Isabella. From the perspective offered by the young King, Edward is a tragic victim and his suffering excessive.

The play thus ends with a denial that the death by poker is an exemplum of poetic justice. This message may have a considerable emotional impact, but there remains a number of unresolved problems relevant to the expectations of the early spectators and their making sense of the action. The ending of *Edward II* is unlike the closing scenes of other contemporary plays, even the more ambiguous and unresolved ones such as that of *3 Henry VI* with the Judas kiss by Richard of Gloucester. It has a number of curious omissions and inadequacies – even apart from the ambiguous suggestions in the final tableau of the Senecan avenger (Kelsall 68–9) – which make it less certain that spectators will accede to the young King's interpretation. The funeral ceremony may be moving but the words of the scene do not bear the weight of the action. Language shrinks in significance as Edward's son oversimplifies, reducing the issues in the final moments of the play to simple sets of antitheses: 'sweet father' and 'wicked traitor', 'monstrous treachery' and 'innocency'. The limiting effect of the language is shown throughout the scene in the reduction of political matters to questions of family relationships. The terms 'son', 'father', and 'mother' serve to explain motives and define actions. To some extent this emphasis on family relationships recalls the words of the virtuous Kent, until his death an advocate for traditional values: 'Either my brother or his son is king, / And none of both them thirst for Edmund's blood' (5.4.103–4). And because of this association, the language gives the impression of a new kind of power: legitimate, orderly, and responsible.

Yet the differences are more important. Whereas Kent has described kingship as part of a providential and natural order, there is no reference to heavenly justice in the words of Edward's son. Kent had petitioned heaven to 'Rain showers of vengeance on my cursèd head, / Thou God, to whom in justice it belongs / To punish this unnatural revolt' (4.6.7–9). But heaven is surprisingly absent from the final scene; and the hell of Edward's death has been translated into the euphemistic 'too soon interred' or 'spilt ... blood'. The omission of heaven is more remarkable still when the ending is compared with those of the other plays. Even the *Jew* ends with the claim of heavenly intervention on the side of the Knights, despite the remoteness of the play's world from a heaven of any kind. In *Edward*, the possibility of some universal significance in the king's fall is glimpsed, only for it to fade away before the end. The new king may seem to act like a king, but the world he inhabits is a smaller one than that of his father. Though he had once, when prince, compared himself with Atlas (3.1.76–8), his language now lacks amplification, be it heroic or royal. The lions and other royal companions have disappeared with the setting at Berkeley of Edward's own sun.

The young King's assertion of legitimate authority thus entails a questioning of the providential order that Edward's death has seemed to affirm. Instead of signalling a restoration of order, the final image of head and hearse suggests that 'manifest signes' are to be viewed with suspicion. The younger Edward may claim that placing Mortimer's head on the hearse is a sign asserting the ultimate victory of Edward's kingly power; but the ceremony is deceptive, and not only because his father failed in the exercise of that power. The spectators observe the young King to be engaged in the making of a myth, complete with emblems he constructs himself. The most instructive parallel here is with Tamburlaine, another master of redefining ceremonies. The survival of traditional political order is seen to depend upon an opportunism more often associated with Machiavellian 'policy'.

The delay in commentary on Edward's death scene, by detaching experience from judgement, has broken the connection between particular and general upon which exemplary rhetoric depends. As in some scenes in *Faustus*, the burden of interpretation has shifted to the individual playgoers, who must make sense of what has been seen in terms of their own ordinary experience. Their individual interpretive narratives may or may not include a belief in providential punishment as intrinsic to the way that things 'are'. But as they watch the play's last moments any confidence the spectators might still retain in an orderly and predictable universe is further tested. By showing how the meaning of exemplary historical events may be constructed, the final scene challenges the certainties of the cautionary tale.

This has unsettling implications for the play, as its effect is to cast doubt upon all the comfortable political commonplaces exemplified earlier in the action. If we reconsider the play from this perspective, we realise how much the meanings of events have derived from the manipulations of political rhetoric, and how often the exempla have been used by one or other of the characters as attempts to relabel what has happened. Redefinition is not confined to the closing scene, but is a process that occurs throughout the play and involves all the main characters. It is seen especially in the confrontations between Edward and the barons: as their conflict proceeds and develops into civil war, the issues are redefined, the essentially selfish motives rationalised, until both sides claim divine sanction for their cause.[23]

This emphasis on the ways that political meanings are constructed is not, of course, something entirely new in *Edward II*. It is an element in the dramatic rhetoric of the *Tamburlaine* plays and that of the *Jew of Malta*. It can be found, as Simon Shepherd establishes, in other less well known plays of the 1580s and 1590s. It becomes, as James Shapiro and others have noted, a particular feature of the early histories of Shakespeare with which *Edward II* is in dialogue. But where *Edward II* is quite different, indeed new, is in its dismantling of the cautionary tale. Other plays, those of Shakespeare among them, continue to refer what happens to some agreed system of values – however conventional or clichéd or even mindless – that offers the spectators a conventional way of making sense of the action. *Edward II*, to the frustration perhaps of many of its spectators (and probably more so of its critics), ultimately does not. The difference can be typified by a small but instructive comparison: between the deaths of Mortimer (*Edward II* 5.6) and the Machiavellian Warwick (*3 Henry VI* 5.2.1–49). There are initially verbal parallels. Mortimer begins by echoing Warwick's dying self-description, speaking of his position in terms of 'Jove's spreading tree' and 'low shrubs'. Since Mortimer is at this moment poised to fall, the echo is ironic. But Warwick's fall is developed as an exemplum of the vanity of earthly glory: 'Why, what is pomp, rule, reign, but earth and dust?' The message is routine, asking of the spectators only recognition and assent. In contrast, Mortimer's fall, though just, and a fitting punishment for his crimes, offers them only uncertainty. It avoids reference to any supernatural power except 'base Fortune' as he contemplates neither hell nor heaven, but 'as a traveller, / Goes to discover countries yet unknown' (*Edward II* 5.6.64–5).

But it is not only the closing scenes of *Edward II* that may have suggested to its early audiences that there might be no exemplary solutions, only unanswered questions. Indeed the uncertainties are anticipated in – and influence perception of – even those exempla that establish a providentialist frame for the action. The redefinitions of the final scene and the manipulations of political rhetoric arise from a playworld that has always been one of deceptive appearances. The funeral ceremony is not the first occasion in the play where what we see and hear does not reflect what is there. But the deceptiveness is not simply a matter of ironic contrast, as it is in the imperfect worlds of early Shakespeare or the popular tradition. *Edward II* may occupy 'a dual world of visual splendor and of secret hypocrisy', as Bevington and Shapiro suggest (267) but, as they also note, the ceremonies repeatedly 'decay' (269). What becomes the most compelling rhetorical pattern of the play is not the contrast between what 'is' and what 'should be' (the traditional and the Shakespearean shaping pattern); it is rather the inevitability of that 'decay'. Edward's scene of triumph (4.3), for example, would appear to invoke suggestions of traditional order. On the sixteenth-century stage, as Fleischer comments, such scenes were visually impressive. They were colourful and elaborate and used the full stage; they often included emblems of Fortune such as chariots (60–4). But the tableau of triumph, like other such exempla in the play (reconcilation, coronation), lasts only a few moments. Then quite suddenly it subsides into anticlimax, with the visual glories dissipating in the banality of Edward's language: 'Why so. They barked apace a month ago; / Now, on my life, they'll neither bark nor bite' (4.3.33–4). That this lack of eloquence is a deliberate rhetorical effect is indicated by Edward's switching a few lines later to the vigour of 'Welcome, a God's name, madam, and your son' with its amplifying imagery of 'bright Phoebus' and 'dusty night, in rusty iron car' (4.3.64–70). The same pattern of inevitable disintegration can be found in each of the play's exempla of order. It is echoed too in the anticlimactic structuring of many of the set-speeches.[24]

The language of *Edward II* falls apart. As in *Faustus*, there are passages where the meanings of words become unstable and unpredictable, and neither character nor audience can make reliable sense. The surfaces of the playworld are not merely deceptive but shifting. Words tend to become isolatable fragments, echoing from scene to scene, changing their reference as they do so. These repetitions (some striking, others unobtrusive) are a marked feature of the verbal rhetoric of the play. When Mortimer asserts his power ('All tremble at my name, and I fear none', 5.6.13) his words sound out a distorted echo of Edward's terror at his impending murder only a few moments before: 'This fear is that which makes me tremble thus' (5.5.104).[25] In consequence, what happens in *Edward II* is that the attempts to control, to manipulate language – to find reasons that 'make white black and dark night day' (1.4.247) – lead to incoherence and loss of meaning. The political confrontations result in a blurring of the differences between the sides; on the battlefield and in victory both parties are reduced to conventional posturing. The extreme instance of the failure of words is the death by poker, where language becomes inadequate to express Edward's suffering. The failure is found too in the silences of the final ceremony: the young King cannot explain more without suggesting more problems for interpretation, and so enjoins the lords – and in effect the spectators – to 'help me to mourn'.

'Help me to mourn.' What is left now is not appropriate judgement but only appropriate feeling, not explication but sensation. The young King's lament is the play's last challenge to the cautionary tale, the final transformation of its exemplary rhetoric. The 'difference' of *Edward II* originates in an exploiting of the traditional – the striking detail, the emotional reinforcement of the lesson – but ends in something new. The audience are called upon to feel before they think, to participate in before they consider the lessons of history. It is this experiencing of a 'manifest signe' as disengaged from its exemplary lesson that makes possible a new kind of tragic understanding, in which suffering may become more than just a 'cautionary tale'.

CHAPTER 5

Framing the action

London life

In the late 1580s *The Jew of Malta* transformed theatrical experience by exploiting – and then dismantling – the framing rhetoric of the late morality. The *Jew* is in some ways the most traditional of Marlowe's plays; in others, the most provocatively subversive. Yet this subversiveness has less to do with its references to Machiavellian philosophy than is generally realised. These references made the *Jew* topical and sensational, but its real novelty at its own moment in history – in about 1589 – lay rather in how it changed the ways that the perspectives of the audience were constructed. Like other plays of the late 1580s and early 1590s, the *Jew* experimented with framing techniques; its experiments, however, were more radical, enabling the spectators to disengage from their accustomed ways of observing and feeling and responding. Where older plays, as well as most contemporary ones, provided an 'authorised version' to guide spectators in making sense of the action, the *Jew* liberated competing voices, opening up new possibilities for performance and interpretation. How this happened is the subject of this chapter.

Framing rhetoric, as suggested in Chapter 2, sets up the boundaries and contexts for theatrical experience, operating through elements such as the 'playworld' or conventional devices and signals. It interacts with the expectations spectators bring with them into the theatre, establishing perspectives that govern what they might notice in the action before them and influencing how they make sense of what they see. Framing rhetoric generates its own expectations: of particular kinds of action and relationships, particular outcomes, particular ways of responding appropriately. Its operation has always been important in the performance of *The Jew of Malta*, since this is a play that creates its theatrical excitement by manipulating audience perspectives on the action, by working to unsettle the expectations aroused even as they seem to be fulfilled. As N. W. Bawcutt comments, the 'many local changes of tone or sudden reversals of direction' are basic to the play's techniques (Introduction 35). At the level of dramatic incident this rhetoric of unpredictability ensures the continuing vitality of the *Jew* in performance. To appreciate the 'newness' of the *Jew* in its time, however, we need to set aside our sense of what is possible on the modern stage. Some of the expectations called upon by the play were more specific to performance in the 1580s, and it is these that will concern us here.

One context for the play's early performances was the playgoing experience of its audiences with the generic expectations this fostered. The *Jew* appealed to an established theatrical taste for plays of lively, outspoken social criticism. It might have a more complex narrative structure than the usual late morality, but it retains significant elements of these earlier plays in its setting, action, and verbal rhetoric – and, importantly, in its concern with social relationships and political behaviour. The playgoers who thronged to the performances of the *Jew* may already have seen a number of such plays, including perhaps Robert Wilson's *The Three Ladies of London* in its original or revived version. Yet for all the novelty of the *Jew* – and the fourteeners of the *Three Ladies* – they would have found much that was familiar.

We can obtain some sense of what might have been familiar to, and enjoyed by, these late sixteenth-century playgoers by imagining a performance some time in the late 1580s. The place is a London playhouse – the Rose, perhaps, or the Theatre. The play presented this afternoon is set in London or somewhere remarkably like that city. Though there is much talk of international trade, the action to be seen on stage has little to do with glamorous exploits in exotic places, but is concerned with the particular detail of the ordinary and everyday: with buying and selling, with courtship and employment, with keeping faith (or, more often, breaking it) and passing judgement. There are satirical vignettes of city life, observed in street and lawcourt, counting-house and brothel. There is a Jew – and at least one Turk. There are characters who lie and cheat and murder, and others who issue pious warnings against wrongdoing. The play demonstrates, repeatedly, that love and conscience are no proof against avarice, and that avarice leads to corruption and violence. But, while the messages may be forceful, the moral lessons are not always tidy. Villainy prospers, organised religion reveals its corruption, and the secular authorities muddle through. The ending of the play, in particular, departs from the earlier morality pattern: there is no last-minute rescue by God's Grace or Heavenly Mercy, no simple apportionment of rewards and punishments.

The play? Our hypothetical performance in the late 1580s could well have been a performance of *The Three Ladies of London*, recently revived to accompany its sequel play. It could just as easily have been a performance of *The Jew of Malta*, at the beginning of its long career in the playhouse repertory. Indeed, it is not impossible that the two plays competed for the custom of Londoners on the same afternoon. Nor were the *Three Ladies* and the *Jew* unique in kind, as plays that can be described in similar terms are not restricted to the 1580s. Some years earlier, many of these elements are to be found in a simple morality such as Walpul's *The Tide Tarrieth No Man* (1576); some years later, most are retained in a play such as Ben Jonson's *Volpone* (1606).[1]

The similarities between the *Jew* and the late morality do not end with these coincidences of place or person or even preaching. In its framing rhetoric the *Jew* retains features of the morality 'playworld' that might well have suggested to its early audiences a familiar moral landscape, and activated in them customary expectations. In the morality, early or late, simple or sophisticated, the playworld is organised around one predictable contrast, in which 'what is' is set against 'what should be'. The particular form this contrast takes in the *Three Ladies* can be seen in the ways the playworld is defined: by continual reference to the 'real' world of London, which is outside the privileged space of the playhouse and to which the audience must return after the performance; and by an assumption that the audience adheres to a particular set of conventional, socially conservative values. The play attacks the practices of society, but it mounts no real challenge to what it assumes to be society's 'profession'.

In presenting 'what is', the morality play resorted to multiple demonstrations of wickedness. The spectators were accustomed to the use of exempla to organise their view of the action, to plays proceeding from a general notion about experience to particular illustrative instances that served to advance the message. Some moralities attempt little more: *Like Will to Like*, for example, consists mainly of a series of comic demonstrations that the wicked will end up in each other's company. *The Tide Tarrieth No Man* is a catalogue of missed opportunities, for the well-intentioned as well as the rogues. The *Three Ladies* has a more developed narrative interest, but it too organises action in this way. The early scenes illustrate 'like will to like' with characters suing for patronage and employment; later scenes exemplify deception and violence, before a third series of alternating scenes shows the contrasts in fortune between the wicked and the well-meaning. At each step the moralising is fulsome, with the audience left in no doubt about how they are expected to make sense of the action.

The *Three Ladies* supplements its exempla with lengthy accounts of contemporary social abuses: the fraudulent practices of the various trades; the exploitation of the poor; the corruption of parliamentary and legal processes; even the defects of contemporary trade policies, illustrated by catalogues of imports and exports. These accounts reinforce the connection between the action of the play and everyday life in London, as do the many small anecdotes calling upon the audience to observe the fine detail of ordinary life. To cite one typical example: the tailor who steals one and a half out of seven yards of material (the player's accompanying gestures can readily be imagined):

> Such Taylors will thrive that out of a doublet and a payre of hose can steale their wife an Aporne [apron]:
>
> > The Dublet sleeves three fingers were too short,
> > The Venecians came nothing neare the knee.
>
> (1515–18)

The other side to the morality contrast, offering the audience a perspective from which to observe and interpret, is an appeal to shared values, social as well as moral. These include a distrust of foreigners and their notions. Simony is a recent import, brought back by English merchants from Rome; Usury has been in service in Venice; and the Italian merchant Mercador, complete with comic foreign accent, proves a worthy henchman of Lucre (he exports good English commodities to buy the foreign trinkets that corrupt foolish ladies).[2] As well as this appeal to xenophobia, there is frequent recourse to proverbial sentiments – Conscience, faced with a four-fold increase in rent because Usury is a follower of Lady Lucre, comments: 'We must have pacience perforce seeing there is no remedie' (835) – and even to sermonising, with Judge Nemo's concluding speech drawing the predictable moral: 'For Covetousnesse is the cause of wresting mans Conscience, / Therefore restraine thy lust, and thou shalt shonne the offence' (1960–1).

In *The Jew of Malta*, the morality contrast persists, along with the exemplary rhetoric. 'What is' in Malta – as in London – is thoroughly sinful. In the spread of wickedness throughout Maltese society, from the Governor's son to the courtesan's pimp, there is even a suggestion of the estates morality, similar to the *Three Ladies*. There may be less time devoted to explicit commentary, but the *Jew* still offers a procession of exempla quite sufficient to satisfy any playgoer of a moralising disposition. Here before the spectator is enacted demonstration after demonstration of avarice, deceit, hypocrisy, and, not least, the 'pestilent Machivilian pollicy' (the phrase is Robert Greene's) that appears to have fascinated the contemporary playgoer and continued to be a selling point for the play, part of the expectations audiences might take with them into the theatre, even in 1633: 'you shall find him [Barabas] still, / In all his projects, a sound Machevill, / And that's his character' (Prologue spoken at Court 7–9).

The morality contrast is echoed in the familiar combination of 'real' life and shared values. The impression of the 'real' in the *Jew* is very much a product of what the audience is directed to see. The action of the play is grounded in a world that appears to be quite precise and prosaic, quite visible and tactile like the riches of Barabas's soliloquy. Bags of gold are counted or carried; they are handed or tossed from one person to another. A large 'pot of pottage' is carried on stage, tasted by Ithamore, and stirred with a ladle. A girdle is used to strangle a Friar and a staff to belabour the body. There are poisoned flowers to smell and a lute to play. There is Barabas *'with a hammer . . . very busy'* – and a cauldron waiting beneath. To these examples of visible objects and actions can be added many others, not actually seen by the audience but evoking exact times, places, and objects. Barabas orders 'three score camels, thirty mules, / And twenty waggons to bring up the ware' (1.1.59–60). Del Bosco defeats the Turkish galleys because the wind rose, 'And then we luffed, and tacked, and fought at ease' (2.2.14). The details accumulate to establish an impression of the familiar and everyday.

This sense of ordinary life, of the 'real' world, is supported as in the *Three Ladies* by a constant appeal to shared values, in particular to the standards of conventional, practical wisdom. The commentaries and sermons of the *Three Ladies* are matched by an abundance of proverbial expressions and biblical allusions. Their repeated use offers the audience a particular perspective on the action that recalls the routine response generated by the morality contrast. Such expressions in the *Jew* may have the effect, as Stephen Greenblatt comments, of suggesting 'all the neatly packaged nastiness' of Maltese society (*Renaissance Self-fashioning* 207); but proverbs and allusions are also, and more importantly, familiar ways of attempting to make sense of experience. They express 'a mode of perception that had its roots in practical life and in the common man's concrete world of objects and ideas' (Weimann 206). Indeed the characters of the *Jew* often seem to be speaking the same 'language' as those in the *Three Ladies*. There is, it would appear, no great distance between Conscience's words cited above, urging 'pacience', and Barabas's 'No, Abigail, things past recovery / Are hardly cured with exclamations' (1.2.238–9); nor between Judge Nemo's earnest message and Ferneze's pious warning that 'Excess of wealth is cause of covetousness: / And covetousness, O, 'tis a monstrous sin!' (1.2.124–5). Much of what the characters assert or advise is, on face value at least, predictable and reasonable, especially for 'men of judgement'.[3]

In Malta as in London outward shows are taken seriously. The routine courtesies are observed, as well as the routine discourtesies. Public dissension is expressed in set phrases: 'Hinder her not, thou man of little faith' (Jacomo, 1.2.339); 'Converse not with him; he is cast off from heaven' (Katherine, 2.3.160); 'Heaven bless me; what, a friar a murderer!' (Barabas, 4.2.195). This stereotyping of attitudes and opinions constructs for the audience the picture of a society that assumes for its inhabitants a defined place and 'profession', including the right to be unrepentantly self-righteous: 'For I can see no fruits in all their faith / But malice, falsehood and excessive pride' (Barabas, 1.1.115–16); ''Tis not our fault, but thy inherent sin' (First Knight, 1.2.110). In their epitomising of the conventional these sentiments are as precise and familiar as the visual imagery of the play. Reinforced by ceremony and (most probably) by costume, they convey an impression of an ordered society with well-defined rules. For all its supposedly exotic setting, the action of the *Jew* occurs within a world that recalls for its early audiences the London of plays such as the *Three Ladies*, and evokes for them a similarly strong sense of the predictable, of ordinary life and conventional values.

Accounting for 'difference'

For much of its action then, *The Jew of Malta* looks, and sounds, like a late morality. The framing rhetoric of the play exploits that similarity, inviting its early spectators to entertain their usual expectations of a certain kind of action on stage and to respond in their accustomed ways. Here presented before them, the echoes of the morality suggest, is no more than the career of 'a sound Machevill', exemplified at length and ending in deserved punishment. But what actually happens in the audience's experience of the play is something quite different. We can obtain some glimpse of this if we revisit one of the parallels between the plays. When Judge Nemo, in closing the action of the *Three Ladies*, warns against 'covetousnesse', he is offering the 'authorised version' that allows the audience to make sense of the action. This is a statement of 'truth'; it is to be read as unaffected by either irony or ambiguity. The wicked may not be punished sufficiently, but their moral status is clear. When Ferneze, disputing with Barabas and justifying extortion, claims that covetousness is 'a monstrous sin', he may sound like Judge Nemo and his statement could certainly be accepted in the same straightforward way, as choric or 'authorised'. But even at this early point in the play it could also be interpreted quite differently, as, let us say, a sign of hypocrisy or an attempt at special pleading. The attention of spectators has already been drawn to Ferneze and the slipperiness of his rationalising rhetoric. They have thus been provided with more than one possible perspective on the action, more than one option for interpretation.

This radical transformation of theatrical experience is overlooked by most critical studies. Indeed many commentaries on the *Jew* begin and end with an explication of its exemplary rhetoric. Some are devoted to collecting examples of avarice and deceit; others have taken up Machevil's veiled invitation to look for his followers, noting especially the suggestion that 'such as love me guard me from their tongues' (Prologue 6). For many years the critical debate (and hence estimates of theatrical experience) centred on whether the play was really 'Christian' or really 'Machiavellian' or atheist.[4] A related approach has been the 'historicist' one of viewing the play itself as an exemplum of social attitudes or ideological constructs. What, the critic asks, does the *Jew* show (or conceal) about Jews or attitudes to them, or about Catholics or foreign places, or about anything marginalised or Other?[5]

These exemplary approaches to the *Jew* exhibit the same inadequacies as the iconographic approaches to Tamburlaine's chariot: their cumulative effect is to establish that interpretations do differ, especially critical interpretations, but not why or how interpretations can differ. In particular, they do not explain how, or if, the Machiavellian 'ideas' mentioned in the play are able to be translated into perceptions that undermine conventional ways of making sense of the world. The *Jew*, after all, may offer just another version of what is wrong with society – and that has always been the ordinary fare of drama. The *Jew* may have introduced daring subject matter to the popular stage in the late 1580s (Robert Greene, for one, expressed shock at the airing of such ideas); but the popular stage then, as usually since, thrived on the topical and sensational and downright voyeuristic. In the next few years an unknown playwright would dramatise the shocking murder of Mr Arden of Faversham by his adulterous wife, and Marlowe would collaborate with others to present the startling career of a German magician. Greene himself would join with Thomas Lodge in bringing to the stage a King of Nineveh who indulges in adultery, incest, and listening to soothsayers – and whose incestuous queen is turned black by lightning right before the audience's eyes – all for the most admirable cause, the prophets Oseas and Jonas keep insisting, of making Londoners aware of their sins.

The more informative critical approaches to the *Jew* have been through performance rhetoric and the theatrical tradition. Many of these studies have dealt with some aspect of framing rhetoric, finding parallels and continuities between the *Jew* and other plays, and offering models of response based in most cases upon generic expectations. The *Jew*, they suggest, may have appealed to its early audiences as tragedy (Beecher); or as something akin to 'black comedy' (J. Smith), or melodrama (H. Levin), or burlesque (Cartelli, 'Endless Play').[6] Other studies relate the rhetoric of the play to some aspect of its theatrical heritage. David Bevington explains its mixture of serious and comic action by locating a traditional pattern of alternation (*Mankind to Marlowe* 219–22). Nicholas Brooke describes the *Jew* as 'a *Cambises*-type play', emphasising its 'rapid changes of theatrical mode' ('Marlowe the Dramatist' 95–6). Several studies treat continuities with the conventional figure of the Vice.[7]

These performance and developmental studies illuminate more of what happens in the play than do the exemplary ones, but, in their quest for categories and similarities few arrive at any adequate definition of the *Jew*'s 'difference'. They do not explain, that is, how the audience was brought to see differently, any more than did my comparison a few pages ago between the playworlds of the *Jew* and the late morality. Many studies resort to versions of the view that the difference lies in Barabas's being a more 'realistic' character than his predecessors in the moralities, a stage half-way (as Bernard Spivack describes him) between the Vice and Iago. And like Spivack, many writers are puzzled when this innovative character – with whom, it is assumed, the audience can 'identify' – does not survive the second act (Spivack resorts to hinting at defects in the author's 'genius', 352). Alternatively, the play is seen as some kind of extreme case, as when Thomas Cartelli develops Stephen Greenblatt's notion of 'absolute play' (*Renaissance Self-fashioning* 219–20). To a sixteenth-century audience, Cartelli argues, the *Jew* would have permitted an unrestrained indulgence in transgressive fantasies; this occurs because it lacks the structures that would lead an audience to resist those fantasies (*Economy of Theatrical Experience* 161–74). The 'fantasy-gratifications' encouraged by the play include:

> the urge towards self-aggrandizement and the humbling of all opposition; the desire to feel secretly all-knowing, to gain power by withholding; the desire to role-play, to change shape at will, and, hence, to escape the confining (and legally enforced) self-definition of everyday life; the urge to release pent-up aggression against traditional sources of surveillance and repression (like the Church); and, more generally, to experience the sheer freedom of moral abandon. (*Economy of Theatrical Experience* 174)

But in the morality tradition something 'transgressive' was always to be expected. The 'fantasy-gratifications' attributed to the *Jew* were already part of the playgoing experience of the early audiences. Indeed the contrast employed in Cartelli's analysis between 'engagement' and 'resistance' is as familiar a feature in studies of the morality as it is in studies of the *Jew*. The role of the Vice, in particular, has often been discussed within some such framework. Robert C. Jones explores the 'dangerous sport' involved in the 'moral interludes' in terms of audience 'engagement' with and 'rejection' of the Vices ('Dangerous Sport'; *Engagement with Knavery* 11–17). And yet in either case – whether we set the *Jew* against Shakespeare or against its predecessors and contemporaries – we need to go beyond locating the *Jew*'s 'difference' in an absence of restraining structures. Some of the *Jew*'s less well known contemporaries offer much better examples of such 'indulgence', patently encouraging audiences in simple-minded and aggressive fantasies. Three instances, aimed (respectively) at the French, the Spanish, and the Catholics, are *The Famous Victories of Henry V*, *The Three Lords and Three Ladies of London*, and *The Troublesome Reign of John, King of England*. On the other hand, and in its immediate theatrical context, the *Jew* provided its first audiences with (if anything) an excess of restraining structures. There would seem to be, in Cartelli's terms, plenty of 'defenses against the unsettling fantasies' of (in this case) 'power, play, and moral abandon' (*Economy of Theatrical Experience* 34, 163). At every step the play calls upon the framing rhetoric of the late moralities and their contrast between 'what is' and 'what should be'. It retains – and draws attention to – many of the devices they employ to keep spectators aware of how they should be viewing the world: the monologue, sermon, and aside; the topical reference, proverbial sentiment, and ironic instance. In exploring the changes the *Jew* brings about in theatrical experience, we need to come to terms with this excess of structures and devices. The simple answer, that excesses just cancel or confuse, takes us only part of the distance.

More is involved, in any case, than setting the transgressive against the received. As Jones comments (*Engagement with Knavery* 5), 'engagement' – which entails an awareness, even a sharing, of viewpoint – should be distinguished from the emotional commitment assumed in 'identification' (he observes that 'we share Iago's level of awareness and Othello's anguish'). More importantly perhaps, Cartelli's model of theatrical experience does not take into account other significant reactions to performance, in particular the keen responses that derive from a play's satisfying or frustrating the particular ways that an audience has learnt to expect and view and make sense: recognition and disappointment to be sure, but also elation and distress, surprise, relief, suspense, and anticipation. To understand the 'difference' of the *Jew*, we need to consider it against the whole apparatus of framing rhetoric in the late morality. Certainly something transgressive was to be expected in the appeal of such plays to an audience, but also something more than that.

In the morality tradition expectations about storytelling and appropriate responses were realised in distinctive ways. The action, mostly, consisted of a collection of incidents determined by the play's thesis and framed generally by the familiar moral landscape of 'what is' and 'what should be'. At the same time, audience expectations were also anchored in the conventional figure of the Vice. In many plays the Vice occupied a central position in the framing rhetoric: he was the focus of expectations, the initiator of exemplary action, and the most prominent interpreter of the playworld. For many years (*Mankind*, written more than a century before the *Jew*, has a Vice-devil figure in Titivillus) and especially from about 1550, playwrights used the Vice as an agent for constructing audience perspectives: for making specific their pictures of 'what is' and reinforcing their lessons of 'what should be'. The convention was still a vital one well into the 1580s and, as Alan C. Dessen shows, lingered in the memory of playwrights and playgoers into the seventeenth century (*Late Moral Plays* 18–22, 137–9). Its usefulness for the playwright can be seen in its extension to popular plays of all kinds. In the romantic adventure *Clyomon and Clamydes*, for instance, the role of the Vice (Subtle Shift, disguised as Knowledge) is small but crucial, connecting the heroic nonsense of the plot to the moral concerns of everyday life. The hero must choose his elevated path of slaying maiden-eating flying Serpents, but the issues for his follower are more to do with surviving in an unfriendly world: weighing up the rewards of honesty and loyalty against the immediate benefits of telling expedient lies and finding the least hazardous master. As Lois Potter comments with reference to *Cambises* and its tales of exotic cruelty, the Vice, however indirectly, 'keeps the audience in touch with familiar moral standards' (248).[8]

But the audience expected more of the Vice than the voice of ordinary experience. Though many figures in the traditional drama interacted openly with the spectators, it was the Vice's relationship with them – developed and sustained by devices such as aside or monologue, or even by remarks to and about individual spectators – that was the key to the performance rhetoric of the morality, in dining hall or playhouse.[9] The use of direct address established the audience contact necessary to fulfil the Vice's multiple roles in the play: manipulator, tempter, entertainer, commentator, presenter. In enacting these, the Vice might switch from aggressive to ingratiating, from taunting the audience to claiming rapport with them. But, as Jones maintains, though this relationship may have involved the 'dangerous sport' of conspiring with the Vice against his stupid or foolish victims, it was not, in the end, subversive. The spectators were brought to recognise both the skill of the performer and their essential kinship with the victims. By including the spectators in the playworld, the devices of direct address thus engaged them in judgement on the action. The Vice might outwit the virtuous, might organise the best entertainment in the play, but such moments tended always, as Jones reminds us, to reinforce the play's didacticism by confronting the audience with its enjoyment of the villainy: 'though the vices may have the last laugh, they never have the last word' ('Dangerous Sport' 47).

In the morality tradition the framing techniques – whether they are found in explicit commentary or direct address, or in other aspects of the playworld – supported a single authorised version of the action. This does not mean that opposing viewpoints were not aired during the play, nor that some temporary subversiveness did not occur. The Vice in particular provided a dissenting voice, as did sundry other characters – even if the latter were usually

presented as unintelligent or unenlightened. At times the voice of the
Vice was wantonly destructive (note Ambidexter in *Cambises*, or
Haphazard in *Apius and Virginia*); at other times, as with
Dissimulation in the *Three Ladies*, it was more insinuating, appealing to an attitude of worldly cynicism. The perspective of the Vice
was, nevertheless, a complementary one, always defined and defining in terms of the values it opposed, and the authorised version was
always ultimately affirmed. This occurs even in a play such as the
Three Ladies where poetic justice operates imperfectly. That the
virtuous suffer and the Vices survive does not alter the moral worth
of any single one of them; it merely confirms the satirical point that
abuses persist in the 'real' world of London.

Introducing the Vice

The Jew of Malta made use of but then dismantled the traditional
structure of framing rhetoric. The voices it liberated were competing
rather than complementary ones. The play disrupted the expectations of its early audiences by casting the Vice (still complete with
much of his customary rhetorical baggage) adrift from the morality
playworld, and casting the playworld itself adrift from morality
complacencies. How this happens is a complex process, parts of
which have been illuminated by other studies.[10] My aim here is to
offer a more comprehensive account, using one of the traditional
devices of framing rhetoric, the introductory Vice monologue, as the
starting point from which to explore the *Jew*'s 'difference'.

The speech by which the Vice introduces himself to the audience
is a convention – indeed a theatrical cliché – of the late morality. It
is located early in the play, following the Prologue or soon thereafter. The Vice, alone on stage, confesses his particular nature and
apprises the audience of his schemes. The message of the introductory monologue will be intermittently reinforced during the play
with comments on exemplary situations. But this is not just a matter
of instructing the audience how to view. In providing a perspective
frame for subsequent action, much of the theatrical impact of the
monologue lies in the degree to which it establishes a sense of
sharing and conspiracy, with Vice and spectators linked in their
possession of 'superior' knowledge about the world, and about the
events of the play to follow. Before this conspiracy can be established, however, the spectators must identify the Vice. The
convention, as Happé comments, depended for its success upon
immediate recognition: the 'Vice is instantly recognizable by his

noises, his language, and probably his peculiar clothing' ('"The Vice" and Popular Theatre' 19).

These conventional features can be illustrated by the introductory monologue of Dissimulation in the *Three Ladies*.[11] The speech occurs early in the action, immediately after a brief encounter between Lady Love, Lady Conscience, and Fame, which poses the question the play will answer: can Love and Conscience survive unscathed in the city of London? The condition of the world soon becomes apparent and the answer starts to take shape: the spectators must realise at the outset that this is a dishonest world where everyone dissembles.

> *Enter* DISSIMULATION, *having on a Farmers long coat, and
> a cappe, and his powle and beard painted motley.*

> Dissimulation.   Nay no lesse than a Farmar, a right honest man,
>   But my toong can not stay me to tell what I am:
>   Nay who is it that knowes me not by my partie coloured head?
>   They may well thinke that see me, my honestie is fled.
>   Tush a figge for honestie, tut let that goe:
>   Sith men, women, and children my name and doinges do know,
>   My name is Dissimulation, and no baseminde I beare,
>   For my outwarde effectes my inward zeale doe declare:
>   For men doe dissemble with their wives, & their wives with them
>   again,
>   So that in the heartes of them I alwayes remayne:
>   The childe dissembles with his father, the sister with her brother,
>   The mayden with her mistres, and the young man with his lover:
>   There is dissimulation betweene neighbour and neighbour,
>   Friend and Friend one with an other.
>   Betweene the servaunt and his Maister, betweene brother and
>   brother,
>   Then why make you it straunge that ever you knew me,
>   Seeing so often I rannge thorowout every degree?
>   But I forget my businesse, ile towardes London as fast as I can,
>   To get entertainment of one of the three ladies, like an honest man.
>   (*Three Ladies* 37–58)

The rhetoric of this speech has distinctive, conventional features. The 1580s spectators recognised Dissimulation as a Vice by attending to various visual and verbal clues. His particular nature is first signalled by his costume. This is suitably equivocal: part-emblematic ('his powle and beard painted motley') and part-disguise ('a Farmers long coat, and a cappe'). His confession then illustrates his appearance: he scornfully dismisses 'honestie' even as he adopts a pose of sincerity. The spectators' recognition of his nature is confirmed as the monologue proceeds, as well as their complicity in what he represents. Inciting and inviting the audience to respond, the speech moves through a succession of tones: mock-apologetic, earnest, confiding, cynical, challenging, swaggering. Dissimulation justifies himself by claiming that everyone dissembles. He claims the audience as his accomplices. He challenges hypocrites: 'Then why make you it straunge that ever you knew me?' The lines give the player an opportunity to make contact with individuals in the audience, to the delight of everyone else present.

The relationship this speech establishes with the audience is typical of the morality Vice. In seeking to enlist the spectators (the Vice as tempter), Dissimulation asserts that they live in an imperfect world. But their conspiracy can never be a wholehearted one, since the very frankness of his confession makes the audience more aware of Dissimulation's 'vice'. The conventional rhetoric of his speech elicits a particular set of responses: the spectators' recognition of what happens every day and (it is anticipated) their knowledge that they should condemn it. In this way the introductory monologue prepares the audience for other, more explicit commentaries later in the play.

The Jew of Malta provided its early audiences with a surplus of the familiar, setting before them not one but three distinct versions of the Vice's introductory monologue: Machevil's Prologue, Barabas's counting-house soliloquy, and Barabas's account of his exploits to Ithamore in the slave-market scene (2.3). Each of these draws upon conventional rhetoric and expectations before offering the audience a fresh way of making sense of the action. Each illustrates a different means by which the play begins to detach the Vice from the morality playworld. In performance, all three versions of the introductory monologue call the spectators' attention to the speaker as 'Vice'. This has been widely noted, especially of Barabas (see Spivack 346–53; Bawcutt, Introduction 10); but what should be emphasised is the diversity of the theatrical signals involved, ranging through physical appearance to demeanour to verbal detail. Machevil in particular is kin to Dissimulation; viewed side by side, the similarities are striking. Like his predecessor, he offers temptation and invites disapproval. His appearance arouses suspicion (an Italianate costume would be a convenient means of helping the audience to identify him); and his moral status is obvious in the references to the Guise, to religion as 'but a childish toy', to laws 'writ in blood'. At the same time, like the Vice, he reaches out to involve the audience: some may protest, but 'Admired I am of those that hate me most'. Like Dissimulation, his speech is one of shifting tones: sincere, scornful, challenging, deferential, arrogant. Then too, he affects a pose of honest cynicism, scorning hypocrites and wishful thinkers. He appeals to worldly wisdom and common practice, to the spectators' awareness that the world is inherently imperfect.

The soliloquy of Barabas that follows also draws upon the conventional rhetoric of the Vice. The speech occurs at the customary position, after the Prologue. The visual cues are strong. The spectator, alert to theatrical signals, would note the details of Barabas's physical appearance that mark him perhaps as a Jew (Maguin), but most certainly as a representative of Evil: a red 'Judas wig' perhaps, and the 'bottle nose' he shares with the Devil of the moralities. Barabas is a grotesque figure. He may be gaunt (the drunken Ithamore claims that 'he lives upon pickled grasshoppers and sauced mushrooms', 4.4.61–2) and meanly dressed ('The hat he wears Judas left under the elder when he hanged himself', 4.4.67–8). He may on the other hand be physically imposing: the role was played, after all, by Edward Alleyn. As Craik notes, 'the hoarder, instead of being represented traditionally as a thin starved creature, is shown usually as a gluttonous profiteer, bloated with ill-gotten gains and carrying about his moneybags and coffers on his person'; he is richly dressed, perhaps wearing 'a furred hood, another mark of the stage usurer' (*Tudor Interlude* 60).[12] These visual signs act in conjunction with the tone of arrogant familiarity, with the appeal to 'men of judgement', with the assumption that the audience shares his purposes, to indicate that he is to be viewed as morality Vice. This impression is confirmed in the play's third version of the Vice monologue, Barabas's account of his past exploits, which reminds the audience once more of the identifying marks of the Vice: the visual clues ('I worship your nose', says Ithamore), the listing of misdeeds, the invitation to conspire, the appeal to shared values (as in the references to foreigners, contemporary wars, and usury).

In each of these three versions, the audience is invited to recall the familiar figures from the popular tradition, with Machevil or Barabas arousing similar expectations of complicity and detachment, of the temporary success of the Vice but his ultimate defeat. At the same time, and for all their appeal to customary experience and usual expectations, these three versions of the monologue dislodged the Vice from his position as chief interpreter of the play-world. Though they retain much of the traditional rhetoric of performance, they generate new, and conflicting, ways for the audience to make sense of the action. The framing perspectives they offer are multiple (Machevil's Prologue), contradictory (Barabas in the counting-house), and finally (at the slave-market) disconnected from any 'morality' concerns.

Machevil's Prologue suggests that there may be more than one authorised way of viewing the action to follow. Machevil may have been recognised by early spectators as close kin to Dissimulation but he is also the heir to a long line of much worthier figures, the Prologues who had introduced the moralities. The Prologue was a traditional device of framing rhetoric, and activated its own set of customary expectations. In earlier plays, the Prologue spoke for the author. It preceded and framed the Vice by explaining the context of ideas for the action, offering the thesis that the play would demonstrate or, in 'explorative' plays, the hypothesis to investigate (Altman 6–8). The residual potency of the convention even today is indicated by the number of critical studies that begin with the Prologue and ask whether the play illustrates or advocates its 'Machiavellian' precepts.[13] Machevil's assertions about the exercise of political power may owe something to the Vice's 'sermon' (Spivack) or 'anti-sermon' (Beecher), but their manner recalls more strongly the pontificating of Prologues such as those to *Apius and Virginia* on chastity and *Cambises* on 'the honest exercise of Kings'. Indeed many earlier Prologues had devoted themselves as Machevil does to rehearsing authorities and learned allusions in a style far more earnest and 'educated' than that of the play itself. Two instances are the prologues to *Cambises* (a display of political learning, which refers to Agathon, Cicero, and Seneca, and cites the example of Icarus) and that to *Like Will to Like*, which justifies the title and action of the play by referring to 'Cicero in his book *De Amicitia*'.

Machevil is thus a more authoritative figure than the traditional Vice, and ultimately a more provocative one. The conjunction of Vice and Prologue in his figure flouts audience expectations, as Jones comments (*Engagement with Knavery* 64). Such a combination was rare in traditional plays: in *A New Interlude of Vice Containing, the History of Horestes* (1567), the Vice Revenge may open the play and hint at some of its concerns, but his speech of little more than twenty lines still functions more as the usual Vice monologue (he taunts individuals in the audience and speaks of preparations for battle). Machevil's Prologue, on the other hand, offered early spectators two superimposed perspectives – in effect, two authorised voices: the inverted moralising of a Vice and (speaking the same words) the straightforward sermonising of a traditional Prologue. Spectators may assent to or abhor his pronouncements;

but whichever (if either) voice they choose to heed, other conventional expectations are necessarily left unresolved. Yet, if the spectators are left uneasy, they may also find themselves strangely exhilarated, strongly expectant, as they watch the entry of Barabas '*in his counting house, with heaps of gold before him*'.

In this attempt to set up multiple perspectives on the action, the *Jew* is of course not unlike many of its contemporaries. As Braunmuller and others have shown, experiments with framing rhetoric in the late 1580s and early 1590s – beginning not long before the *Jew* with plays such as the *Spanish Tragedy* and evident in the early plays of Shakespeare – extended and enriched the inherited morality playworld. Old devices such as the Induction were exploited, becoming more elaborate, as in the discussion between Andrea's Ghost and Revenge that opens the *Spanish Tragedy*, or the opening sequence of Greene's *Alphonsus, King of Aragon*, where Venus is '*let downe from the top of the Stage*' and enlists the Muses 'to describe Alphonsus warlike fame' (111). Later instances develop this kind of opening into a complicated framing fiction, as in Wilson's *The Cobbler's Prophecy* or the Christopher Sly scenes in Shakespeare's *The Taming of the Shrew*: 'Your honour's players, hearing your amendment, / Are come to play a pleasant comedy' (Induction 2.129–30). At the same time, some contemporary plays departed from traditional practice and established the initial framing of the action by beginning *in medias res*. Influenced perhaps by the opening scenes of *Tamburlaine*, they experiment with dialogue for exposition, establishing the conflicting viewpoints of the figures on stage. This technique is used in plays such as *Arden of Faversham*, but it is associated particularly with the history plays – where the setting is often ceremonial, leading to formal statements of position, as in the funeral procession which opens *I Henry VI*. Examples may be found in the *Troublesome Reign*, *Edward III*, and *The Massacre at Paris*. Yet while these experiments with initial framing often introduce multiple voices, these remain in most instances complementary to the play's authorised version.

The *Jew*'s second Vice monologue, the soliloquy of Barabas, increases the impression of multiple voices claiming the audience's attention. But it also signals the means by which competing voices emerge, so that spectators might be led in time to make sense in a different, non-moralising way. Barabas looks and sounds like a morality Vice, with all the conventional expectations and responses that role entails; but he is also presented in other roles: as icon of Avarice, as type of merchant adventurer and Jew, as distinctive character, and as Presenter. The complications that ensue from these overlapping frames are reflected in the ambiguities of the stage image. Barabas's initial positioning on stage does not announce the Vice, but instead a dramatic device of another kind: the dramatic emblem. The Vice conversed with the audience from a position close to them, and the platform edge may well be the appropriate place for Machevil. The 'counting-house', whether a 'discovery-space' is used or not, is probably withdrawn for practical reasons against the frame of the façade, thereby making Barabas's interaction with the audience less immediate until he moves, after his monologue, to check the weather-vane.[14]

Functioning as a complex dramatic emblem, the counting-house appears to present a compelling perspective from which spectators might judge the world of the play: it shows an archetypal miser, foreshadowing the petty world of Malta and its pursuit of riches and Machiavellian self-interest (Zucker 84–7). But icon is at odds with spectacle. Where the iconography suggests that the action might be viewed from the standpoint of traditional, anti-materialist values, the spectacle of the gold itself offers another, contrasting frame. The riches commended to the audience's attention are not entirely to be rejected: the 'heaps of gold' add some glamour to the scene, summoning dreams of 'infinite riches'. It is not impossible that the stage image, together with the cataloguing of orient pearl and precious stones, evoked for its early audiences an impression of heroic endeavour (H. Levin, *Overreacher* 86). Certainly this was the response of a number of writers earlier in the twentieth century before attitudes to venture capitalism changed and the emphasis shifted to matters like the 'frenzied exhaustion of the earth's resources' (Greenblatt, *Renaissance Self-fashioning* 199).

At the same time, and differently again from these ambiguous larger perspectives, Barabas's viewpoint is shown as that of a character in a story. At the end of his speech Machevil had followed the practice of traditional Prologues in shifting from instruction to narrative: 'I come not, I, / To read a lecture here in Britany, / But to present the tragedy of a Jew'. This exhibiting of Barabas as stereotype Jew and merchant accords with both traditional and contemporary practice: most characters on the popular stage before and after 1585 are social types, and many (an increasing number after 1585) are also developed as distinctive or individual. But Barabas himself is also the Presenter. His monologue here, offering a particular viewpoint as central character on the action to follow, anticipates other important characters in later plays who establish the initial framing perspective: Richard of Gloucester, for example, with 'Now is the winter of our discontent', or Gaveston reading and reacting to Edward's letter – or the numerous villains and Malcontents who, as Braunmuller comments, will 'mediate their represented worlds for the audience' for many years to come ('Arts of Dramatist' 83).

What ensures that the multiple viewpoints in the *Jew* are not simply a matter of fostering ambiguities (as in the attitudes to gold) or complementary (as in a play such as 2 *Henry VI* with its fractious nobles balanced against good Duke Humphrey and the otherworldly King) is the effect of its shaping rhetoric. In the *Jew*, there is no one coherent or complete perspective offered to the spectators that they might adopt to make sense of the action. As several studies of the play suggest, the framing perspectives shift as well as multiply: Cartelli, identifying a series of 'false starts', describes the 'insistently shifting ground of the play' (*Economy of Theatrical Experience* 163); Jones traces the play's 'jolting shifts in perspective' (*Engagement with Knavery* 23). In any case, the perspectives suggested in Barabas's counting-house are different from those of Machevil's Prologue. This 'Vice' is detached from traditional expectations in a different way. This is a different Presenter, a different kind of participant in the action. And during his speech, the frames continue to shift; at any one time, one or another perspective will impress itself more on the audience's attention.

Beyond this shifting and multiplying, however, lies a more radical change in framing rhetoric. Where Machevil's Prologue suggests that there is more than one way of making sense of the action, Barabas's soliloquy confirms that some of these ways will contradict each other. The *Jew* in effect offers its spectators not merely multiple perspectives but colliding ones, not merely an enrichment of theatrical experience but a challenge to its coherence. The play's overriding pattern of shaping rhetoric is antithetical. It replaces the conventional distinction between 'is' and 'should' with an insistent opposing. This rhetoric of contradiction is different from the technique utilised in contemporary plays such as the *Spanish Tragedy*, where the death of Andrea is presented from one perspective after another, even as the sympathies of the audience are drawn in one direction (the early scenes of 1 *Tamburlaine* build up a picture of the presumptuous shepherd in a similar way). It does not wait for an accumulation of competing viewpoints (Machevil, then Barabas, then Ferneze), as Cartelli suggests (*Economy of Theatrical Experience* 171–2), but begins to operate early in the play.

The rhetoric of contradiction is hinted at in the manner of Machevil; it can then be identified in the contrasts of the counting house: between icon and spectacle, for instance, or, visually, between the impressive and the grotesque. What is more, the discrepancies between framing perspectives emerge in the words of the scene, distorting the eloquence of Barabas. As his monologue progresses, tensions develop between words and rhetorical structures. The speech moves to its rhetorical climax in a way not unlike the set-speeches of *Tamburlaine*, progressing with rising enthusiasm from 'paltry silverlings' to 'wedge of gold', from pearls and precious stones to 'infinite riches'. At the same time, the words undercut the glamour of these aspirations by their colloquial familiarity and their references to commerce. The tensions erupt in antitheses: between 'trash' and 'wedge of gold', between 'men of judgement' and 'vulgar trade'. Disparities develop between 'infinite' and containable riches: Barabas may refer to distant places and fabulous wealth, but the gestures of the counting-house ('of this quantity') render these treasures tangible and finite. All human activities are reduced to the mercenary – and pearls become as 'pebble-stones'.

The voice of Barabas may sound as authoritative as the voice of the Vice, and he remains the focus of the spectators' attention. But he no longer controls their view of the action. What he says is no longer just the familiar inversion of what is 'authorised'. And the responses he draws upon are no longer just the customary ones. Dissimulation spoke to an audience that could be relied upon to respond along certain lines; Barabas, as Rocklin suggests, speaks to an audience that must attend to learning new roles in their engagement with the Vice ('Experimental Dramatist' 140). And yet the tensions created by the *Jew*'s rhetoric of contradiction are not primarily between sympathy and detachment or even indulgence and restraint, but between opposing ways of making sense. The 'new' challenge for the 1580s spectator was not 'Do you dare to indulge?' – which was the traditional challenge of the Vice and his 'dangerous sport' – but 'Do you dare to interpret?'

Dismantling the frame

Complication, shift, and contradiction: these strategies begin to dismantle the traditional structure of framing rhetoric and to transform theatrical experience. They dislodge the Vice from his interpretative role, casting him adrift to continue the organising of mischief. They unsettle preconceptions, converting a world that recalls the predictable world of the moralities into one that challenges accustomed ways of feeling and responding in the playhouse. In this process, both sides of the morality contrast are subverted. The spectators discover that in the world of the *Jew* – and despite the self-righteous posturing of its inhabitants – no one can be entirely sure of 'what should be'. At the same time, the play also challenges any comfortable sense of 'what is', of the 'real' world assumed in the morality play to be the reference point of the action.

In its questioning of 'what should be', the *Jew* at first draws upon familiar, entirely-to-be-expected ironies. The ironies inherent in the role of the Vice have been mentioned. More generally, the morality play had undertaken the task of defending 'true' Christianity, whether against Catholics or against Protestants or worldlings or unbelievers. Indeed one critical approach to the *Jew* sees the play very much in these terms. G. K. Hunter, for example, contends that by stressing Barabas's role as Jew the play calls upon a traditional framework of responses, conditioned by theology and activated by biblical allusions, in which the Jew was the opposite of the Christian, preferring material possessions to spiritual enlightenment, and therefore liable to be charged with an assortment of errors, crimes, and inherent sins ('Theology of *Jew*' 214–18). Barabas, like the Vice, is obviously to be condemned, but this is for his religion as much as his wickedness.

But Barabas, like the Vice, is also an important instrument of satire. His commentary on the deeds of the Christians exploits the contrast between their 'profession' and their actions; his failure as Machiavel (he trusts Ferneze) highlights their greater proficiency. This particular kind of ironic inversion, referring to shared values but inverting expectations, was not new. It was familiar to the audience from earlier plays, including the *Three Ladies*. The most notable instance there is that of the charitable Jew Gerontus, who is fully aware that 'many of you Christians make no conscience to falsifie your fayth and break your day' (1245–6); but nevertheless gives up all claim to the money Mercador owes him rather than have the defaulting merchant renounce his Christian faith. In case the audience misses the point, the moral is drawn by the (infidel) Turkish judge: 'Jewes seeke to excell in Christianitie, and the Christians in Jewishnes' (1754). But the instance is hardly unsettling. As Douglas Cole comments, the 'Christian' Jew is presented as wholly admirable and the ironic contrast is straightforward (133). The exemplum merely confirms the moral superiority of the true 'Christianitie' that society professes.[15]

The *Jew*, nevertheless, goes beyond such simple morality equations to offer an additional, potentially subversive perspective. Its rhetoric of contradiction destabilises conventional ironies, so that the demonstrations of contrast (between Jew and Christian, between profession and practice) repeatedly twist. The spectators are offered an additional perspective frame that complicates their making sense: that both Jew and Christian are essentially the same. This is demonstrated repeatedly, in word and deed. It is especially so of their attitudes to 'heaven', which both parties use as a convenient court of appeal. It sanctions their lies: 'heaven can witness it is true, / That I intend my daughter shall be thine' (Barabas to Mathias, 2.3.255–6). It deals appropriately with enemies: 'As sure as heaven rained manna for the Jews, / So sure shall he and Don Mathias die' (Barabas, 2.3.250–1); 'Wonder not at it, sir, the heavens are just' (Ferneze, 5.1.55). And then, both Jew and Christian are shown to have the same besetting sins: 'This is the life we Jews are used to lead, / And reason, too, for Christians do the like' (Barabas, 5.2.115–16). Barabas begins as the exemplar of Machiavellian self-interest – '*Ego mihimet sum semper proximus*' (1.1.188) – and in subordinating everything and everyone else to his own ends he progresses from miser to murderer. But the same egoism is echoed in the actions of the Christians – and with the Christians, too, it issues in a callousness that views mass-murder as a convenient means to an end: 'Why, then the house was fired, / Blown up, and all thy soldiers massacred' (Ferneze, 5.5.105–6).[16]

The contradictions extend to the figure of the 'good Jew'. Abigail is generally noted as such, and her role seen as comparable to that of Gerontus in the *Three Ladies*; for Cole, 'the traditional Christian order is vindicated by the contrasting perceptions and choices of Abigail' (143). But these perceptions and choices are never shown simply, without qualification. Lady Love and Lady Conscience are scorned as poor and naive by the wicked characters, and after their respective 'falls' rebuked as sinful by the virtuous, but these judgements are quite predictable and consistent within the playworld. Abigail, despite her attractiveness, is repeatedly presented in contexts that detract from her goodness and beauty. She is motivated by love and a sense of duty; but her good intentions result, ironically, in violence and death. Nor is this only because the Machiavels take advantage of her naivety, since Abigail herself is also shown to deceive and betray. To the moral confusion in her actions is added the ambiguity of her beauty, which is always brought to the audience's attention in a context of exploitation. Her father in hopes of recovering his gold sees her as 'the loadstar of my life' (2.1.42); and even Mathias, for all his apparent sincerity, speaks of her on his first entrance as 'the rich Jew's daughter' (twice – 1.2.364, 380). Above all, it is her sexual charms – an aspect of her 'Jewishness' (Sanders 344–5, Goldberg 236–7) – that others compete for. The friars welcome her to the nunnery as a 'moving spirit' (1.2.327); Barabas plays upon the lechery and avarice of Lodowick in discussing her as a 'diamond'; and even her true love Mathias signals his less-than-honourable intentions with his allusions to the 'tale of love' and 'the sweetest flower in Cytherea's field' (1.2. 367, 377).[17]

The 'good Jew' is finally depreciated in the presentation of her death, with the action oscillating between pathos and farce. Abigail herself speaks sincerely, and her life in the nunnery has been exemplary ('chaste and devout, much sorrowing for my sins', 3.6.12–14); but when she dies no one wastes any time or sympathy on her. Mathias and Lodowick are lamented at length, and ceremoniously; Abigail is briefly regretted, but only by the lecherous Bernadine in a callous twisting of her final words: 'Ay, and a virgin, too, that grieves me most' (3.6.41). Any lingering pathos is dissipated by the treatment of her body, dragged off as an object to be disposed of: 'First help me bury this' (45). To the Friar she has become merely 'this' – not 'this virgin', 'this nun', nor even 'this body'. In ways such as these, the contradictory perspectives of the *Jew* complicate and disturb response to the shared values necessary to the morality play-world. By casting doubt upon the certainties of 'profession', or even upon the hope of goodness, the *Jew* subverts one side to the basic morality contrast.

The complementary side to this contrast, the spectators' comfortable sense of the 'real', is also undermined by the *Jew*'s insistent rhetoric of contradiction. This employs, but goes beyond, the traditional alternation in the morality between serious and comic action (see Bevington, *Mankind to Marlowe* 197–8). One aspect of this rhetoric surfaces in the play's use of violence, and involves the exploitation of what James L. Smith identifies as the techniques of 'black comedy' (14–18). Basing his comments on the Royal Shakespeare Company productions of 1964 and 1965, Smith emphasises the comic effects produced by the speed of changes and reversals and the 'collision' of contradictory emotions:

> Much of this scene [the killing of Bernardine and deceiving of Jacomo] depends upon the crudest slapstick and 'mugging'. But the hackneyed music hall routines are more than mere clowning, and the 'side-splitting'

laughter derives its sadistic punch from the diabolical ingenuity of the villains and the gleeful irreverence with which a human body is thrown about the stage like a sack of potatoes. (15–16)[18]

'Black comedy' usefully defines the effect of the play's passages of violent farce. The term, as Smith acknowledges, is a new label rather than a new technique. Nicholas Brooke had earlier identified its main features in describing the *Jew* as 'a *Cambises*-type play', or one 'which can move between the polarities of straightforward serious-ness and outright farce' ('Marlowe the Dramatist' 95). But, while instances of black comedy do occur in the moralities, its effect in these earlier plays is somewhat different. The scenes of violent farce are often used explicitly to underline a moral message; in any case they are never far removed in the action from the affirmation of conventional values.

In the *Jew*, on the other hand, the impact of such scenes is usually more ambiguous. Contradictory responses are exploited, severing the link between violence and moral lesson. Smith points to the duel and its sequel, the lamentation of the parents, as an effective passage of black comedy, presenting 'the same event as both violent farce and poignant "tragedy", all within the space of forty lines' (17). But the oppositions are not limited to kinds of action. Both parts of the scene – farce as well as tragedy – offer additional, opposed ways of viewing. The 'poignant' mourning (which should nevertheless be acted very seriously) has definite comic undercurrents. The matching speeches of the bereaved parents call for ritualised and repetitive gestures, but also ones that may be somewhat too emphatic, as in Katherine's 'Lend me that weapon that did kill my son, / And it shall murder me' (3.2.23–4); or in the climactic speech of Ferneze, with its use of the conventional language of love poetry, complete with refer-ences to 'one sacred monument of stone' (30), 'my daily sacrifice of sighs and tears' (32), prayers to an apparently deaf heaven (33), hands and hearts (35). All of this is less than appropriate for the pair of young men, one of whom had already planned to betray his friend before Barabas tried to sell him a 'diamond'.

The dislocation of emotions associated with black comedy points to a more general dislocation and distortion in the playworld that is not restricted to moments of violence. Time after time, the words do not fit and customary expectations are confounded. Coburn Freer, noting the *Jew*'s 'stylistic multiplicity', comments also that it refuses 'to mesh character and voice, event and language' (158). One of many possible instances is the scene where Barabas seeks his gold at midnight (2.1). He is at first a 'tragic' figure, his grief amplified by imagery of darkness, disease, and disfigurement; yet he is at the same time only melodramatic, since recovery of his treasure is surely not as significant as the Exodus and hardly requires an invocation to the God of Israel. And then, after his greed has been demonstrated as both passionate and grotesque, the scene ends with an overflowing into the ridiculous as Barabas '*hugs his bags*' and imagines himself hovering in the air with the lark, 'Singing o'er these, as she does o'er her young, / "Hermoso placer do los dineros"' (2.1.63–4). Instances such as these give some point to the comments of Joel Altman, who discusses the play in relation to traditions of writing that encouraged virtuoso display, describing it as 'an exercise in wit run wild' (353).

But the rhetoric of contradiction is not limited to words. The ordinary life of Malta, which seems so precise and tangible, can suddenly give place to the absurd (Pilia-Borza's greeting of Ithamore: 'saluting me in such sort as if he has meant to make clean my boots with his lips', 4.2.33–4); to fantastic action (Barabas 'thrown' over the walls); and even to an occasional excursion into fable (the three-part test by which the Jews can choose how much money to forgo; or Ithamore's dismissal of the duel: 'And so they met, and as the story says, / In doleful wise they ended both their days', 3.3.23–4). The effect, as Zucker notes, is often to combine 'story-book villainy and intrigue' with a 'distance from normal ethical judgments' (84). At such times, the spectators are offered an additional perspective on the action. The world suggested is one adrift from the everyday 'realities' of the morality playworld, but retaining its own rules and rituals and narrative logic. It is a world that belongs to the privileged space of the playhouse, allowing its spectators an indulgence in fantasy, a freedom from the rules of ordinary existence quite exceeding their limited, authorised complicity with the Vice. In this additional playworld the action becomes very much – but never completely – as Cartelli describes it: a 'complicated theatrical game, played for the sheer pleasure it brings in making fantastic pastime of the freedom of the stage' (*Economy of Theatrical Experience* 173).[19]

This option for making sense of the play – the possibility, in effect, that the action makes no sense in 'morality' terms – is associated particularly with the third version of the Vice monologue. It arises less from any multiplying of perspectives or indeed from any failure of restraining structures (Cartelli's view) than from the play's insistent rhetoric of contradiction. The sense of an alternative, fictional world existing at first beside, but then cast adrift from, the complacent morality playworld develops sporadically in the early part of the play, before it takes definite shape in the slave-market scene (2.3).

This scene is pivotal. Viewed simply from the perspective of the traditional moral consensus, the slave-market has considerable impact as satire. It is similar to (even if notably more complex than) that of Lucre's purchasing of Lady Conscience in the *Three Ladies*. Abandoning her struggle with poverty, Conscience accepts Lucre's overpayment for her brooms; in consequence, she is suitably 'spotted' and must guard the house of adultery. Neither Love nor Conscience, the scene demonstrates, can survive in the mercenary city. In the *Jew*, the slave-market likewise marks a point where the city becomes corrupt beyond redemption. All honourable motives disappear as Barabas pursues his revenge and Ferneze his political and financial advantage. The slave-market itself, standing in silent witness to much of the action, implies the devaluation of human worth to mercenary terms: as the Second Officer comments, 'Every one's price is written on his back, / And so much must they yield or not be sold' (2.3.3–4). Lodowick asks 'And what's the price?' (65) of the 'diamond' that is Abigail, and Barabas uses the language of commerce to assert the inevitability of his revenge: 'The account is made, for Lodowick dies' (243–7).

> *Lodowick.* Well, Barabas, canst help me to a diamond?
> *Barabas.*   O, sir, your father had my diamonds.
>   Yet I have one left that will serve your turn.
>   *I mean my daughter – but e'er he shall have her,*   Aside.
>   *I'll sacrifice her on a pile of wood.*
>   *I ha' the poison of the city for him,*
>   *And the white leprosy.*
> *Lodowick.* What sparkle does it give without a foil?
> *Barabas.*   The diamond that I talk of ne'er was foiled,
>   *But when he touches it, it will be foiled.*   [Aside]
>   Lord Lodowick, it sparkles bright and fair.
> *Lodowick.* Is it square or pointed? Pray let me know.
> *Barabas.*   Pointed it is, good sir – *but not for you.*   Aside.
> *Lodowick.* I like it much the better.
> *Barabas.*   So do I too.
> *Lodowick.* How shows it by night?
> *Barabas.*   Outshines Cynthia's rays;
>   You'll like it better far o' nights than days.
>
>   (2.3.49–64)

This is the exemplary rhetoric of the morality, replete with reminders of 'what should be'. Malta's decadence is manifested in its debasement of sexuality. When Barabas offers Lodowick his 'diamond' he is acting more as the procurer than the merchant, and the language retains sexual overtones even when he becomes, in aside, the fanatical Jewish avenger – with the expressions 'serve your turn', 'foiled', 'it', and 'white leprosy' (most likely the second stage of syphilis – Henke 2.315). In Malta the 'sweetest flower' perishes; and the fruits of corruption survive to poison, deceive, and 'stink like a hollyhock' (4.4.40). That is the condition of the world, and Christian is no better than Jew. As such passages show, it is both within and because of the ordinary life of the city that the Machiavel can thrive. Machiavellianism in Malta – and by extension London – is not simply a matter of adhering to a set of reprehensible precepts, though reference to these made the play provocative and topical; it is more a succumbing to ancient vices, a moral state before it becomes a political programme.

But this is not the only way the audience are led to see and make sense of the action. Lady Conscience's 'fall' leads predictably to her deserved punishment: imprisonment and (in the sequel play) a stone seat labelled 'Remorse'. There is no such inevitability about the *Jew*. If the playworld is predictably corrupt it is also increasingly unpredictable, so that possibilities and expectations multiply. Passages such as this can be viewed earnestly as satire, but they also suggest a liberating extravagance. Although the restraining structures persist, the morality contrast between 'what is' and 'what should be' loses its definition. The action is at once familiar and grotesque, with the ordinary practices of society (buying and selling, arranging marriages, the routine courtesies and discourtesies) set against instances of the absurd and distorted. Chasms open up between words and actions and responses. The opposing elements are sharply defined: 'respectable' commerce or obscene soliciting, obsequiousness or aggression, gravity or farce. Barabas's asides call audience attention to these contrasts, but they also enlist the audience, not so much for a traditional judgement on the action as for the excitement of participating in an outrageous revenge. There is a cutting loose from the 'real', with the action that ensues demonstrating in the characters, and cultivating in the audience, a failure to feel appropriately. In this, the new rhetoric of the *Jew* challenges the exemplary method of the moralities. Lady Conscience's 'fall' relies for its theatrical effect upon the evoking of customary and predictable responses, with no significant variation or contradiction being anticipated. In the *Jew* the challenge to, even the suppression of, appropriate feelings enables violence to be accepted and the laughter of black comedy to be liberated. At such moments the theatrical experience is too extravagant to be accounted for simply in the usual terms as a tension between approval and disapproval, identification and alienation, or even 'engagement' and 'resistance'.

At this point in the play there is 'dangerous sport' indeed. The centre-piece of the slave-market scene, framed between passages that show the selling of Abigail and the gulling of the young men, is the play's third version of the Vice's introductory monologue.

> *Barabas.*   Hast thou no trade? Then listen to my words,
>   And I will teach thee that shall stick by thee:
>   First, be thou void of these affections,
>   Compassion, love, vain hope, and heartless fear;
>   Be moved at nothing, see thou pity none,
>   But to thyself smile when the Christians moan.
> *Ithamore.*   O brave, master, I worship your nose for this!
> *Barabas.*   As for myself, I walk abroad o' nights,
>   And kill sick people groaning under walls;
>   Sometimes I go about and poison wells;
>   And now and then, to cherish Christian thieves,
>   I am content to lose some of my crowns,
>   That I may, walking in my gallery,
>   See 'em go pinioned along by my door.
>   Being young, I studied physic, and began
>   To practise first upon the Italian;
>   There I enriched the priests with burials,
>   And always kept the sexton's arms in ure
>   With digging graves and ringing dead men's knells;
>   And after that was I an engineer,
>   And in the wars 'twixt France and Germany,
>   Under pretence of helping Charles the Fifth,
>   Slew friend and enemy with my stratagems.
>   And after that I was an usurer,
>   And with extorting, cozening, forfeiting,
>   And tricks belonging unto brokery,
>   I filled the jails with bankrupts in a year,
>   And with young orphans planted hospitals,
>   And every moon made some or other mad,
>   And now and then one hang himself for grief,
>   Pinning upon his breast a long great scroll
>   How I with interest tormented him.
>   But mark how I am blest for plaguing them:
>   I have as much coin as will buy the town!
>
>   (2.3.169–202)

This speech is sometimes described as marking a reversion to morality methods. Spivack argues this, commenting that Barabas becomes from this point onwards merely 'the homiletic demonstration of serialized villainy' (348).[20] Certainly the speech, together with Ithamore's comments, retains references to those features by which the Vice can be recognised. The improbable claim to excessive villainy is quite traditional, as is the suggestion that Barabas is play-acting to deceive a new victim. This time too, Barabas may occupy a platform position, closer to the audience and the traditional location of the Vice, rather than being placed as an icon '*in his counting-house*' against the tiring-house façade. The monologue thus poses the possibility that Barabas may, after all, be no more than the Vice, that he may, at last, be able to be contained within the familiar, traditional pattern of responses.

But any such reassuring impression is short-lived. The morality technique is recalled, of inverted but authorised commentary, but the consequence is again to emphasise the *Jew*'s difference from its predecessors. The sudden shift into, and then out of, the monologue suggests that this is a world where nothing can be taken for granted. Added to this is a change in the way the audience is called upon to view the action. Barabas as Vice may have moved forward on the platform, but the speech is no longer simply directed at the audience, with the Vice framing the action and intimating how he will deceive his next victim. The Officers and Slaves may have left the stage, declaring that it has been a 'reasonable market' (they may of course still be leaving when Barabas launches into his account), but Ithamore remains to become an on-stage audience, mediating initially between Barabas and the spectators, framing the third version of the monologue with his comments ('O brave, master, I worship your nose for this!') and responses ('Faith, master, / In setting Christian villages on fire', 2.3.175, 204–14).

The monologue is, in effect, relocated within a fictional play-world, where the audience does not need to make sense of the action in morality terms but simply respond to the demands of the story. If Barabas's claims are (to say the least) extravagant, then that is quite compatible with the other extravagances of this alternate playworld. One consequence is that the possibilities for viewing and response multiply. Bawcutt notes some of them: 'Is the catalogue of crimes he recites to Ithamore ... a piece of genuine autobiography to be taken at face value, or a pretence designed to indicate to Ithamore what kind of behaviour is expected from him, or a kind of bravura display that hovers on the borders of fact and fantasy?' (Introduction 23).[21] The answer is, perhaps and potentially, all of the above. The specta-tors, like Ithamore, must decide whether to accept the speech as exemplary rhetoric, or assent to it as a fiction detached from the morality frame. They are, in effect, called upon to construct their own perspectives on the action.

After Barabas

After Barabas the rhetoric of performance would never be the same. The Vice had been a theatrical success story: a long-lasting and especially vital dramatic convention. Before the mid-1580s, his prominence on the stage had been challenged only by the occasional Clown like Simplicity in the *Three Ladies*. Other experiments with the convention – the arrival of the 'public' Vice to supplement the Vice-as-entertainer and the Vice-as-tempter (Dessen, *Late Moral Plays*), and the use of multiple Vices – had enriched but not essentially altered the framing rhetoric of the morality tradition.[22] And yet by 1595 the 'Vice' had become merely an old-fashioned comic figure, his role as the chief representative of evil usurped by a new generation of 'Machiavellian' villains: Aaron the Moor (*Titus Andronicus*); Richard of Gloucester; the adulterous Suffolk (*Henry VI*) and Mortimer (*Edward II*) and Mosby (*Arden of Faversham*).[23] The key to this sudden and remarkable change, I would suggest, was not simply a change in theatrical fashion or venue (Jones, 'Dangerous Sport' 63), nor the impact of the actor Tarlton (Weimann 187), nor the multiplying of perspective frames as plays moved from demonstration to narrative.[24] What mattered was the new rhetoric of the *Jew* and its dismantling of the morality frame. Evil, no longer contained, was set loose in the world of the play. Cast adrift from his special position as authorised interpreter of the morality playworld, the traditional Vice disappeared, even though his descendants retained a deal of what had once been the Vice's rhetorical baggage, including the catalogue of misdeeds that had once featured in the introductory monologue.

But theatrical conventions also reflect prevailing views of 'reality', or 'how things are'. *The Jew of Malta* signalled more than the exit of the Vice from the popular stage. What the play offered was a new way of coming to terms with experience, with, in particular, the possibility that there was more than one kind of interpretative narrative that spectators might use in making sense of the world, 'real' or theatrical. Viewed from one perspective, of course, the play still draws upon the traditional moral consensus: like the more effective of the late moralities it is a compelling satire on the deficiencies of a supposedly Christian society, a quite traditional and conventional challenge to 'how things are'. Viewed another way, however, the play challenges these conventional beliefs and attitudes, undermining any comfortable sense of 'what should be'. And then from another viewpoint still, the action becomes fantasy or 'play', adrift from moral judgement, freed from the old dichotomy of rule and transgression. By offering no single, consistent, or authoritative frame of reference, the *Jew* enabled (though it did not compel) its first audiences to disengage from their accustomed ways of viewing and responding in the playhouse.[25]

Along with the Vice then, the spectators were also set free. The play's rhetoric of contradiction encouraged them to disagree – and that is something quite new and different in the late 1580s context. *The Jew of Malta* transformed theatrical experience by dismantling the framing rhetoric of the morality with its 'authorised versions' and complementary voices. The spectators are called upon to respond to an unstable and unpredictable world that renders judgement uncertain. It is a playworld that may seem very different from, but in its confusions is not unlike, the later playworlds of *Doctor Faustus* and *Edward II*.

CHAPTER 6

Looking at Angels

=====

Not 'Shakespearean' but 'debatable'

The traditional narrative of dramatic character tells of the advent of a new kind of character in the 1590s. This is usually labelled the 'Shakespearean', and is considered to be quite different from the limited figures of earlier plays. The new character is defined in terms of its essential nature, as being 'individual' and 'complex'; as having become more like a 'real' person (like 'us', that is); as having achieved 'self-expressiveness' and 'interiority' and 'subjectivity'. The humanist subject has arrived, though not (one must admit) to universal applause.

Marlowe's role in this narrative is not to be Shakespeare, even if his characters are also seen as representing the new 'individual'. His protagonists are described typically as larger-than-life, as 'dramatizations of ... heroic impulses'; as 'overreaching heroes who conveyed the simultaneous grandeur and cynicism of this brave new Elizabethan world and its unbridled colonial appetites'. They are at the same time the victims of their own energies: controlled perhaps by their 'repetition compulsion'; or 'ravished' by desire. On the stage they depend, we are told, on 'self-conjuration'; on 'declaration' rather than Shakespearean 'embodiment'. In the traditional narrative of character they are merely a distraction: briefly the focus of attention and imitation for their *style* of self-assertion, but old-fashioned within a few years. They are mocked by the young and clever ('The stalking steps of his great personage, / Graced with huf-cap termes and thundring threats'), and their rhetoric dismissed as flying 'from all humanity'. And yet, they also survived on the popular stage as 'potent embodiments of Elizabethan emotions' until the closing of the theatres.[1]

The traditional account, with its culmination in the 'Shakespearean' character, has been under siege for many years: initially because of problems with defining the 'real', but more recently because of revisionist challenges to the timing and even the fact of change. Perhaps, some suggest, this new 'interiority' was the same old interiority to be found in many medieval writings. Perhaps, others maintain, this kind of character with its 'imaginary interiority' could not properly exist in the sixteenth- and seventeenth-century theatre, and the notion of the humanist subject had to wait for later readers and critics to be articulated.[2] For some time now, the critics have circled each other like predatory birds, while notions many of them consider illogical, undesirable, or simply old-fashioned linger as cultural commonplaces and as strategies for performance. The discussion has become unproductive, made more so because many commentaries have been sidetracked by the obvious, relying on the conspicuous differences between (in most cases, post-1600) Shakespeare and earlier texts, and paying insufficient attention to the differences that emerge in the playtexts of 1585–95.

This chapter suggests that the narrative of dramatic character needs to be rewritten. It shifts the focus of discussion from essential nature to performance, from the labels appropriate to the figure on stage to the rhetoric that shapes the relationship between figure and spectators, leading them to observe and interpret in particular ways. This relationship has always been an important aspect of theatrical experience: assigning particular attributes and motivations is an element in the spectators' – and almost invariably the readers' – making sense of the action before them. Marlowe's larger-than-life protagonists may have astounded and challenged and enthralled their first spectators, but – especially from the perspective of the 1580s and the popular tradition – they do not represent his most influential contribution to the development of dramatic character. That, I argue, was a new way of presenting character on stage, a new, transforming rhetoric of character. Marlowe's place in the narrative of character should be seen not as marginal but as seminal, with Faustus in particular showing the way to Hamlet.

The new rhetoric, as so much else that was notable in late sixteenth-century drama, emerged in the years between 1585 and 1595. It is anticipated, at odd moments, in plays such as *The Spanish Tragedy* and *Titus Andronicus*; yet it finds its first full expression not in any play of Shakespeare but in Marlowe's *Doctor Faustus*. The new rhetoric made possible something quite different on the late sixteenth-century stage: what might be termed a 'debatable' character. The label indicates that divergent views of a character's motivation become possible.[3] It points not so much to a change in the 'kind' of character as to a significant shift in audience and reader response: from an attention to ethical concerns to an interest in individual psychology. The new rhetoric of dramatic character called upon audiences to observe the action differently and to ask different questions about the figures on stage. Traditionally, these questions had focused upon questions of 'should' or 'should not': should the character indulge his appetites or slaughter his opponents or take revenge? The point of interest with some characters now became 'why': why is the character unable to repent or too ready to kill or reluctant to take revenge? Philologus (the despairing Calvinist hero of *The Conflict of Conscience*) is supplanted by Faustus, Cambises (the appalling tyrant) by Macbeth, and Hieronymo (the avenger) by Hamlet.

The impact of this new rhetoric persists in our own responses to sixteenth- and seventeenth-century plays. Four hundred years after they first appeared on the stage, we are still asking 'why' about Faustus and Macbeth and Hamlet, even when we accept as more or less transparent the 'character' and motives of a host of other personages: not just minor, forgotten figures such as Lady Conscience (*The Three Ladies of London*) and King Rasni of Nineveh (*A Looking Glass for London and England*), but substantial presences such as Queen Margaret (*Henry VI*, *Richard III*), and Titus Andronicus – or even Hieronymo and Barabas and Richard of Gloucester. These figures are certainly distinctive and memorable, but it is their deeds and dilemmas that we question, not any intrinsic 'nature' they might possess. 'Debatable' characters, on the other hand, still attract contesting opinions, informed by our individual powers of observation and notions of psychology.

Joining the debate

Why do we debate some of these dramatic figures and not others? The answer to the question has usually been in terms of essential nature, with changes to dramatic character supported by reference to some general historical narrative. Earlier accounts spoke of an increasing or evolutionary 'realism', or the illusion of realism: this can be seen in studies such as Bernard Spivack's on the Vice convention or in Robert Weimann's observations about a new 'realistic mode of characterization' (200) that offers 'a new sense of the interdependence of character and society' (197). Another significant emphasis has been on the character as 'individual', in line with the received notion of the Renaissance as the triumph of individualism. Commentaries have generally drawn upon the changed emphases in philosophical discourse from about 1600, as seen in writers such as Montaigne, Bacon, Descartes, and Locke; and these have been revisited and reassessed by the newer historicists. Some studies argue for the influence of particular cultural developments: Protestantism, for many, is seen as associated with more 'individual' characters on stage because it stressed individual conscience and interpretation and religious experience (Diehl, *Staging Reform* 90–3; Sinfield 159–60). Or, at a less articulate level, the aggressive energies of mercantilist trade are transferred, Stephen Greenblatt argues, to the individualistic theatrical energies of characters such as Tamburlaine (*Renaissance Self-fashioning* 194). Others find more general parallels. As A. R. Braunmuller comments:

> Changing dramatic techniques [in presenting character] in the 1580s and 1590s are part of complex cultural phenomena – the 'interiorization' of experience, the creation of models for human individuality – that appear everywhere from ethical argument (over usury, for example) and economic behaviour (joint-stock companies, for instance) to religious controversy and parliamentary debate. ('Arts of Dramatist' 69)

The problem with all these accounts of change is that they do not explain what makes the audience's relationship with Faustus different from that with Lady Conscience on the one hand or Richard of Gloucester on the other. It is not simply that Faustus is somehow more 'realistic' or 'individual' – even if the Prologue to *Faustus* does suggest that the story is to be seen as something more 'real', or closer to everyday life, than accounts of royal dalliance or heroic exploits far away. The physical presence of Conscience on stage is quite 'real' in this everyday sense; and Richard is nothing if not 'individual'. There are of course difficulties with the notion of 'realism' (or the 'illusion of realism') as found in critical writings. Theoretical objections have been urged for sixty years or more, from L. C. Knights's attack in 'How Many Children Had Lady Macbeth?' upon A. C. Bradley and anyone else who would praise Shakespeare's characters for being 'real as life' ('"character" ... is merely an abstraction from the total response in the mind of the reader or spectator, brought into being by written or spoken words', 4) to the more recent, far-reaching assault on 'humanist' ideas and values, in which 'character' is subsumed by signifying practices or subjected to the 'decentring of man' (Dollimore).[4]

Theoretical deficiencies aside, 'realism' – especially of the kind

familiar on the stage since the late nineteenth century – is also an
inadequate marker of change in describing sixteenth-century performance practice. There were significant continuities within the
popular tradition and no neat distinctions between what we would
call 'realistic' and 'non-realistic' characters. In late moralities such as
the plays of Robert Wilson (these were written in the 1580s and
early 1590s), the characters may bear abstract labels, but their
theatrical impact relies upon the precise observation and imitation
of everyday life. Indeed, as Alan C. Dessen suggests (*Late Moral
Plays* 135–7), late morality characters on stage would have looked
more like 'realistic' social types than abstractions; and the playgoers
may have noticed little difference when individually named figures
arrived on stage.[5] After about 1585 the action of plays was more
likely to be contained within a narrative than a didactic frame, but
that in no sense presupposed any especially naturalistic conventions.
For many years performance retained elements of the older 'demonstrating' style, with its regular use of choric statement, for example,
or direct address or role-playing. There may have been fewer
abstractions in the cast list, but the representative 'type' remained an
important figure on stage. Most characters could still be described
as exemplary rather than individual, as depending (in Leech's terms)
upon 'declaration' rather than 'embodiment'.

Attempting to categorise characters as more or less 'real', moreover, fails to take into account the range of contemporary responses
to the drama. While contemporary theatrical practice (direct
address, for example) put into question the distinctions we are familiar with (illusionist/non-illusionist), contemporary assertions about
the drama made use of contested and shifting notions of the 'real'.
There were accusations against playing of 'feigning' or 'idolatry' and
defences of moral efficacy, with each side assuming a different relationship between the theatrical and the real. But being 'real' or 'true
to nature' was also a rhetorical claim, with playwrights offering a
succession of competing, more authentic versions of 'real' life. The
Prologue to *Faustus* calls upon everyday life, but then a very similar
claim had been made about ten years earlier for the late morality
The Three Ladies of London and its story of Lady Conscience. In
spurning the mythical, heroic, and pastoral, Robert Wilson may well
have had in mind romances such as *Clyomon and Clamydes*, just as
Marlowe had in mind late moralities such as the *Three Ladies* when
he claimed in *Tamburlaine*'s Prologue to offer more direct experience of the senses ('you shall hear the Scythian Tamburlaine ... /
View but his picture'). A few years later, of course, Hamlet advised

the Players to remember 'the purpose of playing', which he defined as 'to hold as 'twere the mirror up to nature' (3.2.20–2); and Ben Jonson commended 'the true artificer' as not running 'away from nature', while holding up to scorn the rhetoric of 'the Tamerlanes and Tamerchans of the late age' as flying 'from all humanity' (*Timber* 542).

What these assertions show, apart from the rhetorical clout there was assumed to be in appealing to 'commonsense' notions of the real or everyday or natural, is that the rhetoric of dramatic character was changing. The dramatic conventions that satisfied an audience as representing the 'real' on stage (or what an audience was prepared to accept as 'real') were different in 1590 as compared with 1580, and different again in 1600. The dominant element in this process was not so much any movement towards 'debatability' as the increasing 'complication' of dramatic character. By the 1590s the figures on stage – responding at least in part to the theatrical one-upmanship of playwrights and companies – had become more various in kind, more distinctively 'individual', more individually complicated than the characters of the late morality.[6] This greater complexity is reflected in the elaboration and amplification of the Senecan set-speech noted by Wolfgang Clemen and A. R. Braunmuller. As the latter comments, audiences expected more information and 'playwrights elaborately developed their characters' verbal analysis of their own actions' ('Arts of Dramatist' 69).

But 'complication' does not of itself provide a sufficient explanation for the different relationship that becomes possible between an audience and Faustus. We learn a great deal about Richard and Hieronymo, or for that matter Tamburlaine and Barabas. They are more interesting, satisfying, and entertaining than any figures on stage before them. Yet we also remain in little doubt about their 'characters' and motives. We consider the meaning of what they do (what, that is, their deeds exemplify) rather than the nature of how they 'are'. The same response applies to the many richly elaborated or overdetermined characters in later plays (Ben Jonson's Volpone is but one instance): our interest in them remains primarily ethical, not psychological. Complication was the dominant trend in the late sixteenth-century drama, but it led to Volpone rather than Hamlet. There was no inevitability about the arrival of the 'debatable' character.

Another long-standing commonplace of criticism – along with 'realism', 'individuality', and 'complication' – has been the 'fact' of a late sixteenth-century change in dramatic character. In the past

twenty years or so, however, general narratives of the Renaissance
have diversified, as have attitudes to humanism, and revisionist
critics have challenged the traditional narrative. Perhaps, as one
group of 'cultural materialist' writers suggest, there was no late
sixteenth-century change. Perhaps the new 'Shakespearean' character ('realistic', 'individual', and endowed with 'interiority') did not
exist in the sixteenth- or seventeenth-century theatre – and the
notion of the humanist subject had to wait for eighteenth-century
readers and critics to be articulated. This view was anticipated by
Catherine Belsey in *The Subject of Tragedy*, in contending that the
humanist subject with its 'imaginary interiority' (48) did not properly arrive on stage until the Restoration (in response then, she
maintains, to 'the interests of the bourgeois class which came to
power in the second half of the seventeenth century', 7). For Belsey,
the drama from 1576 to 1642 is transitional, trapped between two
conflicting modes of apprehending the world, the 'emblematic' and
the emerging 'illusionistic' (26–33). Other writers are more extreme;
Francis Barker, for example, argues that even in *Hamlet* 'interiority'
is but 'gestural', and 'subjectivity' a matter of 'historical prematu-
rity' (163).[7]

But it is not only the 'cultural materialists' who dispute the 'fact'
of a late sixteenth-century change. Other writers deny or downplay
change in emphasising continuities with the classical or medieval
past. In *Character: Acting and Being on the Pre-modern Stage*,
Edward Burns argues from a 'rhetorical' perspective that 'modern'
notions did not appear until the eighteenth century, and that the
'classical' concept of character persisted in sixteenth- and seventeenth-century playtexts. Characters in these plays are part of the
ethical demonstration of the text: their 'nature' is coterminous with
their deeds and their social role or position (85–6). Their 'individuality', he suggests, inheres in their distinctiveness, not in any sense of
an inner self (139, 154).[8]

A different challenge – based upon another kind of cultural continuity – is found in 'new medievalist' commentaries. Perhaps, they
suggest, sixteenth- (or for that matter eighteenth-) century 'interiority' was not 'new', but belonged instead to a long-standing cultural
tradition. As David Aers remarks, medieval courtly literature offers
many examples of a 'concern with inward states of being'; and this
preoccupation is also 'a fundamental aspect of mysticism and the
literature of self-examination and self-fashioning in late-medieval
culture' ('Whisper in Ear' 190).[9] This does not mean, of course, that
these interests and preoccupations were necessarily translated to the

popular stage with its different audiences and different expectations. A sixteenth-century romance such as *Clyomon and Clamydes*, for example, does not attempt the moral and psychological complexities of the contemporary, non-dramatic romances of Sidney and Spenser. These, as Brian Gibbons notes (213–17), had little influence on popular dramatists before the Jacobean period. At the same time, and at a more general cultural level, Aers provides a useful reminder that 'the whole medieval penitential tradition involves a fundamental and perfectly explicit distinction between *inner* and *outer*, between that which is within and passes show and that which is without, the external act' ('Whisper in Ear' 185). As this suggests, a number of the conventional oppositions between 'old' and 'new' characters cannot be sustained, because they simply do not discriminate. Characters such as Richard II (to cite a commonplace example) do not suddenly acquire a sense of inner authenticity by being able to contrast the 'external manners of lament' with the 'substance' of an 'unseen grief / That swells with silence in the tortur'd soul' (*Richard II* 4.1.296–9). The dichotomies usually found in such speeches – substance/shadow, inner/outer, reality/appearance – are not new: they are cultural commonplaces, and the ordinary material of morality drama. They do not of themselves indicate any particularly 'humanist' subjectivity or interiority.

None of this, however, much advances our understanding. The preoccupation of these revisionist narratives with 'subjectivity' and 'interiority' – with the essential nature of character rather than the relationship between character and audience – ensures that they are no more adequate than the traditional studies they repudiate. Neither revisionist approach (deferring 'change', stressing continuities with the past) comes to terms with the arrival on stage of the 'debatable' character. Neither approach explains, that is, why spectators can see a figure such as Faustus or Hamlet as 'debatable' when they do not see earlier figures in that way. The distinction between new and old (often formulated as Shakespeare versus the rest) is a persistent one in both performance and critical practice, even if it is sometimes obscured in critical theory.[10] In particular, relocating the 'difference' from earlier text to later reader does not solve the problem. Burns's eighteenth-century reader or critic may have discussed Hamlet's 'essential nature' but would not, I suggest, have debated the psychology of Lady Conscience or Cambises.

Finding words for certain concepts may need to wait upon particular philosophical discourses, or upon particular shifts in political power, but that does not preclude earlier, less articulate changes at the level of theatrical experience, where audiences see and make sense of the action before them. In the case of the 'debatable' character, the interpretive narratives familiar to modern readers may be anachronistic, as some critics suggest, but they respond, I would contend, to 'something there': some element in the play's dramatic rhetoric, a particular structuring of experience that was initially potent in performance but still encoded to some degree in the written text. The more absorbing question is not, after all, whether 'humanist' or eighteenth-century responses are in some way 'wrong' in fact or philosophy – or whether they are anticipated in the reading of fourteenth-century poems – but how they become possible. That possibility derives less from 'character' or 'subject' or 'essential nature' than from changes in late sixteenth-century dramatic rhetoric.

Addressing the theatrical past

The first of the new 'debatable' characters was Marlowe's Faustus. In his case the new rhetoric of character operates sufficiently, though not always consistently, to transform the traditional relationship between spectators and figure on stage. They are brought to look differently at the figure before them, with the effect that they are prompted to make sense of Faustus for themselves, in terms that is of their own notions of psychology rather than, necessarily, in terms of any authorised version or interpretive narrative offered in the play – the Prologue or Epilogue, for example, or even Faustus's farewell to the Scholars. It is this looking differently that signals a new rhetoric of character.

My concern here is not so much to stake out a position in the debate on Faustus's 'character' – to offer, that is, another 'reading' – as to seek those traces in the text that register a change in the relationship between audience and character. As Max Bluestone once remarked, viewpoints on Faustus 'diverge as sharply as views of doctrine' ('*Libido Speculandi*' 40). From one perspective of course Faustus remains just another conventional figure: readily typed (fool, 'unsatiable speculator'), his career an old-fashioned cautionary tale.[11] Then again, the character is complex enough to satisfy the 'commonsense' expectations of the 1590s audience. But his presentation before an audience is by no means coherent: when Faustus makes important choices, the action ranges from the up-to-date Senecan set-speech which opens the play, methodically surveying his career options like Gaveston or Richard of Gloucester; to the routine psychomachia late in the play where Mephistopheles threatens arrest and Faustus submits like a typical morality character; to the complex debate with himself in the final soliloquy. At the same time, and despite these inconsistencies, the play constructs the impression both that Faustus has a 'character' that 'persists recognizably in each new appearance' (States xv) and that he perceives and acts for reasons particular to himself.

A key to the newness of Faustus can be found in perhaps the least likely of places: Marlowe's use of the old-fashioned psychomachia. The new theatrical experiences that made debate possible, that transformed the relationship between audience and character, depended, in the first instance, upon an addressing of the theatrical past. For its early spectators, and like *The Jew of Malta*, *Faustus* defined itself against specific dramatic conventions of the late moralities and the ways that audiences had 'learned to see and respond' (Williams).

> *Faustus.*   Commend me to my dearest friends,
>   The German Valdes and Cornelius.
>   Request them earnestly to visit me.
> *Wagner.*   I will, sir.   *Exit.*
> *Faustus.*   Their conference will be a greater help to me
>   Than all my labours, plod I ne'er so fast.
>
>   *Enter the* GOOD ANGEL *and the* EVIL ANGEL.
>
> *Good Angel.*   O Faustus, lay that damnèd book aside
>   And gaze not on it, lest it tempt thy soul
>   And heap God's heavy wrath upon thy head!
>   Read, read the Scriptures. That is blasphemy.
> *Evil Angel.*   Go forward, Faustus, in that famous art
>   Wherein all nature's treasury is contained.
>   Be thou on earth as Jove is in the sky,
>   Lord and commander of these elements.
>
>   *Exeunt* [ANGELS].
>
> *Faustus.*   How am I glutted with conceit of this!
>   Shall I make spirits fetch me what I please,
>   Resolve me of all ambiguities,
>   Perform what desperate enterprise I will?
>
>   (1.1.66–82)

The Angels arrive early in the play, before the consultants in magic, before Mephistopheles or Lucifer, before Pope or Emperor or Clowns, before any of the Shows. Faustus has opted for magic, and the old machinery of the psychomachia promptly appears. Here, for all its late sixteenth-century garb of Protestant scripture-reading and humanist conflation of deities and unabashed materialist dreams, is none the less the same old contest for the human soul between the forces of good and evil.

Or so it would appear. Most commentators describe the angelic psychomachia as a simple old-fashioned device for showing spiritual and/or psychological conflict. What this view overlooks, however, is the theatrical impact of the Angels on the playhouse stage: what it meant, that is, for the early spectators to see and hear the Angels physically present before them. In that context, the early scenes with the Angels were not brief, leftover scraps of morality play but something new and potent. They did not simply indicate that Faustus is in conflict but also made it possible for the spectators to interpret his actions in different, non-traditional ways.

By 'different' ways of interpreting I mean more than challenges to conventional thinking, more than dissatisfaction with the Epilogue and its comments about 'forward wits' and 'hellish' falls. Individual contemporaries may have experienced the play as 'atheistic' or disturbing, prompting, perhaps, the rumours about Marlowe's opinions that Thomas Beard exploited (see above, Chapter 4) or the apocryphal stories of 'one devil too many' (Chambers 423–44). Modern writers may unearth in the text subversions or inversions or transgressions of various kinds: an angelic conspiracy (Minshull, 'Dissident Subtext' 202–3); the 'dull and feeble bleatings' of the Good Angel (Brooke, 'Moral Tragedy' 99); the exposure of religious discourse as 'theatrical' (Grantley 235). But these 'readings' of the play are, in effect, only consequences of the new way of interpreting the play allows, a new way that is characterised by a momentous change in the relationship between audience and figure on stage. It is an insight into this change that is offered by Faustus's encounters with the Angels.

To appreciate the contemporary impact of the Angel scenes, we should set aside much of our own experience of modern productions of the play – and a great deal of modern commentary. Most critics have made the Angels intelligible to readers today by subordinating them to modern notions of the psychology of Faustus. They are no more, it often seems, than projections of his inner conflict. For Robert Weimann, they are but 'dramatic metaphors' superfluous to the 'temptation [which] arises within the hero's own breast' (183–4); for Catherine Belsey, 'shadowy figures whose very existence might be an illusion' (*Subject of Tragedy* 43). Even those who mention the Angels as visible figures on the sixteenth-century stage tend to side-step promptly into the mind of Faustus. G. M. Pinciss expresses a typical view: 'Whether they are reflections of Faustus's own mental processes or independent of them, these allegorical figures objectify the inner conflict in the hero; through them the contest for his soul is dramatized' ('Cambridge Years' 257).[12] The directors have followed suit and staged illusory or 'psychological' Angels. In some notable modern productions, the Angels have become mere objects, mere voices. Thus John Barton in 1974 (Royal Shakespeare Company production, Edinburgh and London) showed the Angels as aspects of Faustus's consciousness, entirely dependent upon him. Ian McKellen as Faustus held a white doll and a black puppet, manipulating them and supplying the voices. Christopher Fettes in 1980 (Fortune Theatre, London) dispensed with distinctive figures or visual signs: the angelic voices were supplied by Faustus's fellow scholars as they sat, robed in black, at a long refectory table (Tydeman 75, 81–2; Michael Scott 29).

Where modern 'Angels' are generated by the mind of Faustus and illustrate his 'character', sixteenth-century Angels were provided to offer guidance to the audience; as Leo Kirschbaum comments, the Good Angel is 'the voice of God, the expounder of things as they are' (231).[13] They were not an illusion, but there to be seen: unmistakably physical presences on the playhouse stage, like the four Angels that attend the figure of London in the prologue to *The Three Lords and Three Ladies of London*: two '*before her, and two after her with bright Rapiers in their handes*'. To early spectators the Angels would have looked like something quite familiar: angelic figures certainly, but also the heirs of the Virtues and Vices of the morality. The early spectators saw three figures grouped in some conventional way on stage, with the Angels visually separate, both from each other and from Faustus. They were identifiable immediately by their costumes and possibly by what they carried. We can imagine them with wings perhaps, the Good Angel with 'yellow silk hair' and carrying a bible; the Evil Angel indicated by some grotesque visual detail and carrying the instruments of despair, the dagger and rope halter.[14]

In their significant grouping with Faustus the Angels called upon a lengthy cultural tradition. The psychomachia was an established way of leading readers and spectators to make sense of both reality and human behaviour. For more than a thousand years – in religious art, in sermons, in poetry – it had offered a view of human life as a continuing contest for the soul between the forces of good and evil (Spivack 60–95).[15] In the drama, this set-piece conflict between allegorical figures had faded by the 1580s;[16] but (and this is not generally noted) the rhetoric of the psychomachia survived into the late morality plays as the dominant rhetoric of character, inherent in the way the audience is led to make sense of relationships and conflict and decision-making. What structures the audience's view of action and impulse on stage is the experience of opposed voices. Reality – or how things 'are' – is shaped as a series of contests: between good and evil (the definition of these varies with the version of established truth appealed to), and, by extension, between their consequences or corollaries – between Conscience, for instance, and Sensual Suggestion, between Faithful-Few and Despair, between Policy and Pride.[17]

In the late moralities, and this may have been more apparent in performance, the rhetoric of opposed voices was not restricted to separate figures on stage. Plays were inventive and varied in the ways they presented conflict, even with allegorical figures. These might engage the protagonist in discussion, and then continue the discussion when he left the stage; they might act in dumb show to represent his spoken thoughts. They were by no means static or distant figures: they whispered in ears and touched faces and waved objects in front of characters. There were, in effect, various techniques available in popular dramatic practice to show Faustus troubled by inner voices.

This variety can be illustrated in a single scene from *Apius and Virginia*, an interlude written some twenty years or so before *Faustus*.[18] In this, Judge Apius succumbs to the persuasions of the Vice Haphazard and his own intense lust, and makes a damnable decision: to 'deflower' the beautiful Virginia. At this point, two figures emerge from the Judge: his (inconvenient) Conscience and his (capacity for) Justice, both carrying emblematic properties: '*Here let him make as thogh he went out and let Conscience and Justice come out of him, and let Conscience hold in his hande a lamp burning, and let Justice have a sword and hold it before Apius brest*' (428.1–4). As the figures stand near him, Apius speaks for them ('And Justice saith Judgement wold have me condemned ...'). The Vice Haphazard is unimpressed by Apius's account and remarks: 'These are but thoughts, man!' (437). When Apius, unrepentant, leaves the stage with the Vice, the Virtues lament their condition and point to its cause, elaborating upon what Apius has said: 'I spotted am by wilfull will, / By lawles love and luste' (Conscience, 462–3); 'And yet hath filthy lust supprest / My vertues in one houre' (Justice, 472–3). Thus in about fifty lines the Virtues have been presented first as physically part of and then as separate from the protagonist, then as spoken thoughts, and lastly as independent figures. A later scene presents the voice of virtue in yet another form, when the Judge's Conscience is heard to speak offstage: as the stage direction instructs appropriately, '*Here let* Conscience *speake within*' (559.1).[19]

Increasingly, the opposed voices of the traditional rhetoric of character were incorporated into the speeches of individual characters – as reported experiences or adopted roles, or even as unseen presences on stage. But this was no sudden change, and indeed the mixture of presentational techniques persisted well into the 1590s. In the 1560s Apius explains what Conscience and Justice 'say', even before they begin speaking. In *The Tide Tarrieth No Man* (printed 1576) the Vice Courage reacts to the death of his friend Greediness by '*reasoning with himselfe*': 'My thinkes these newes are not true which you tell. / Yes, truely, he dyed in a great madnesse' (p. 77).[20] In about 1590 the Usurer scene in Lodge and Greene's *A Looking Glass for London and England* shows an Evil Angel 'tempting' the wicked, despairing Usurer, with the Usurer's experience shown primarily as a contest involving unseen voices, but also as reported thoughts and mimed action: 'In life no peace: each murmuring that I heare, / Mee-thinkes the sentence of damnation soundes, / Die reprobate, and hie thee hence to hell' (p. 217). At this point the Evil Angel, the visible counterpart of these 'murmurings', mimes his 'tempting'. Silently, he offers the dagger and halter the Usurer himself had brought on stage. No Good Angel is to be seen, but three lines later the Usurer becomes aware of the alternative choice as 'a voice amidst my eares / That bids me staie: and tels me that the Lord / Is mercifull to those that do repent' (p. 217). His decision to repent is then expressed as self-debate, using a new set of opposed voices: 'May I repent? oh thou my doubtful soule, / Thou maist repent, the Judge is mercifull'.[21]

What these instances, both early and late, suggest is a problem inherent in the label 'interiority', especially as it has been used in the critical debate about the 'Shakespearean' character. Long before Marlowe or Shakespeare the popular drama provided access to some kind of 'interiority'. These conflicts are located within the minds of Judge Apius and the Vice Courage and the Usurer, and there is no differentiation in the nature of the conflict as the action slips seamlessly from one mode of representation to the next. There was, in effect, no sudden, one-way shift from the externalised conflicts found in the morality play to the internalised conflicts found in the Shakespearean soliloquy – despite this being the commonplace view in developmental studies. Belsey, for example, argues that: 'As the literal drama discards allegory, and morality personifications give way to social types, concrete individuals, the moral conflicts externalized in the moralities are internalized in the soliloquy and thus

understood to be confined *within* the *mind* of the protagonist'
(*Subject of Tragedy* 43). Actual dramatic practice was different:
both ways of representing a character's inner experience (externalised, internalised) could exist – interchangeably – in plays within
the theatrical experience of the 1590 playwright or spectator. They
were the ordinary, conventional ways of showing inner conflict.[22]

This conventional 'interiority', however, did not provoke debate
about the 'essential nature' of the figure on stage. Whether the
opposed voices were seen or unseen, the traditional rhetoric of character in the moralities drew upon a customary way of responding to
characters in performance. As Edward Burns suggests, the spectators
are called upon to recognise their own deeds and dilemmas in the
action before them and apply the lessons both to themselves and to
wider social contexts; the audience, he comments, is constructed as
'subject' (54). Thus the figure of Conscience in a number of plays is,
importantly, 'your' – and everyone's – Conscience; a Vice-figure
such as Ambidexter offers himself as reflecting 'your' double-dealing
and the practices 'you' can observe in society. Even when the figure
on stage becomes more 'individual', the individual 'character'
remains no more than the sum of its opposed voices, fitting neatly
within its exemplary frame. The particular natures of Judge Apius
and the Usurer are of no significance beyond what they reveal of the
effects of lust and avarice and despair – and when they arrive at
some unpleasant and appropriate end, we feel no impulse to debate,
or even question, the motivation that has led them there.

It is this traditional rhetoric of character, as well as the ordinary
expectations of their popular audience, that the Angels of *Faustus*
insist upon with their familiar visual rhetoric. As figures conventionally grouped with but visually separate from Faustus, they act as
interpreters, offering the spectators a metaphysical frame to make
sense of the action. As opposed voices, they represent aspects of
Faustus, but they also offer alternatives, urge decision, and call upon
the spectators to make sense of the scene in the traditional way: as
relevant to their own moral choices. Standing on stage, the focal
point of these angelic exhortations, Faustus becomes not the particular person but a particular instance that represents the continuing
contest between good and evil.

And yet the Angels also bring something new. They may look and
indeed sound like fragments of morality play, but in what they make
possible for the spectators, the Angel scenes in the first half of
Faustus are significantly different from other angel scenes (the B-text
judgement scene included) and other instances of the psychomachia.

What is 'different' and unexpected in the Angel scenes is not the Angels – they remain conventional, unambiguous figures throughout – but how Faustus is seen to respond to them. Even as the Angels suggest that he is an exemplary figure, Faustus begins to escape from the exemplary frame.

In leading the audience to focus on Faustus, what the visual rhetoric draws attention to is his lack of awareness, and that departs from conventional practice. The audience hears what the Angels say, but it sees that Faustus neither hears nor understands them adequately. His responses can be traced moment-by-moment in the language of these brief encounters: they are observable as a fluctuating and erratic attention to the Angels and a limited awareness of what they say. When he does respond, it is most often to fragments of their speeches, to individual words and phrases, and seldom to whole statements or to their meanings. It is only after the fourth appearance of the Angels, midway through 2.3, that he exhibits any real comprehension.

He can be observed as least attentive during their first two appearances. In the first, Faustus stands asorbed in the book of magic, while the Good Angel ensures that the audience understands the implications of what they see: 'O Faustus, lay that damnèd book aside / And gaze not on it, lest it tempt thy soul / And heap God's heavy wrath upon thy head!' (1.1.72–4). But Faustus, it seems, is entirely unaware of the Good Angel. Nor does he respond directly to the Evil Angel. The relationship hinted at is more like an affinity of imagination, with the words of the Evil Angel echoing and confirming Faustus's aspirations with their references to 'that famous art', 'all nature's treasury', and 'lord and commander' (75–8). Faustus stands silently until the Angels leave. His comments then ('How am I glutted with conceit of this!', 80) reflect the Evil Angel's suggestions of wealth and power. A similar lack of attention marks the Angels' second appearance:

Good Angel.   Sweet Faustus, leave that execrable art.
Faustus.   Contrition, prayer, repentance – what of them?
Good Angel.   O, they are means to bring thee unto heaven.
Evil Angel.   Rather illusions, fruits of lunacy,
      That makes men foolish that do trust them most.
Good Angel.   Sweet Faustus, think of heaven and heavenly things.
Evil Angel.   No, Faustus think of honour and wealth.
                                                     Exeunt [ANGELS].
Faustus.   Of wealth?
      Why, the seigniory of Emden shall be mine.

                                                     (2.1.15–23)

Once again the spectators see Faustus standing on stage, absorbed perhaps in his own thoughts, unaware (it would seem) of the angelic presences. Both Angels advise Faustus to 'think', both answer his question, 'Contrition, prayer, repentance – what of them?', with rhetorically balanced appeals, but they are in effect debating each other. While the audience is made aware of the contest between opposed voices, Faustus responds only to 'wealth', the final word of the Evil Angel.

This defective awareness is usually seen as indicating some flaw of character, rather than being considered in the context of early performances and the past experience of early audiences. Wilbur Sanders, for example, suggests that it reveals Faustus's 'blindness to the real issues at stake' (217); Douglas Cole that it stresses 'the Doctor's own will and responsibility in acting against his own best interests' (237).[23] In context, however, this imperfect awareness becomes an important theatrical signal. Behaviour like that of Faustus may not be unprecedented in the morality tradition – though we cannot be certain when many plays do not survive – but it is sufficiently unusual to breach audience expectations. What the spectators observe with *Faustus* is no simple, traditional exemplum of spiritual blindness, in which the character does not 'see' but the disability lasts only long enough to illustrate the point.[24]

The consciousness of morality characters – however their inner conflict is conveyed – is not in general distinguished from that of the audience. What the spectators see and hear, the figures on stage see and hear. They listen not to fragments and phrases but to whole speeches. They listen to what is said, whatever form is taken by the rhetoric of opposed voices. The Usurer hears 'each murmuring' as clearly as he hears the 'voice amidst mine eares' – and as clearly as the audience hears them. He is aware first of the reprobate's damnation and then of the Lord's mercy – just as the audience is aware. In *Apius and Virginia*, the Judge is shown to be fully conscious of his options. When Conscience and Justice 'come out' from him, Apius himself explains to the spectators what they have just seen, reports the views of both Virtues, and informs the audience of the inevitable consequence of his actions: 'that [the] fier eternall my soule shall destroy' (436).

The decisions of morality characters may be misguided or stupid, but they are invariably conscious ones, their 'reasoning' explicit and the audience suitably informed. Thus in *The Conflict of Conscience* the protagonist Philologus endures without speaking a protracted discussion between his 'Conscience' and a Vice-figure (Sensual)

Suggestion. When he then leaves the stage in the latter's company his words and actions indicate that a wilful choice has been made: 'My Conscience speaketh truth mee think, but yet because I feare / By his advice to suffer death, I doo his wordes forbeare' (1897–8).[25] Morality characters may vary in understanding (some require the whole play to 'see' the point it is making) but they do not vary in their awareness.

The theatrical signal of Faustus's imperfect awareness becomes even more exceptional when set against the adjoining action. In the soliloquies that preface the Angel scenes or develop from them, the audience is led to see Faustus as fully conscious of his opposed voices. Before the Angels appear in 2.1, for example, he is shown to be aware of the elements of his spiritual conflict, and responsive – like any morality figure – both to statements that present as thoughts ('Despair in God, and trust in Beelzebub') and to those that present as heard 'external' voices ('Abjure this magic, turn to God again!'). But when the Angels speak, his awareness changes. There is, as the audience can observe, a discontinuity in his responses to spoken thoughts and those to speaking figures, a switching between his full awareness of opposed voices and his imperfect listening to the Angels. This abrupt shifting, into the Angel scene and then out of it, disrupts what appears to be the traditional rhetoric of character. The view of the audience is realigned, their relationship with Faustus transformed.

In the presence of the Angels Faustus can be viewed as 'detached', his experience suggested as in some way disconnected from – and extending beyond – the old rhetoric of conflict. In early performances of the play the process of detachment may not have been complete. The spectators viewing the Angel scenes may still have 'identified' with Faustus in the old way, recognising him as a figure that represented them in the eternal contest between good and evil. They could, that is, attend to the angelic messages and make sense quite traditionally. From this viewpoint his motives and actions are, transparently, damnable. At the same time, however, they could set aside the angelic messages, suspending ready-made judgement, and focus on the details of Faustus's behaviour. They may still have 'identified' with the figure on stage, but in a new way. As with passages such as the bond-signing, their attention is now drawn to the individual moments of his non-representative experience. And the responsibility for making sense of what they see is shifting to individual members of the audience.[26]

The exemplary effect does not necessarily disappear. In looking at

Angels, we may still ask, 'What does this scene demonstrate?' – but our main interest has become, 'Why does Faustus behave in this way?' We make sense of the action in terms of our own notions of psychology. That the early audiences may have made sense in terms of sixteenth-century notions, while we make sense in terms of more recent ones, is not the point. The angelic psychomachia in *Faustus* refashioned the conventional rhetoric of character, giving the audience access to new, non-traditional perspectives on the figure before them.

Anticipations of the 'debatable' character

It is this possibility of detachment from interpretive frames – and of being more than the sum of his opposed voices – that sets Faustus apart from his near contemporaries as much as from his predecessors in the late morality. The traditional rhetoric of opposed voices continues to flourish in the drama before 1595, remaining part of ordinary or 'commonsense' expectations about character.[27] Moments of crisis produce vigorous self-debate. A familiar example is that of Richard III, afflicted by his 'coward Conscience'.

> What do I fear? Myself? there's none else by;
> Richard loves Richard: that is, I and I.
> Is there a murderer here? No. Yes, I am!
>
> (*Richard III* 5.3.183–5)

The voices here are especially combative, though by no means unusual. Some years earlier, Hieronymo's voices had registered his conflicting impulses as he toyed with the familiar implements of despair:

> This way, or that way? Soft and fair, not so:
> For if I hang or kill myself, let's know
> Who will revenge Horatio's murder then?
> No, no! fie, no! pardon me, I'll none of that:
> *He flings away the dagger and halter.*
> This way I'll take, and this way comes the king,
> *He takes them up again.*
> And here I'll have a fling at him, that's flat.
>
> (*Spanish Tragedy* 3.12.16–21)

The rhetoric of opposed voices also governs moments of decision. Many of the soliloquies and asides in pre-1595 drama are structured as debate. A simple example is Hubert's soul-searching in *Troublesome Reign* when the King instructs him to put out the eyes of Prince Arthur:

– I faint, I fear. My conscience bids desist.
'Faint' did I say? 'Fear' was it that I named?
My king commands; that warrant sets me free;
But God forbids, and he commandeth kings.

(1 Troublesome Reign 1511–14)

Other instances can be more elaborate, rehearsing each argument in detail, progressing step-by-step until the decision is reached. Most retain the impression of separate voices within the character, if only by using the structure of question and answer. Some preserve the sense of voices emanating from elsewhere. In *Troublesome Reign*, Philip of Faulconbridge, the figure who becomes the Bastard in Shakespeare's *King John*, first hears his own voice as detached from himself, then the same message as a 'hollow echo' in Nature, before his 'trance' or 'dream' (258, 259) is interrupted by the voice of his commonsense experience:

– *Phillippus atavis edite regibus.*
What sayst thou, Philip? Sprung of ancient kings?
Quo me rapit tempestas?
What wind of honor blows this fury forth?
Or whence proceed these fumes of majesty?
Methinks I hear a hollow echo sound
That Philip is the son unto a king;
... Birds, bubbles, leaves, and mountain's echo – all
Ring in mine ears, that I am Richard's son.
Fond man, ah, whither art thou carried?
How are thy thoughts yrapt in honor's heaven?
Forgetful what thou art, and whence thou cam'st?

(1 Troublesome Reign 260–6, 273–7)

A similar effect is achieved elsewhere by the use of quoted texts. Hieronymo, seeking arguments to counter the biblical injunction against revenge, consults the book of Seneca he carries in his hand: '*Vindicta mihi!*' (*Spanish Tragedy* 3.13.1–44). Each of the three Latin quotations he cites is developed by explication, advancing the argument another step. The same methodical approach (as well as similar stage business) lies behind the opening soliloquy of *Faustus*, though Faustus goes beyond Hieronymo's straightforward explication.

None of these instances from plays contemporary with *Faustus* asks the audience to respond to the figure on stage as 'debatable'. The focus of these speeches is still ethical (what the character should do) rather than psychological (why the character is behaving in this way). Unlike Faustus in the presence of the Angels, all of these characters -Richard, Hieronymo, Hubert, Philip – are fully aware of their 'voices'; and their experience does not extend beyond them. Nor are these figures detached from the play's interpretative frame. Even Richard's obsessive, self-conscious egotism is presented for view as part of a firmly established pattern of acknowledged good, acknowledged evil, a pattern reinforced visually in this scene by the two tents set up on stage.

Similar comments could be made about the self-debates of other contemporary characters. Indeed, most of the instances of inner conflict – the troubled consciences – belong to the villains, like the 'fearful thoughts' of York (*2 Henry VI* 3.1.331) or the 'disturbed thoughts' of Mosby (*Arden of Faversham* 8.1); and as such they invert conventional values rather than detaching from them. Most even follow a predictable pattern: a listing of arguments for what they 'should' do (as with the morality Vice, the audience is constantly reminded of received values), followed nevertheless by a decision to persist in evil and then another listing, this time of plans for more villainy. The key to their projected behaviour is often a traditional 'dissembling': 'Peace, John, here comes the legate of the Pope; / Dissemble thou, and whatsoe'er thou sayst, / Yet with thy heart wish their confusion' (John, *2 Troublesome Reign* 309–11); ''Tis fearful sleeping in a serpent's bed, / And I will cleanly rid my hands of her. / But here she comes, and I must flatter her' (Mosby, *Arden of Faversham* 8.42–4); 'But I must make fair weather yet awhile, / Till Henry be more weak, and I be strong' (York, *2 Henry VI* 5.1.30–1); 'Why, I can smile, and murder whiles I smile ... / And set the murderous Machiavel to school' (Richard of Gloucester, *3 Henry VI* 3.2.182, 193).

Among all these, there is little sense that they act as they do for any reason other than ingrained wickedness (rather as if Faustus took no notice of the Good Angel because he was predestined a reprobate, and that is the only way of explaining his actions). Of the villains, Mosby is perhaps most affected by inner conflict: 'Continual trouble of my moody brain / Feebles my body by excess of drink' (*Arden of Faversham* 8.3–4). He regrets his new social position ('My golden time was when I had no gold', 11) to the degree that he imagines himself as a *de casibus* figure ('Each gentle starry gale doth shake my bed / And makes me dread my downfall to the earth', 17–18). But he is quite explicit about what drives him, and feels no urge to repent: 'The way I seek to find where pleasure dwells / Is hedged behind me that I cannot back' (20–1). Having arrived at this point, he then reconfirms his decision to murder Arden (23), and proceeds at once to plan the elimination of his accomplices, including his 'serpent' lover, Alice Arden (24–44).

If the 'debatable' character is anticipated in plays contemporary with *Faustus*, it is not in their highly conscious, explicitly argued self-debates, nor in the conventional inversions of villainy. There may be substantial continuities between the traditional rhetoric of opposed voices and the 'debatable' rhetoric of the mature Shakespearean soliloquy, but the one does not simply evolve into the other. Narratives of dramatic character often argue this; Michael Mooney, for example, suggests a direct line from the Vice to Hamlet through Richard III.[28] Despite their theatrical energy, however, the descendants of the Vice develop into complicated characters rather than necessarily 'debatable' ones. The 'debatable' character may assume the position of the Vice as focus of audience expectations and chief interpreter of the playworld, but this represents a significant displacement of framing perspectives: where the Vice inverts playworld values in order to affirm them, the 'debatable' character is detached from, and often at odds with, the 'authorised' values of the playworld. There is no straightforward path of development from Apius or the Usurer or Richard of Gloucester to the soliloquies of Hamlet or Macbeth, but rather a process of realignment and transformation, to which Faustus provides the key.

It is the 'detachment' of the character from the interpretative frame that makes 'debatability' possible. In other contemporary plays, however, such 'detachment' tends to be temporary, and to occur at moments of heightened emotion where perceptions are disturbed. The increasing emotionalism of the playhouse drama after 1585 is often linked with late sixteenth-century change in dramatic character. Emotional excess becomes common at this time, and the figures on stage have increasingly more to say about what they feel. This 'self-expressiveness' has been seen as pointing to the 'new' character. Simon Shepherd, for example, identifies an over-flowing of emotion as marking the arrival of the humanist subject. He instances *Titus Andronicus* as introducing a new kind of response to the figure on stage:[29]

> In place of a critical relationship with a split subject, the audience is offered a view into the non-problematic, depoliticised subjectivity of the central fictional character; and this view feels satisfyingly full because everything is expressed. The passive audience overhears it all, it gets something for nothing. (Shepherd 83)

Shepherd argues that earlier plays had restrained the expression of emotion within conventional limits; indeed, one key device that signalled extreme emotion was simply silence or an inability to speak (76).[30] The key to the 'depoliticised subjectivity' of Titus and later characters is an emphasis on 'emotional expression which satisfies a need' rather than on persuading the onstage audience or giving narrative information (82). This 'subjectivity' Shepherd examines in *Titus Andronicus* 3.1, where the imagery of earth and sky, sea and deluge 'works to fill the world with Titus's emotion' (82). In all this, the 'point' of Titus's lamenting 'is the revelation of personal emotion: the expression is fluent and full, the inner Titus seems totally knowable' (83).

Shepherd's argument is worth attention because 'self-expressiveness' is commonly seen as a feature of the Shakespearean character. The instances he selects, however, lead in fact to a quite different conclusion: they suggest, in effect, that the 'new' character requires more than sheer quantity of emotion. The spectators may be able to immerse themselves passively in Titus's outpourings, just as (see Cartelli) they might indulge their aggressive fantasies in the eloquence of Tamburlaine or the 'moral abandon' of Barabas. But that need not bring them to debate Titus's inner nature. The reasons for his distress are all too apparent, and it is in the nature of his playworld that injury and loss are felt keenly. His 'filling the world with emotion' can be seen merely as a particularly vigorous instance of traditional rhetorical amplification; and his identification with nature another reworking of images familiar from Senecan plays and Petrachan poetry – and, on the popular stage, from the lamentations of Hieronymo. But if this eloquence reveals (as Shepherd contends) the 'inner Titus', then there is not much to discover. The spectators are led to focus not on his individual psychology but on his appalling situation. That is the centre of theatrical attention: during this particular scene (3.1) Titus must plead for the life of two sons, endure the sight of his daughter Lavinia minus tongue and hands, compete with his brother and remaining son to cut off a hand first, and then take delivery of two heads and a hand. And in case the spectators have failed to grasp the horror of all this, the scene ends with a sensational group exit bearing the properties – with Lavinia having to carry off the severed hand between her teeth. The moral is plain: Titus is indeed, as his surviving but banished son says, 'The woefull'st man that ever liv'd in Rome' (3.1.289).

It is not, however, the volume of Titus's emotional outpourings that hints at some new kind of 'interiority', as Shepherd suggests, but several moments here and elsewhere in the play where he becomes 'detached', where (as Faustus in the presence of the Angels) he sees and hears differently from others in the playworld – and from the watching playhouse audience. The most significant one occurs in 3.1 where, alone on stage, he laments the loss of his sons. The scene has begun with a procession of '*Judges and Senators, with Titus' two sons, bound, passing on the stage to the place of execution, and* TITUS *going before, pleading*'. Some ten lines later '*Andronicus lieth down, and the Judges pass by him*'. Titus fails to notice that the procession has departed, and continues to plead to the tribunes for nearly twenty lines. His son Lucius must remind him (twice) that he is merely recounting his 'sorrows to a stone':

> *Titus.* Ah, Lucius, for thy brothers let me plead:
>   Grave tribunes, once more I entreat of you, –
> *Lucius.* My gracious Lord, no tribune hears you speak.
> *Titus.* Why, 'tis no matter, man: if they did hear,
>   They would not mark me, or if they did mark,
>   They would not pity me, yet plead I must,
>   And bootless unto them.
>   Therefore I tell my sorrows to the stones.
>
>   (3.1.30–7)

For Shepherd, the statement 'yet plead I must' (line 35) indicates that Titus's speeches are 'emotional expression that satisfies a need' (82); why else, he suggests, would Titus continue to plead when there is no one present to persuade? In its theatrical context, however, what Titus's comment signals is a shift in his perception – and a return not to 'self-expressiveness' but to the measured, 'public' rhetoric of the scene's opening. Just before this statement, Titus has acknowledged at last what is obvious to Lucius and the offstage audience (that the tribunes have indeed gone): 'Why 'tis no matter, man' (3.1.33). The extended comparison between tribunes and stones that follows ('Therefore I tell my sorrows to the stones', 37–47) is rhetoric of persuasion. It serves less to indulge his emotions than to amplify – for Lucius and the spectators – the grounds of his complaint: as patriotic hero, Titus deserves better from Rome than persecution or stony indifference.

What has preceded this shift in rhetoric, however, is potentially more 'debatable'. The audience has seen Titus left behind by the procession, lying on the stage, weeping into the dust. The stage picture presents a dramatic emblem of grief or abasement or loss of fortune, which his speech then, it would seem, proceeds to amplify: 'For these, tribunes, in the dust I write / My heart's deep languour and my soul's sad tears' (12–26). But Titus begins to detach from his emblematic frame. While elaborating upon his tears, he continues to address the departed tribunes. He does not perceive as the spectators perceive, a disparity stressed when Lucius, entering '*with his weapon drawn*', reminds him that he lacks an (onstage) audience ('no man is by'), and Titus still persists: 'Grave tribunes, once more I entreat of you' (31). This defective awareness recalls that of Faustus in the presence of the Angels, and like Faustus's, brings into question any simple interpretation of the action. Why, the passage suggests, does Titus as particular individual lament so keenly? The play offers no coherent answer, ironic or otherwise. What is more, it avoids setting the grief of Tamora (for the son sacrificed by Titus) against the grief of Titus (for the sons and daughter destroyed by Tamora's revenge).

Other moments in *Titus Andronicus* – and, for that matter, moments in other plays where strong emotion distorts the character's perceptions – anticipate the 'debatable' character. At times this 'different' seeing may overwhelm any framing perspectives, and extend beyond any conventional use of disturbed speech. This may also happen in the *Spanish Tragedy* 3.13, where Hieronymo is confronted with the Old Man.[31] It is Don Bazulto's 'humble supplication' for his murdered son that provokes in Hieronymo at first recognition ('Whiles wretched I in thy mishaps may see / The lively portrait of my dying self', 84–5) but then, beginning after '*He draweth out a bloody napkin*', a series of irrational perceptions and actions, lasting for some seventy lines. Hieronymo becomes distracted, giving away his possessions, tearing up legal papers with his teeth, and playing 'catch me if you can'. He addresses the Old Man first as a fellow-sufferer, then as Horatio his murdered son, then as a Fury sent to spur him to revenge. At last his frenzy abates, and Hieronymo returns to perceiving as the audience does. Once again he recognises the old man as a mirror of himself: 'the lively image of my grief' (162). The emblematic frame is restored. In the intervening lines, however, and as with Titus, the audience is led to ask why grief leads him as particular individual to act in this way. Is he deranged by grief or the urge to revenge or, for that matter, by his sense of duty?

In plays contemporary with *Faustus*, these anticipations of the 'debatable' character are occasional and temporary. More often, the moments of 'different' perceiving are framed explicitly as *exempla* in the traditional way, and offer emotional reinforcement to some authorised version. The audience are informed, let us say, that the distraction they witness illustrates the effects of grief, and the figure on stage remains tidily within the frame. The process of containment occurs with most instances in contemporary plays of distorted 'seeing'. When Philip of Faulconbridge (*Troublesome Reign*) hears voices on the wind, he is in a 'trance' or 'dream', as other characters inform the audience. When Zabina goes mad and brains herself on the cage (*1 Tamburlaine* 5.1.301–19) the incident is but part of a 'bloody spectacle' with a *de casibus* message: 'Those that are proud of fickle empery ... / Behold the Turk and his great emperess!' (353–5). When Shakespeare's King John dies incoherent, the audience's view of his 'raging' has already been prepared for by the framing commentary of Prince Henry:

> Death, having prey'd upon the outward parts,
> Leaves them invisible, and his siege is now
> Against the mind, the which he pricks and wounds
> With many legions of strange fantasies,
> Which, in their throng and press to that last hold,
> Confound themselves.
>
> (*King John* 5.7.15–20)[32]

Uncertain signs

Characters such as Hieronymo or Titus, or for that matter Edward II, are occasionally 'debatable'. There are, that is, moments in plays contemporary with *Faustus* where characters are seen to 'detach', where they begin to perceive separately and make sense 'differently' from others in the playworld.[33] Faustus's more general 'debatability', on the other hand, does not depend on moments of distraction or strong emotion. In this too he challenges 1590s 'common sense' about dramatic characters. Whether fully conscious or half-aware, Faustus does not see as others do. What the audience sees in the Angel scenes as stable and transparent – angelic figures, angelic voices – he sees as confusing and arbitrary. His experience cannot be accounted for simply in terms of allegorical figures or the rhetoric of opposed voices. There are disparities, incoherencies, excesses – and indeed the sense of an 'interiority' (individual, non-representative, 'debatable') separate from the playworld and its framing rhetoric.

The disparity between audience-view and Faustus-view is perhaps more obvious in the Angel scenes; but his 'separate-seeing' is a persistent feature of the play. It operates even at times when he appears to be as fully aware as any morality figure, or any other contemporary hero or villain. One notable instance of 'separate-seeing' occurs during the survey of career options that opens the play, when he omits the second part of each biblical text, ignoring their assurances of redemption and forgiveness. The action assumes that an audience will be aware of the defects in his argument. This is an important moment for the critical debate over Faustus's 'character'. 'Why?' we ask. Is the omission caused by arrogance, perhaps, or stupidity or inadvertence or ignorance – or, as Danson suggests, a limiting 'literal-mindedness' ('Christopher Marlowe: The Questioner' 18–27)? Is Faustus already damned? Has Mephistopheles turned the pages, as he claims in the B-text (5.2.98–101)? I leave the debate to others. What concerns me here is that our impulse to debate – an impulse that signals a realignment in the way the audience relates to the character – arises again from an instance of 'separate-seeing'.

What compounds the 'separate-seeing' of Faustus and compli- cates his making sense of the playworld is the nature of signs in the play. The audience observes Faustus as the inhabitant of a world of semantic instability, of ambiguity and equivocation, of inversion and parody. Max Bluestone suggests that 'conflict and contradiction inhere everywhere in the world of the play' (*'Libido Speculandi'* 55).[34] In this, *Faustus* is not necessarily different from its contempo- raries. Ambiguous playworlds were common in sixteenth-century drama, especially after 1585. Indeed older plays had regularly exploited disparities between being and seeming (this was after all one important function of the Vice). The spectators at a performance of *Tamburlaine* or *The Jew of Malta* or Shakespeare's *Henry VI* plays are challenged to interpret uncertain and ambiguous signs, just as they are with *Faustus*. But with Faustus they must also watch as – 'detached' and 'separate-seeing' – he encounters and makes his own sense of the playworld.

This uncertainty of signs is usually interpreted as pointing to the play's contesting ideologies, or, reflected at the level of character, to the conflicting elements in Faustus's nature.[35] But Faustus in perfor- mance becomes more than an illustration of ideologies, more than a reflection of the playworld he inhabits. The spectators cannot – or need not – make sense of his 'difference' only in terms of these perspectives, nor, for that matter, in terms of the play's obvious ironies. We may, as David Bevington and Eric Rasmussen suggest, be 'invited to sympathise with a protagonist who discovers to his cost the ambiguous power of speech' (Introduction 39); but Faustus's difficulties with words are by no means confined to his conversations with Mephistopheles and comments such as 'Why, this is hell, nor am I out of it' (1.1.78). Certainly in this instance, but also elsewhere in the play, and cumulatively, the boundaries of meaning shift and slide. Even terms 'as essentially different as *heaven* and *hell* blur together in the figure of ... "Heavenly Helen"' (Forsyth 19). Words impede the apprehension of 'reality'. They resist the attempts of Faustus (as much as of the audience) to label and define. The semantic equivocation begins with the Prologue and its association of both magic and theology with 'sweetness'. Thereafter the instability is general: Faustus, Wagner, Mephistopheles, and the Clowns all play to a greater or lesser degree with the meanings of words. Indeed the process of redefining seems at times to be inherent in the rhetorical structures of much dialogue and many set-speeches: the interplay of question and answer, of statement and counter-statement, facilitates exchanges such as 'made for men ... made for me' (2.3.9–10); ''Tis but a surfeit, sir ... / A surfeit of deadly sin' (5.2.11–12). The shifting surface of the language in the more serious scenes is reflected in the word-play of the comic episodes, as in Wagner's verbal games of 1.2 or the joking about false legs and hay horses in 4.1.

The effects of this shifting are evident in the moment-by-moment adjustments to theatrical experience that make possible the 'debatable' character. Once again, the Angel scenes offer an insight into the process. The audience watches Faustus as he stands imperfectly aware, but it also watches Faustus as he attempts to make sense of what he sees and hears. His struggle is especially acute in the third and fourth appearances of the Angels (2.3), those moments when he comes close to repentance. That he does not succeed results from the semantic instability he is observed to encounter in his world. In the two crises, early and mid-scene, he struggles to find firm ground but invariably – and, it appears, inevitably – fails:

> Good Angel.   Faustus, repent yet, God will pity thee.
> Evil Angel.   Thou art a spirit. God cannot pity thee.
> Faustus.   Who buzzeth in mine ears I am a spirit?
> Be I a devil, yet God may pity me;
> Ay, God will pity me if I repent.
> Evil Angel.   Ay, but Faustus never shall repent.
>
> Exeunt [ANGELS].
>
> Faustus.   My heart's so hardened I cannot repent.
>
> (2.3.12–18)

Here, in the third appearance of the Angels, the choices are clearly defined, for the spectators at least: they see and hear unambiguously. For Faustus, however, the Angels are only partly apprehended and their words confusing. He responds only to parts of the speech of each Angel, reassembling the 'buzzing' of the Evil Angel into words but echoing the Good Angel's rhythm and phrasing. He is unable to make firm, unalterable sense of the connections between the words: in the confusion of 'be I' and 'if I', of 'will' and 'cannot' and 'may' and 'never shall', he cannot see clearly. When the Evil Angel, departing, suggests that 'Faustus never shall repent', he accepts the dismal verdict.

The same struggle to make sense of words is crucial to the outcome of the mid-scene crisis. The Angels' words are no less unambiguous, the aural patterning ('repent') no less intense:

> *Mephistopheles.*   Think thou on hell, Faustus, for thou art damned.
> *Faustus.*   Think, Faustus, upon God, that made the world.
> *Mephistopheles.*   Remember this.   *Exit.*
> *Faustus.*   Ay, go, accursèd spirit, to ugly hell!
>   'Tis thou hast damned distressèd Faustus' soul.
>   Is't not too late?
>
> *Enter* GOOD ANGEL *and* EVIL [ANGEL].
>
> *Evil Angel.*   Too late.
> *Good Angel.*   Never too late, if Faustus can repent.
> *Evil Angel.*   If thou repent, devils shall tear thee in pieces.
> *Good Angel.*   Repent, and they shall never raze thy skin.
>   *Exeunt* [ANGELS].
> *Faustus.*   Ah, Christ, my Saviour,
>   Seek to save distressèd Faustus' soul!
>
> *Enter* LUCIFER, BEELZEBUB, *and* MEPHISTOPHELES.
>
> *Lucifer.* Christ cannot save thy soul, for he is just.
>   There's none but I have int'rest in the same.
>
> (2.3.72–85)

The words continue to switch from speaker to speaker, changing direction in each new context: 'damned', 'hell', 'repent', 'distressèd Faustus' soul' – and 'too late'. The effect of these insistent repetitions is to produce a crescendo of emotional tension that leads to Faustus's prayer ('Ah, Christ, my Saviour, / Seek to save distressèd Faustus' soul!', 82–3), and heightens the shock of the Devils' entry that follows. Even then, when Lucifer speaks, it is the words of Faustus's prayer that he recasts anew: 'Christ cannot save thy soul, for he is just' (84).[36] The echoes transform. Justice appears to have been done, the law upheld. Faustus accepts the claim, it seems, because he cannot see past the confusion of words to the reality beneath. Unlike Mephistopheles, he has never 'tasted the eternal joys of heaven'. And the angelic voices echo: 'too late ... too late'.

Faustus's struggle can be observed more generally in the play, from his opening self-debate, with its insistent impulse to redefine (the 'end of physic', for example, shifts from 'our body's health' to the fame Faustus has achieved through mass cures, 17–18); through the soliloquy that precedes the second Angel scene: 'Now, Faustus, must thou needs be damned' (2.1.1–14), with its sharply opposed voices and shifting associations of 'love' and deity; through the bond-signing, with its distorted perceptions ('*Homo fuge!*'); to the desperate pleading of the final soliloquy. At each stage, the spectators are able to see his 'inner' conflict as the sum of his opposed voices and as exemplifying the age-old struggle between good and evil, as leading to damnation perhaps or protesting against heavenly power; but they are also brought to view his conflict as the product of an individual and separate seeing. Faustus is observed as a figure who sees and hears quite differently from them, and differently again from others in the playworld. He encounters his world rather than merely illustrating it.

The more fully 'debatable' character emerges in Shakespeare's plays a few years after *Faustus*, with figures such as Richard II.[37] Richard's encounter with his playworld is very different from that of Faustus, but the rhetoric of his character has important similarities – as does the relationship constructed between audience and figure on stage. Richard, like Faustus, detaches from conventional frames, sees separately, and struggles to make sense of his situation. Unlike Titus or Hieronymo, his 'detachment' is more than temporary. It becomes fully apparent mid-play, in the scene where he returns to his kingdom only to be met with the news of Bolingbroke's successful invasion (3.2). As each item of bad news is announced, the scene develops into an illustration of the falls of princes, climaxing in: 'For God's sake let us sit upon the ground / And tell sad stories of the death of kings' (Richard, 155–6).

But this is no set-piece dramatic emblem. Richard's comments extend beyond the *de casibus* lamentations typical of such scenes (the scene of Edward's capture in *Edward II* is a case in point, with its emotional ballasting of the theme). And he does more than amplify and illustrate his opposed voices: the belief in a special, kingly nature ('Remember who you are', Aumerle, 82); and the promptings of despair ('of comfort no man speak', 144). In attempting to make his own sense of the situation, Richard reinterprets the commonplaces, and the audience is brought repeatedly to view his figure as detached. Where other characters (including Bolingbroke) are essentially choric, descendants of the *Henry VI* playworld with its mouthing of political clichés, its brawling and duplicity, Richard is innovative, even radical. In his 'separate-seeing' he challenges conventional thinking by taking it seriously, not as a mere matter of 'respect, / Tradition, form, and ceremonious duty' (173) but as literally present to him as particular individual. This is brought to audience attention especially in what he terms his 'senseless conjuration' of the 'dear earth' (6–22): 'So weeping, smiling, greet I thee, my earth, / And do thee favours with my royal hands' (10–11); or later in the scene, where his reflections on the 'death of kings' prompt an insistence on his common humanity: 'I live with bread like you, feel want, / Taste grief, need friends – subjected thus, / How can you say to me, I am a king?' (175–7).

The suggestion here of excess, of departure from conventional expectations, is accentuated by the uneasy responses of those around him. Richard's difference from others in the playworld is signalled by gesture and visual separation, but he is also seen to be aware of the gap in making sense between himself and his onstage audience: 'Mock not my senseless conjuration, lords' (he hastens to insist that 'This earth shall have a feeling', 23–4). The lords do not comment on this statement, even though they respond to Richard's speeches generally with 'ceremonious duty'. Further marking the separation between themselves and Richard, they retreat into flattering reassurance, 'Fear not, my lord. That Power that made you king / Hath power to keep you king in spite of all' (Carlisle, 27–8); or into sententious advice: 'My lord, wise men ne'er sit and wail their woes, / But presently prevent the ways to wail' (Carlisle, 178–9). At the same time, their remarks betray a certain impatience with his speech-making: perhaps all this business of saluting the earth and sitting in the dust proceeds from 'fear'; perhaps someone who makes a claim to 'majesty' should act, not 'sit and wail'.

The emphasis shifts in this scene from Richard's situation to his psychology. He is not merely at odds with his followers, nor does he simply exemplify one version of monarchist theory. What the audience observes of Richard is a persistent impulse to make his own sense, to find some image or formula that will fix his identity in terms of both kingship and mortality. What he is observed to encounter is a world of uncertain signs, in which nothing ever remains the way he defines it. He apprehends signs 'differently' from others in the playworld. For Richard as for Faustus, words are unstable, their meanings prone to shift as they recur in one context after another, and as they switch between literal and metaphorical levels of meaning: 'subjected thus' (to hunger, grief), Richard asks, 'How can you say to me, I am a king?' (176–7).

Richard's 'debatability', like that of Faustus, develops from an attempt to impose order upon an experience he can no longer control. Before, during, and after his confrontations with Bolingbroke, he constructs versions of what-should-be reality that – like the scholar's dreams of magic power – the playworld cannot sustain. Despite this, he persists in his effort to make sense. In prison, not long before his death, the thought of Bolingbroke may 'unking' him and reduce him to 'nothing'; but he then qualifies that sentiment in 'But whate'er I be' and continues his struggle to define. For Richard, the language of power slides inexorably into the language of identity.

> Then am I king'd again, and by and by
> Think that I am unking'd by Bolingbroke,
> And straight am nothing. But whate'er I be,
> Nor I, nor any man that but man is,
> With nothing shall be pleas'd, till he be eas'd
> With being nothing.
>
> (5.5.36–41)

Debatability

The Angels in *Faustus* address their theatrical past, challenge the 'common sense' of their theatrical present, and signal, for the future, a transformation of the rhetoric of character. This chapter has argued that we should reconsider our notions of the 'Shakespearean' character, as well as our narratives of late sixteenth-century change. In the rhetoric of dramatic character there was no sudden one-way shift from the externalised to the internalised presentation of 'inner' conflict. Nor was there a straightforward evolution from the opposed voices of the traditional rhetoric of character to the 'debatable' rhetoric of the mature Shakespearean soliloquy. Between Apius and Hamlet lie the anticipations of Titus and Hieronymo, and the new rhetoric of Faustus.

The term 'debatable' has been used here to signal a new rhetoric of character, and to sidestep the critical impasses associated with labels such as 'realism' or 'individuality' or 'complexity', or even with concepts such as 'interiority' and 'subjectivity'. Too many of the conventional oppositions between 'old' and 'new' characters cannot be sustained. Some simply do not discriminate. In late sixteenth-century plays all significant characters – traditional and 'debatable' – became more individual and more complicated. In any case (as writers such as Aers have suggested) characters like Richard II or Hamlet do not suddenly acquire a sense of inner authenticity by being able to contrast the 'external manners of lament' with the 'substance' of an 'unseen grief'. Differences such as these are cultural commonplaces; they do not of themselves indicate any particularly humanist 'subjectivity'.

No single device produces the 'debatable' character, though the uncertainty of signs would seem to be an important precondition. As the instances of Faustus and Richard suggest, 'debatability' emerges in ambiguous and unstable playworlds. Other factors, however, are less predictable. Faustus's 'detachment' depends less upon any specific technique (it does not, for example, arise directly from the use of psychomachia or soliloquy) than upon the constructing of a different relationship between spectator and character. Various devices or conditions may trigger 'debatability', at least temporarily; but many of these were also part of the traditional rhetoric of character. Visual separation on stage is sometimes a signal (like the sight of Hamlet at Claudius's court), but the device had been used conventionally to denote an interpreter or social outsider or chorus: Ambidexter (before 1570) or Simplicity (1580s) or Henry VI (1590s). Emotional excess may be associated with 'debatability', but in earlier plays it had led conventionally to disturbances of speech and sometimes perception (Shepherd 75–6). Even lack of explicit motivation, in the context of the lengthy self-explanations in late sixteenth-century plays, has sometimes been seen to open a character to debate (this has been suggested of Alice Arden)[38] but insufficiencies of this kind are also common in earlier plays. When Lady Conscience decides to follow Lady Lucre, her conversion is abrupt: Lucre overpays her for the brooms and Conscience suddenly becomes her follower, 'And sith every one doth it, why may not I doe it too' (1362). In such a case we do not need to be told that money can corrupt even the most virtuous. We rush to fill the interpretative gap with the most obvious and conventional reason that the play-world affords.

The 'debatability' that is produced by the new rhetoric of dramatic character in the 1590s does not so much change the 'essential nature' of dramatic characters as enable an audience to interpret some of these figures differently. 'Debatability' is, importantly, additional. It involves more than offering multiple perspective frames for the spectators to make sense of a figure on stage, more than an increasing complication. It brings to the playhouse stage not so much a new 'inner' consciousness as the sense of a 'separate' consciousness. The new rhetoric of character produces detachment, dislocation, separation. Exemplary frames remain relevant, but the figure on stage no longer fits neatly within them. The character appears to be 'separate-seeing', to perceive and make sense 'differently' from others in the playworld – and indeed from the watching audience. It is this new 'encountering' of the playworld that gives the impression of a new 'interiority' or 'subjectivity', of an individual, non-representative consciousness that responds to the events of the play, not in any particularly organised way (step-by-step perhaps), but as moment-by-moment experience.

How, then, should we locate the 'debatable' character within our more general narratives of the Renaissance? There are two ways of answering this question. The 'debatable' character could of course join the 'Shakespearean' as an illustration of cultural change. In its 'separate-seeing' the 'debatable' character may reflect, for example, the Protestant stress on individual access to religious experience, what G. K. Hunter terms 'the sense of the unique centrality of individual consciousness' ('Revolution and Continuity' 37). Or it may remind us of Montaigne's turning from 'the exemplary, the universal, or the edifying' to follow 'the contours of the changing reality of one being, himself' (C. Taylor 179). Or, more widely, the 'separate-seeing' may relate to that 'relativity of perception' seen generally as characterising the new science, the new philosophy (Elton 26–8). Again, in its new 'interiority', the 'debatable' character may anticipate the writings of Descartes, in which the self becomes the source and shaper of knowledge, instead of responding to some higher order of ideas (Ideas) and valuations located elsewhere (C. Taylor 186). A new 'Cartesian' character? Perhaps. But no less possible or impossible than a new Protestant character – or for that matter a new Machiavellian, or Freudian, or Marxist, or humanist, or even a deconstructed or decentred one.

The other answer to locating the 'debatable' character in our general narratives recognises that such labelling may be a secondary process. The story we tell about a character is shaped by the rhetoric of performance, and not merely by cultural conditions or discourses. As this chapter has argued, the effect of the 'debatable' character was less to do with *what* people thought than with *how*, in the late sixteenth-century playhouse, they came to make sense in a different way. The 'debatable' character signals an epistemological shift in popular theatrical experience. Whatever cultural developments outside the theatre this shift may have paralleled or anticipated, the change is not manifested in any developed sense in the London playhouses before the arrival of Marlowe's Faustus. And he took the stage several years before Richard II – and perhaps ten or more before Hamlet.

CHAPTER 7

Managing the space

―――

Spectacle

Theatrical space always matters in an audience's making sense, even if its influence is not always recognised. The conventional expectations of late sixteenth-century spectators included certain understandings about the rhetoric of space, as they did about visual signs or cautionary tales or the theatrical clichés of the late morality. In the management of space too, the period between 1585 and 1595 brought rapid changes. The usual explanation for these is the building of the playhouses, but this obvious answer needs some amending. It originates, as do other narratives of the drama, in a looking backwards from Shakespeare. The non-Shakespearean texts tell a different story, with Marlowe's plays, in particular, providing new directions, new possibilities.

Marlowe's plays are notorious for their spectacle, for striking images, memorable moments. In most accounts, these are the visual counterparts of the grand personages and the 'mighty line'. The Prologue to *1 Tamburlaine* promised the audience that it would see and hear things 'stately' and 'astounding', and the extravagance of the action did not disappoint: the contemporary imagination was haunted by an emperor in a cage and a conqueror's black streamers. Later, there were to be other compelling sights: a chariot with its hapless 'jades', Barabas's fall into the cauldron, Edward's death by poker, the ambushing of the Admiral, the devils and fireworks of Faustus. For many, these moments epitomise the performance style of Marlowe's plays. Michael Hattaway, labelling this style as 'iconic' (and referring also to Shakespeare's *Henry VI* plays), remarks that such plays 'depend on scenes that follow one another with a strong architectonic rhythm, on moments that must have been realised by bold visual effects, formal groupings that tend toward tableaux, archetypal personages, frozen moments that would lodge in the spectators' minds' (57).

There were memorable and 'frozen' moments aplenty, but that is only part of the story. Less sensational perhaps, but potentially more wide-reaching in their effects, were the changes that the early stagings of Marlowe's plays brought to the relationship between spectator and stage action. Instead of being (in effect) a spectacular diversion, these performances reshaped the language of theatrical space: first by exploiting elements of staging tradition, then by providing new options for the management of space in the playhouse. Theatrical space, traditionally reflective, now became, additionally, refractive, with audiences offered new emotional dimensions to their experience in the playhouse. These changes are connected of course with the other aspects explored elsewhere in this book: the increasing complication of visual signs and framing rhetoric, for instance, or the new perspectives on character. This chapter will focus more directly on the rhetoric of theatrical space, and specifically on the changes that occur in the staging of ceremonies.

Theatrical space

The theatrical space that concerns me here is the space that confronts the spectator: the space visible on stage and bounded by the physical structures of the playhouse. There is a constant interaction between this visible space and the reported or imagined space offstage, although onstage space is never a simple reflection or extension of the offstage. It may be 'designated' (Hilton 14) or 'inscribed' (Ubersfeld, *Lire le théâtre* 75) with meanings and values that originate elsewhere, but onstage space is additionally space set apart, with its own limits, possibilities, and indeed conventions. It will have its own particular rhetoric, and arouse its own distinctive expectations. There are, that is, rhetorical effects attributable specifically to performance in space, rather than to the words of the playtext or to any imitation or appropriation of cultural practice.[1]

Attending to the rhetoric of onstage space – disengaging for the moment from the offstage and metaphorical – is contrary to our usual habits of criticism. Very few studies address the particular rhetoric of onstage space at any length. For one thing, the common emphasis upon the 'bare stage' of sixteenth-century playhouses encourages the assumption that what can be imagined is always more significant than what may be seen. Many comments on

'theatrical space' thus pay little heed to the action on stage viewed
by an audience, but look instead to the words of the playtext to
create their images of the play. To cite one typical example, in
Renaissance Self-fashioning Stephen Greenblatt insists that the
Marlovian stage is characterised by an 'essential meaninglessness of
theatrical space' (195), so that 'all places are alike' and blur into one
(197), with the characters set within a vacuum. Such descriptions
might engage the imagination of readers, but they tell us little about
the theatrical spaces that sixteenth-century playgoers might actually
have seen.

Most comments on location and setting – which potentially
involve visible theatrical space – also show the same turning aside
from performance to words. Typically in these comments, 'the
concept of place existed only so far as it was perceived by the characters or, to put it more briefly, place is a state of mind' (Hattaway
197, on *Titus Andronicus*). If we are interested in how sixteenth-
century spectators, rather than characters, made sense of the space
before them as they watched the performance, we must turn to
drama theorists (but these are very general), to studies of staging and
stagecraft (but most deal only with Shakespeare), or (with considerable reservations) to studies that treat the cultural dimensions of
theatrical space. At the same time, we need to look beyond any
simple equating of world with stage. Despite the interest of new
historicist critics in social and political performance, there has been
little attempt to explain how more complex areas of cultural space
were, or could be, realised on stage in front of a sixteenth-century
audience – or, conversely, how the rhetoric of stage space during
performance might modify the perception of cultural spaces trans-
posed from elsewhere. Stephen Greenblatt may propose 'a whole
spectrum of representational exchanges' in the 'circulation of social
energy' (*Shakespearean Negotiations* 8), but many references to
staging in historicist commentary still involve straightforward cases
of imitation and analogy, with onstage events seen as taking on the
qualities of offstage practices.[2]

What was the traditional rhetoric of space? Studies of staging
suggest that the sixteenth-century playgoer arrived at the Theatre or
the Rose with expectations about the use of theatrical space that
were quite different from those of a theatregoer today. Indeed
modern productions and modern stage conventions, with their
stronger sense of the set as framing the action, can be misleading
when we attempt to reconstruct the past. In the traditional language
of theatrical space shared by sixteenth-century playwright and play-

goer the figure of the player was the most significant term. Bernard Beckerman comments that this was a drama 'which in production relied almost wholly upon the voice and movement of the actor', and that 'in the Elizabethan drama, particularly in the Shakespearean, a character enters not *into* a place but *to* another character' (*Shakespeare at the Globe* 174). G. K. Hunter suggests that the drama offered a 'landscape of persons' rather than persons in a landscape ('Flatcaps and Bluecoats' 24). The scenes of a play were established by the players themselves taking up positions in the playing space, with visual significance being activated first by the figures themselves. Hunter focuses on signs of status, stressing costume and 'typed social behaviour' (37). Further meanings are signalled by the relationship of players to each other and by their positioning in relation to the physical features of the playing space.[3]

How figures were positioned in the 'landscape of persons' was influenced by long-standing visual conventions. Traditionally, both vertical and horizontal dimensions had been used in grouping and movement. Vertical placement might signify an association with hierarchy of some kind, as in the iconography of heaven, earth, and hell found in the medieval cycle plays; while horizontal placement – in effect, holding the spectators apart from or adjacent to the action – was associated with degrees of audience implication or participation, as in the direct address practised by the Vices. One extensive discussion of traditional placement is that of Robert Weimann in *Shakespeare and the Popular Tradition in the Theater*. He describes the staging conventions of the popular tradition as based upon the medieval combination of *locus* and *platea* staging, with the later flexibility of the platform stage deriving from the 'traditional interplay between *platea* and *locus*, between neutral, undifferentiated "place" and symbolic location' (212). In Weimann's analysis, the *locus* – often elevated, as with the pageant-wagon – and hence likely to have some vertical, hierarchical significance, is associated with localised and self-contained action, with socially elevated characters and formal statements, with assertions of 'order'. The *platea* – on the same level as the spectators – is associated with unlocalised action, with more 'proletarian' characters and direct address, with disorder and the questioning of accepted values by the Vice and his predecessors.

The spacing of figures in the 'landscape' was similarly a matter of convention and expectations. The distance – the onstage space, in effect – between figures may indicate quite specific relationships, as modes of behaviour in the world outside the theatre are mimicked on stage. This imitation (or approximation or impression) can be seen most readily in the application of proxemic codes, which govern the way that the physical distances between characters signal the nature of their relationships: personal, social, and political.[4] Observing the codes of distance is always important on the stage, and it was especially so in a culture where space between persons was (like costume in Hunter's examples in 'Flatcaps and Bluecoats') a significant marker of social difference; and in a theatre where rehearsal was minimal and production relied upon each player knowing his 'place' in conventionally established patterns of blocking.[5]

But this traditional language of theatrical space was flexible as well as conventional. It had developed in circumstances where playing spaces were varied: marketplace or open area, pageant-wagon or booth-stage, temporary amphitheatre or inn-yard, the hall of a town corporation or a great house.[6] Even after the building of the playhouses, the diversity persisted. Each playhouse, each playing space was different: Andrew Gurr, setting the square stage of De Witt's drawing of the Swan against the 'elongated hexagon of the Rose's brick foundations', notes the 'radical variety in the design of stage areas' in the early playhouses ('Bare Island' 35). Stages also differed in size: the stages of the Theatre, the Fortune, and the two Globe playhouses were more than twice the area of the Rose stage (or for that matter those of the private playhouses, the Blackfriars and the Cockpit-Phoenix).[7] Despite these variations, acting companies managed to present plays at more than one London venue; and most of them were also involved at some time in provincial touring.[8]

Although the conventions for positioning players and organising theatrical space did not depend upon the specific architecture of the playing area, players had always improvised or taken advantage of their 'stages' to strengthen vertical and horizontal effects (the constant adaptation of techniques to circumstances is stressed by Southern 591–5). The ground-level area in front of an outdoor platform might be pressed into service; or a ladder propped behind the rear curtain of a booth stage; or a low platform utilised in hall-playing for certain characters or parts of the action. Southern notes a 'traverse' or curtain before the hall screen as first mentioned in the 1520s; a low 'footpace' or stage set in front of the screen as in use from the 1550s; and proposes, in the 1580s playhouse, processional action which moves through the audience in the yard and up on to the stage platform.[9]

This process of adaptation explains some of the differences

between earlier and later plays in their management of theatrical space, but by no means all. A difference in venue might account for the differences between a hall performance of *Cambises* in the 1560s and a playhouse performance of *Clyomon and Clamydes* in the 1580s. But the differences accelerate after 1585. The staging of *Clyomon and Clamydes* is more similar to that of *Cambises* ten years or so earlier than it is to that of a play such as *Richard II* ten years or so later.[10] One index to this variation is the presentation of tournament and royal display. In *Clyomon and Clamydes* the rituals of knightly combat are presented straightforwardly, as the way such things might be expected to be performed; in *Richard II* they become distorted and ambiguous. As Bevington comments of the latter in *Action Is Eloquence*, 'the elaborate chivalric symbolism and the providential assumptions of trial by combat ... are at odds with the morally complex issues posed by the murder of Thomas of Woodstock' (123).

The differences are obvious, but how they might have happened has not been sufficiently explained. As with other aspects of the rhetoric of popular drama, there is no detailed account of the changes in managing space during the transitional time from 1585 to 1595 – though there are lengthy accounts of medieval staging (as in Wickham and Weimann), interlude staging (Craik, Southern), and especially Shakespearean staging (Beckerman, Bevington, Gurr, Styan, Thomson). Most studies of late sixteenth-century staging are, in any case, more interested in continuity than change, a consequence perhaps of the need to enlighten modern readers encumbered by modern expectations. These studies might mention earlier plays including the late moralities, but do so primarily in order to illustrate conventional features that persist: items of stage 'business', particular visual signs, and the various accretions of theatrical practice. Where change is the issue, developmental studies tend to locate the key changes in or at the time of Shakespeare's plays. Of the 1580s they notice only the arrival of the 'University Wits'; of 1580s plays, typically only the metadrama of the *Spanish Tragedy*, the spectacle of *Tamburlaine*, and the obsolete trappings of *Doctor Faustus*.

Many developmental studies are further restricted in their explanations of change by their allegiance to particular interpretative narratives. When Weimann describes how traditional staging modulates into Shakespearean practice, he turns away from exploring the management of space and towards mainly verbal considerations: levels of language, for instance. He employs the notion of

Figurenposition, defined as 'the actor's position on stage, and the speech, action, and degree of stylization associated with that position' (224), to explain how some characters in later plays (Hamlet, for example) can establish a special *platea*-type relationship with the audience by their use of 'ordinary' language (proverbs, for example), even though they are otherwise *locus*-characters – being socially elevated and part of the play's illusionist action (208–52). But the explanations are less impressive than they sound. It is only part of an answer to suggest, as Weimann does, that the spectators in the playhouse will feel closer to Faustus because he is accompanied on stage by popular but old-fashioned allegorical conventions in the form of the Angels, or closer to Hamlet because he sets 'himself apart from the more self-contained dialogue by using couplets, wordplay, and similar illusion-breaking speech patterns' (230). None of this explains sufficiently how the management of space changed, or for that matter how spectators might begin to see differently.

The explanation for change most favoured by staging studies is the arrival of the playhouse. At first glance the solution is attractive; considered more carefully, however, it becomes apparent that the playhouse may account for only some of the processes of change, not all. Certainly the architecture of the playhouse did allow more opportunities to experiment with the positioning of figures in the 'landscape'. Vertical arrangements could now be amplified by the constant presence of a decorative tiring-house façade which, along with any 'heavens', gallery, under-stage space, and occasional scenic device, offered a means of revitalising medieval iconography or establishing new images of secular power. Horizontal placement could be accentuated too, in particular by the sheer size of the stage platform, extending in some cases to the centre of the playhouse.[11]

The impact of the playhouse on staging practice is conveniently illustrated by Robert Wilson's 'London' plays. As Southern comments, there is a clear difference in the staging requirements between *The Three Ladies of London* (first played in the early 1580s) and the sequel play *The Three Lords and Three Ladies of London* (1588). He suggests that the earlier play 'may well be meant for simple presentation in the old Interlude tradition; it has no reference to any sort of stage'; the second, with its more elaborate action making use of different playing levels as well as the stage posts, is 'a play which is unmistakably devised for direct public playhouse presentation' (545).[12] These differences point to a shift in assumptions about theatrical space. Earlier plays, and these include the various interludes and moralities Southern discusses in his classic study, kept their performance options open: they might call for particular techniques or special effects, but they adapt flexibly to different performance spaces. Later plays (and this marks a movement towards the fully developed Shakespearean model favoured by studies of the sixteenth-century stage) retain that flexibility but, as most studies suggest, they also take active advantage of the physical features and resources of the playhouse to develop a new rhetoric of theatrical space. From the late 1580s especially playtexts begin to register a different thinking about space, as playwrights calculate the effects (to take one small set of examples) of placing Belimperia above the stage to let fall a letter, or Abigail and Jessica to drop bags of treasure, or Juliet to invite adoration. None of these instances would have been impossible to stage earlier, but each one depends on an acute sense of the visual relationship between platform and façade.[13]

But this is only part of the story. The example of Wilson may have another corollary: that the new playhouses did not have much impact until the late 1580s. David Bevington describes the acting companies as 'eager to exploit the spatial dimensions of their new home' (*Action Is Eloquence* 101), but just how soon this opportunism translated into new approaches to theatrical space is uncertain, as there are few extant playtexts from the 1570s and early 1580s, and the evidence in these is equivocal. *Clyomon and Clamydes* has stage directions that may indicate upper-level action and machinery to raise and lower, both features of later playhouse production; but hall staging had already developed techniques for presenting what would become upper-level action in the playhouse.[14] John Pikeryng's *Horestes* (printed in 1567, performed at court) stages the siege of a city twenty years before such action became a feature of playhouse productions such as *2 Tamburlaine* or *1 Henry VI*. The stage directions include the instructions '*let ... Clitemnestra speake over the wal*' (marginal, beside lines 834–7); '*fling him of the lader and then let on* [one] *bringe in his mother Clytemnestra but let her loke wher Egistus hangeth*' (beside lines 943–53); and '*Take down Egistus and bear him out*' (beside lines 966–70). These instructions envisage a theatrical 'house' perhaps, or just a simple curtain and ladder; at this time and place they are not exploiting a tiring-house façade.[15]

In Robert Wilson's case, and despite his considerable experience in the theatre (he was a playwright and leading actor by 1583 when he was selected as one of the Queen's Men), it seems that as playwright he did not take much advantage of the physical resources of the playhouse until the late 1580s with the staging of the *Three Lords*. The instance may of course be misleading. There undoubtedly were other performances experimenting with the architecture before this time and these may have been recorded in playtexts now lost. Several other texts of the late 1580s and early 1590s, however, also give the impression of a sudden, excited realisation of the playhouse's possibilities, and a sudden access to new techniques. They include Kyd's *Spanish Tragedy*, *2 Tamburlaine* (with its sieges of Balsera and Babylon), the spate of English history plays, and even morality survivals such as Lodge and Greene's *A Looking Glass for London and England* with its prophet Oseas '*set downe over the Stage in a Throne*' (p. 133), and its 'brave Arbour' rising '*from under the* [ground]' (p. 150).

The connection between playhouse staging and Shakespeare's management of theatrical space is explored in David Bevington's *Action Is Eloquence*. This focuses on Shakespeare's plays and hence does not directly address change in general before 1595. It does, nevertheless, offer a useful starting point for discussion. Bevington notes continuities with the past in Shakespeare's use of theatrical space, but is also concerned to emphasise the differences. He distinguishes between the 'morally absolute antitheses' of earlier drama and the 'stance of ironic complexity' he identifies in Shakespeare's plays (159). Shakespeare's technique, he contends, is 'iconoclastic' in that it frequently retains the traditional language of space to present ritual or ceremonial action while at the same time discovering 'ambiguity beneath the reassuring exterior of symbolic certitude' (123). This ambiguity is often achieved by positioning and movement in relation to the façade – which could represent both the medieval 'theatrum mundi' – 'a world of hierarchy and cosmic pattern that is often under assault' – and the frame for neoclassical comedy – 'a world of illusion, escape, and rebellion against authority' (108). Bevington suggests that the differences betweeen earlier and Shakespearean plays result from an exploiting of playhouse architecture, from a fusing of two inherited languages of the façade: 'one [the medieval, or popular] embodying a symbolic pageantry of moral example and the other [the neoclassical] an illusory mirroring of social manners' (100). In consequence, there is an 'unceasing dialectic in Shakespeare between a visually structured world of seemingly fixed meaning and one of ambiguous transformation' (191).

Bevington's contrast between 'morally absolute' and 'ironic

complexity' is useful for suggesting how theatrical space operated before and 'during' Shakespeare. And indeed Shakespeare's contribution to change before 1595 is undeniable: the innovations Bevington notes in the use of the façade appear in his earliest plays, in *The Comedy of Errors* and *The Taming of the Shrew* as well as the first group of history plays and *Titus Andronicus*. But Bevington's preoccupation with the façade and vertical movement obscures other parts of the picture. Although he comments that the 'Spatial meaning of above and below is defined always in relation to the main stage, the realm of human action' (115), he says little about the actual management of space on the platform, or how (in Weimann's terms) *locus* might merge with *platea*, or what leads to the 'planning in depth' that J. L. Styan identifies as characteristic of Shakespeare's 'stagecraft' (*Shakespeare's Stagecraft* 18). Indeed, in responding to the playhouse, the playwrights not only took advantage of its physical resources; but they began also to manage space across the platform differently, enriching the inherited 'landscape of figures', complicating the relationships both between players and between players and spectators. Important instances of this second kind of response are to be found in plays after 1585, but especially in Marlowe's plays.

Ceremonial space

The traditional staging of ceremonies accords with Bevington's 'morally absolute antitheses'. Conventional opinion assumed that the natural state of society was orderly and hierarchical, even if the young were breaching sumptuary legislation, or Puritans taking more notice of their consciences than the Church authorities, or increasing numbers of the restless heading for London and the corruptions of city life. Ceremonies were an important part of the action in most sixteenth-century plays. Early audiences expected playwrights and players to imitate, adapt, or approximate examples of proper ceremony in the world outside the theatre – 'real life', literary, or pictorial – though many instances they saw on stage also drew upon past theatrical practice.[16] In the theatre playgoers might see enacted the rituals of royal court and lawcourt; of procession and tournament and execution; of social etiquette and economic exchange; and (with important restrictions on what might be staged) of religious observance.

The rhetoric of space in these ceremonies was essentially reflective. Their staging depended on shared expectations, which included

not only certain verbal formulae and set behaviours but also particular spatial conventions. Ceremonies, it was assumed, use a
particular kind of 'landscape' complete with proper spacing. Formal
meetings, and for that matter formal confrontations, employ a
symmetrical blocking of players just as they will also use balanced,
often antithetical speeches. Important personages are identified by
their elevation; kings for example properly occupy the 'state', which
may have been raised one or more steps above the stage platform
and the characters of lower rank.[17] Because distinctions of status
were important in sixteenth-century society – and ceremonies
outside the theatre affirmed those distinctions – the audience was
alert to signs of status: where a character is placed in a procession
perhaps, or where he stands on stage. As Hunter comments: 'In a
system so tight, so ordered, so punitive as the Elizabethan social
system the smallest shift of priorities made a disproportionately loud
signal of rejection or disaffection' ('Flatcaps and Bluecoats' 35).

The breaching of ceremony signals disorder. At such times, the
organisation of theatrical space changes. Blocking may become
asymmetrical, with shifting positions on stage and irregular
distances between figures. A king may enter unattended, or characters move apart from their proper ceremonial places. In *Clyomon
and Clamydes* the quarrel between the knights originates when
Clyomon 'steals' Clamydes's knighthood. Clamydes is kneeling in
readiness to be dubbed a knight when Clyomon manages to inter-
pose himself: '*as the King doth go about to lay the Mace of his head,
let* Clyomon *take the blowe*' (262–3). His breaching of the ceremony
is accompanied by abrupt changes of position, with rapid movement
first from outside the ceremonial space ('Clyomon *with subtill* Shift
watching in place', 261–2), and then offstage ('*and so passe away
presently*').[18] The action of many plays similarly involves a ceremony that is in some way challenged or disturbed: funeral (*1 Henry
VI, Richard III*); marriage celebration (*Troublesome Reign*, *2 Henry
VI, Massacre at Paris*); trial and judgement (*Famous Victories*);
swearing allegiance (*Troublesome Reign*); victory and triumph
(*1 Henry VI, Edward II*); coronation (*1 Henry VI*); and a second coronation, during which '*five moons appear*' (*Troublesome Reign*).[19]

The traditional staging of ceremony also allowed scope for the
decidedly non-ceremonial – the mock-heroic, the restless energies
and unruly humour of the Vice – without detracting in any essential
way from the earnestness of the occasion, or from the assumption
that the audience would interpret the ceremony unambiguously. The
solemn trial of the Ladies Love, Conscience, and Lucre in *The Three*

Ladies of London is preceded by the comic business of the Clown Simplicity's being stripped of his clothes and whipped for the crimes of others: '*Lead him once or twice about, whipping him and so Exit*', 1840–1). Despite this episode, the trial then proceeds with all due solemnity.[20] Another opportunity for the comic is sometimes afforded during ceremonial entrances, especially when space is cleared in the crowd for the progress of important personages. When Alexander is to return to the stage in *Clyomon and Clamydes* to adjudicate in the quarrel between the knights, the Vice Subtle Shift enters first, '*like a Wiffler*'. While a real-life whiffler might carry a sword, Shift probably wields a dagger, the traditional implement of the Vice: 'Rowme there for a reckning, see I beseech you if thale stand out of the way' (1676–7). After reminding the audience of the issues at stake, he concludes with bawdy innuendo: 'Well here they come, roome for the King, heres such thrusting of women as it grieveth mee' (1692–3).[21] And yet the antics of Shift have no observable impact on the serious business of the scene, either on Alexander's entry or on the preparations for the combat of Champions.

These straightforward instances of ceremony did not disappear after 1585, but are found in many plays, those of Marlowe and Shakespeare included. They rely on the audience to make sense in the traditional way, establishing a framework of received values, of moral absolutes, against which the action may be judged, with positioning and spacing used to reinforce images of order. Conventionally, ceremony is used to illustrate and amplify the narrative. Thus the impressiveness of Alexander's procession in *Clyomon and Clamydes* offers visual proof of his power ('King or Keysar, who hath not fixt his knees to me on ground?', 381);[22] and in *Famous Victories* Henry V's victory at Agincourt is confirmed when the French nobles swear allegiance to him (the action shows the 'Duke of Burgondie' and 'prince Dolphin' kissing his sword, 1519–29). At times, perhaps, ceremony may be not much more than an excuse for spectacle, as in *Alphonsus, King of Aragon* where Alphonsus confronts Amuracke the 'great Turke': '*Enter Alphonsus, with a Canapie carried over him by three Lords, having over each corner a Kings head crowned*' (1587–9) – the severed heads (it is soon made clear) of Amuracke's followers. On the other hand, ceremony often provides a memorable visual focus for the issues of the play or the conflicts between characters. The ceremonies of knightly challenge in *Clyomon and Clamydes* intensify the contest between the heroes and their notions of 'honour'. The elaborate sequence of ritual confrontation and battle in the *Three Lords* makes plain the superiority of London-English values over those of Spain. Bevington notes this focusing – and ultimate resolution – of conflicts as the key to Shakespeare's use of ceremony (*Action Is Eloquence* 137).

Enriching space

Changes in the staging of ceremony between 1585 and 1595 illustrate Bevington's shift from the 'morally absolute' to 'ironic complexity'; but they also provide evidence of alternative, and often more radical, ways of managing space that originate not so much in any feature of playhouse architecture as in what was inherited – the figure of the player in the 'landscape of persons'. In performance, these ways exploit the dimensions of the stage platform rather than the framing possibilities of the façade. In doing so, they activate more of the spatial possibilities of the playhouse, which – as the players move around the platform, or from outer edge to façade – had itself afforded spectators a wider range of perspectives on the action than other sixteenth-century playing places.[23]

Irony had always been present in the traditional staging of ceremony, at least potentially, in breaches and challenges and disturbances as well as in comic diversions. But it was irony of a particular kind: inverse, complementary, contained – the negative example that serves to direct audience attention to the received values that ceremony promotes. The 'stance of ironic complexity' which developed after 1585 may have included elements of these traditional ironies, but its focus was quite different. As Bevington comments about ceremonial confrontations in the *Henry VI* plays, 'The extensive symmetries ... cannot determine right from wrong; instead, they testify to an increasing savagery made all the more terrible by the ritual form in which the massacres are staged' (*Action Is Eloquence* 123). The point of the irony in such scenes is not simply to illustrate traditional notions of order, but to challenge abuses and violations (137–9). Bevington associates these qualities of 'ironic complexity' and 'ambiguity' with Shakespeare's exploitation of the playhouse façade and its potential for both 'medieval' and 'neoclassical' meanings. But the shift from 'absolute' to 'ironic' can only be partly explained in terms of this more complex framing. It was not in any case limited to Shakespeare's plays. Before 1595 (and before most of Shakespeare's plays) the options for staging and interpreting ceremony had already multiplied.

The first of the new and different ways of managing space developed from the traditional 'landscape of persons'. The placement of

figures across the platform changed, locating the 'landscape' differently in the performance space. Older plays – *Cambises* (hall staging,
1560s), *Clyomon and Clamydes* (playhouse, 1570s–1580s), even
The Three Ladies of London (playhouse, early 1580s) – share
similar patterns of movement and positioning. Strings of simple
meeting or confrontation scenes are interspersed with pauses for
direct address, after which the Vice or Clown moves from his position close to the audience to intervene in the action. The traditional
expectations of audience engagement apply: the spectator, these
plays assume, will relate more readily to Ambidexter or Subtle Shift
or Simplicity positioned at the edge of the playing area or moving
among the audience than to the (most often) physically more distant
figures of Cambises or Alexander or Mercadorus.[24] Plays after 1585
are less predictable. In some, there are sudden changes in the movement and positioning of figures in the 'landscape'. The staging of
The Jew of Malta, for example, depends upon successive shifts in
positioning as characters (Machevil, Barabas, Ferneze) move to
engage with the audience, with each move serving to frame a character or characters positioned closer to the façade. In performance
these abrupt movements and reframings dislocate audience expectations, making it less possible for them to settle upon any tidy or
secure interpretation.[25]

More generally, a number of plays after 1585 experiment with the
conventions of horizontal placement, in particular with the effect of
positioning characters at the edges of the playing area, relocating (in
effect) the extremities of the 'landscape'. J. L. Styan notes the 'downstage' choric commentator who criticises upstage behaviour as a
feature of Shakespearean staging, citing Horatio, Emilia, Kent,
Banquo, and Enobarbus (*Shakespeare's Stagecraft* 100–3). The practice owes something to the tradition of Vice and Clown, but becomes
more complex and unsettling after 1585 in plays such as Marlowe's
Edward II. In *Edward II*, the margins of the stage are repeatedly set
against the centre. One after another the characters enter alone in
advance of the group, or detach themselves from the main group in
the 'landscape'. Although some move towards the façade or the rear
of the stage (Isabella's duplicity is shown in this way), in most
instances they move to the platform edge, there to comment on the
action. At such times the audience tends to share the perspective of
the marginal observer in viewing the main action at stage centre.
Thus the spectator sees the first court scene (1.1) from the viewpoint
of Gaveston and his comments of 'Well done, Ned'; and sees
Isabella's victory (4.6) from the viewpoint of Kent, who has entered

'*alone, with a sword and target*'. This framing of the action by antagonistic or alienated witnesses is later a feature of the staging of *Hamlet* and several of Jonson's plays, *Sejanus* in particular with its procession of commentators.

A second way of moving towards 'ironic complexity' was by enriching the theatrical space within the 'landscape of persons'. In part, this can be seen as a general process allied to other changes in the drama. Multiplying narrative frames or elaborating dramatic character had the effect of complicating the relationships between individual figures in the 'landscape'. The space between players was thus inscribed with a greater range of meanings, and hence signified more than a simple adherence to ceremonial distances or an obvious breach of ceremonial rules.[26] An example of this richer inscription of space can be found in the banquet scene early in the *Spanish Tragedy*. Horatio, the son of Hieronymo, is rewarded for his valour in battle when the King bestows on him the honorable duty of cup-bearer (1.4.130–1). The honour is reaffirmed later in the scene when the King pledges Hieronymo in reward for the dumb show and '*Takes the cup of* HORATIO' (174.1). The positioning of figures on stage supports the ceremonial relationship between the royal party and Horatio: Horatio must stand in attendance while they sit at the banquet table. But there are other relationships between characters that this positioning calls to audience attention; and the very space between characters is inscribed with them. Seated at the King's table while Horatio stands are his rival for honour, the King's nephew Lorenzo, and his princely rival for love, Balthazar. The difference in placement between Horatio and the other young men underlines their differences in rank, reminding the audience of the unequal rewards for their valour allotted to Horatio and Lorenzo, and giving visual weight to the view of Lorenzo and Balthazar that Horatio should not presume to love Lorenzo's sister. Immediately before the banquet 'enters' they have seen her awarding Horatio her glove (1.4.101). When they later discover proof of that love, they murder Horatio for being too 'ambitious proud' (2.4.60), for not adhering, that is, to the proper distances.

The impact of this scene for an audience derives from effects that are particular to the 'landscape of persons': the relative positioning of figures, for example, and the distances between them. Elsewhere in the play Kyd exploits the physical resources of the playhouse, in particular the upper playing level; and this exploitation is generally considered to be his most innovative contribution to staging and theatrical space.[27] In the banquet scene, and apart from the framing presence of Andrea and Revenge, the architecture is not necessarily of much relevance to the rhetoric of theatrical space. A decorated façade may have heightened the sense of ritual and formality, but what the scene's notable spaces lead the audience to apprehend is the conflict festering within that 'landscape' – and anticipating Revenge's reply to Andrea in the next scene: 'I'll turn their friendship into fell despite, / Their love to mortal hate, their day to night' (1.5.6–9). This enrichment of space – with complex relationships inscribed in the spaces between the players – becomes typical of many plays after 1585, an important element in their 'ironic complexity'.

To understand the other, more radical developments in the rhetoric of space, we need to turn to the plays of Marlowe. These, of the extant plays between 1585 and 1595, offer the most useful insights into how the management of theatrical space changed, and how spectators were enabled to see differently. Marlowe's plays exploit, enrich, and ultimately transform the staging of ceremony. Initially, however, and despite 1 Tamburlaine's promise of new theatrical experiences, they relied upon an intensification of the traditional. Much of their ceremony could only be labelled innovative in terms of its frequency, complexity, and excess. Indeed, both Tamburlaine plays are noted generally for their ritualisation of stage action.[28] They feature processions and ceremonies at every stage of the political and personal journey: enmity and alliance, courtship and coronation, triumph and defeat, death and lamentation. They draw upon the conventional signs of power and loss of power, along with the conventional spatial signals of elevation and abasement. Positioning and distances are ceremonially determined, with the sense of ritual retained even when processional entries modulate into confrontations – between Tamburlaine and Bajazeth and their followers, for example, or Sigismond and Orcanes, or Tamburlaine and Callapine. On these occasions action is suspended while the characters declaim, and the space between the players defines their roles as they strike ritual postures at its boundaries.

The Tamburlaine plays may exploit playhouse architecture, especially Part Two, but their 'ironic complexity' develops primarily from the constant accumulation of diverse meanings within the 'landscape of persons'.[29] More so than in the Spanish Tragedy, this complexity depends upon the enrichment of space in the 'landscape'. Horatio's positioning at the banquet locates him in terms of several relationships, and draws attention to the interwoven threads of the narrative. It is far less complex, however, than a positioning such as that of Tamburlaine in the chariot. This elevation is an extravagant invoking of the customary space allotted to important personages: the conqueror is positioned above the other players on stage and, with the raised stage platform, an additional distance above many of the spectators. The image suggests all the conventional ironies of rule, and these are reinforced soon afterwards by the sight of at least two other figures that provide ironic visual parallels with Tamburlaine's elevation: the Governor of Babylon, hanging 'in chains upon the city walls' (2 *Tamburlaine* 5.1.108) before being used as target practice; and Amyras, ascending to the chariot with 'broken heart / And damnèd spirit' (5.3.206–7). But the conqueror's chariot is quite different from these. It is not simply a momentary special effect as they are, merely part of a fixed ceremonial tableau. Tamburlaine remains elevated in the chariot while he scorns the 'jades', distributes Turkish concubines, invokes Samarcanda, dreams of apotheosis, besieges Babylon, burns the books found in the temples of Mahomet, calls upon God, experiences a sudden 'distemper', suffers the torment of a burning sickness, confronts a new threat from Callapine, reviews the map of his conquests, and resigns his place to his son Amyras. His distance above and apart from others thus accumulates varied meanings during performance, even as it is also potentially inscribed with the weight of literary, theatrical, historical, and contemporary analogues.

The most innovative feature of spatial rhetoric in the *Tamburlaine* plays, however, lies in a shift towards a more 'rhetorical' organisation of space. Traditionally, the spatial language of ceremony had established a framework of received values against which the action might be judged. Thus Alexander in *Clyomon and Clamydes* draws attention to the conventional ironies the audience might see in the stage image by appending some conventional reflections on mortality to the account of his triumphs: 'And yet *Alexander*, what art thou? thou art a mortall wight, / For ever thou hast got or wonne by force in fight' (382–3). Ceremonies in *Tamburlaine* sometimes have this kind of reference (the conventional ironies are retained in Tamburlaine's transfer of power to Amyras, for example, or the flawed ceremonies associated with Mycetes and Callapine); but the primary purpose of ceremony becomes 'rhetorical' or persuasive.

This 'rhetorical' effect is seen especially in the escalating extravagance of vertical positioning (indeed, when the chariot arrives it impresses, initially, as the climax to a series of elevations). In Part One, when Tamburlaine ascends to his throne by means of his unfortunate footstool, the movement relies upon traditional spatial language, but its effect is to show Tamburlaine himself as master of ceremonies, appropriating the signs of power, able to redefine himself as 'the chiefest lamp of all the earth' (*1 Tamburlaine* 4.2.36) and his opponent as 'base villain' (19); when Bajazeth protests the conventional dangers of 'ambitious pride' he is promptly returned to his cage.[30] Tamburlaine in effect redesigns the 'landscape of persons'. The effect of such scenes – for all their use of traditional elements of ceremony – is less to do with promoting conventional notions of order, far more to do with a new kind of theatrical experience in which spatial meanings are assigned by eloquence and persuasion. The spectators who witness these events may still take note of the old exemplary lessons, but may also be moved to admire, to make sense of what they see in less traditional ways.

Refractive space

Marlowe's later plays are more radical still in their management of space within the 'landscape of persons'. The *Tamburlaine* plays and the *Spanish Tragedy* had offered spectators new ways of making sense by superimposing first narrative and then rhetorical values upon the older spatial patterns of ceremony. The plays after *Tamburlaine* augment the relationship between audience and action by extending the 'refractive' qualities of space on stage. The term perhaps needs some comment. In the traditional staging of ceremony, the space between the figures in the 'landscape' is essentially reflective, an extension or illustration of the words and action. The *Tamburlaine* plays may be innovative in attaching ceremony to rhetoric, but their onstage spaces remain reflective. The distances that audiences see between Tamburlaine and his opponents mirror in a straightforward way the differences in their status.

But space does not always lie passively on the stage, waiting to reflect. Increasingly after *Tamburlaine*, theatrical space in Marlowe's plays becomes 'refractive'. The meanings suggested by words and action are liable to change direction in some way, to be distorted or complicated through the effects of performance in space. At such times, ambiguities arise from the rhetoric of space within the 'landscape' itself, rather than from the words or any architectural framing or any imitation of the ambiguities in 'real-life' ceremonies. This 'refraction' may be accompanied by straightforward ironic reversals, but goes beyond them to suggest something additional, something other than ceremonial order or even its inversion. Indeed, it is the 'refraction' of space rather than 'ironic complexity' that accounts for many of the ambiguous effects Bevington notes in Shakespeare's plays. For that matter, 'refraction' is also an element in that kind of theatrical space in Shakespeare's plays which Barbara Hodgdon identifies as 'poetic': the 'comprehensive spatial poetry which becomes an active presence within the play, clarifying and defining not only the actors' attitudes and responses but those of the audience as well' (45).[31]

In plays before 1585 it is the comic, non-ceremonial moments that foreshadow refractive space: the antics of Subtle Shift or Simplicity redefine onstage space as disorderly, even absurd. But the effect of such moments is often fleeting, often overtaken immediately by a switching back to the ceremonial. After 1585, the reflective mirror of ceremony itself begins to distort, and cumulative patterns of refractive space begin to provide additional dimensions to staging and response. The process is not limited to Marlowe's plays, but they offer early, important examples. The action of *The Jew of Malta* depends largely on ceremonies, not in this case those of royal display or conquest but instead the many rituals of ordinary life: buying and selling, enticement and pledge, flattery and imprecation, arraignment and mourning. The confrontation between Barabas and the Knights early in the play is fully as ritualised as those of *Tamburlaine* with its three-part 'test' and formal responses. Yet even as these ceremonial exchanges take place, the space between Barabas and the Knights becomes refractive. It operates less to reflect their self-righteous words or even inversely, to illustrate the disruption of received values, than to point to the deceptions it conceals on both sides.

In *The Jew of Malta* the onstage space between players is inscribed with the power to deceive. As in the *Tamburlaine* plays the characters are fixed in roles or ritual postures, but the effect is quite different. Most of the memorable spaces between characters could be described as 'deceiving', drawing attention to deception or misinterpretation: typically, on one side of the 'landscape' stands a character who is deceiving the character or characters on the other side of the space. In such instances the space seems to enforce its own patterns of action, with the fixing in roles or postures serving largely to discourage intimacy or the comparing of notes. Deception flourishes because there is little attempt to cross the intervening space. Characters hide behind their public roles, as does Barabas confronting the Knights, or offering his daughter to each young man in turn or all his wealth to the Friars. Ferneze too deceives, confronting Barabas or springing the trap on the gallery.

The Jew of Malta offers new possibilities for the spatial rhetoric of ceremony. The relationships between the figures in the 'landscape' have changed. The ceremonies have become in a sense irrelevant, the ceremonial spaces detached from conventional notions of order. The influence of such moments may be observed in the staging of scenes in *3 Henry VI* and *Richard III* that include Richard of Gloucester, another heir to the Vice. Richard also operates within refractive space, deceiving those across the 'landscape': this can be seen, for example, in his 'Judas kiss' that pledges loyalty to his brother by kissing his baby son (*3 Henry VI* 5.7); or in his appearance '*aloft, between two* Bishops', feigning reluctance to accept the crown (*Richard III* 3.7.93.1). Some years later, the spectators will watch as the refractive, deceptive space constructed between Iago and his victims progressively invades and destroys the ceremonial space that has defined the actions and nature of Othello.[32]

The refractive qualities of theatrical space are developed in *Edward II*, but quite differently from the *Jew* or *Richard III*. *Edward II* retains traditional, reflective staging in a number of important scenes, where ceremonial spacing is used conventionally to show instances of both order and disorder. Indeed, most accounts of the play define the action in these terms. David Bevington and James Shapiro, for example, describe *Edward II* as alternating 'visually between large scenes of aborted ceremonial, involving sizable groups of contending factions, and contrasting scenes of isolation when we are virtually alone with a soliloquizing figure in prison or some sort of adversity' (267).[33] The ceremonies of *Edward II* are indeed brief. They 'decay' (as Bevington and Shapiro label the process) or disintegrate suddenly, with that disintegration shown reflectively on stage by increasing horizontal distance across the platform. Confrontations such as the first court scene, or those which follow the throne-sharing or the return of Gaveston from Ireland, show a progressive movement apart of the contestants, punctuated by sudden irruptions of violence as swords are drawn and threats are made.[34]

To see theatrical space in *Edward II* as simply traditional and reflective, however, disregards another important spatial pattern that defines the play's 'landscape of persons'. This alternative, refractive space is present on stage side by side with the reflective, ceremonial spaces, and may significantly affect the audience's view of the action. Bevington and Shapiro describe the play visually as alternating between 'scenes of aborted ceremonial' and 'contrasting scenes of isolation'; yet, if we look at the space between players in the ceremonial scenes, the isolation suggested as one side to the alternating contrast is often there as well, visible on stage, in the midst of the crowd, insisting on the sense of loss and loneliness that is at the heart of the play's emotional experience.

Indeed the play's most significant, and memorable, spaces on stage are those that direct audience attention to the distance between the individual and the group, between the observer and the observed. These spaces separate the figures in the 'landscape', denoting dissension between characters, expressing menace or hostility, or drawing attention to the isolation and obsessions of the individual. Edward himself – as Richard II and Hamlet later – is repeatedly seen at some physical distance from the other characters. He is visibly detached even during processional entries, as in the opening to 2.2, where the Queen and Lancaster comment upon his demeanour: 'Look, Lancaster, how passionate he is, / And still his mind runs on his minion' (2.2.3–4). In an earlier scene he has entered '*mourning*' (1.4.303.1); later he '*rageth*' (5.1.85.1). But the King is only one of a succession of isolated figures. Consider Gaveston standing aside from the unruly court in the first scene; or the lords commenting on Edward and Gaveston as they share the throne; or Mortimer, at the moment of ritual reconciliation, walking apart from the lords who kneel to Edward (1.4.352); or Kent, setting himself at a distance from those who 'kiss as they conspire'; or Isabella, withdrawing to one side as Mortimer interviews Matrevis and Gurney; or Lightborn, waiting upon the jailers as they construe the riddling letter.

The separating space between figures in the 'landscape' offers persistent images of estrangement, reinforcing the 'scenes of isolation' and foreshadowing the lonely torment and death of Edward – where the King, so often seen apart, at last makes his own sense of his experience, separately, as suffering individual. In the play's ending, in the young King's grief and anger and in the old King's funeral, the spectators must once again come to terms with the distance – a separating space indeed – between individual and ceremonial or exemplary experience. Throughout, the relationships between characters in the 'landscape' have been suggested as more, or other, than ceremonial. The rituals proceed, but they do not fit what is happening; nor do they provide any real answers. They are different from Shakespeare's ceremonies, which may be fragile – Bevington describes them as 'more often desecrated than properly fulfilled' – but still representing 'an ideal of ordered behaviour' to strive for (*Action Is Eloquence* 172). Compared with Shakespeare's history plays, *Edward II* may lack 'a strong vertical sense of a cosmic and hierarchical world existing multidimensionally above and below the sphere of human action' (Bevington and Shapiro 265); but what the play gains from its refractive spaces is an additional dimension to experience in the playworld: an extra, emotionally charged dimension to the way that the spectators will relate to and make sense of the action.

Theatrical space in *Doctor Faustus* also signals additional meaning about the nature of existence in the playworld. Most commentators emphasise vertical contrasts in staging. Bevington and Rasmussen, summing up what amounts to received opinion, suggest the 'dominance of the vertical dimension' as reflecting the verbal imagery of aspiration; and indeed, they comment, all aspects of staging 'contribute to a vertical and antithetical balance around which the play is visually organised' (Introduction 42).[35] This vertical 'balance' may of course account for much of the management of space in the play. The B-text in particular may rely on action being viewed against the playhouse façade, and on making use of the 'heavens' above the platform and the 'hell' beneath to reflect the options of salvation and damnation – and, with devils 'above', to offer ironic reflections upon Faustus's career.[36] The sense of the vertical may also have been strong at those moments when Faustus is alone on stage, especially if the player moved out on to mid-platform or platform edge from the 'study' or discovery space area. In such a position he is detached visually from the façade for many in the audience, but exposed, as his words suggest and the spectator might imagine, to universal forces – vast, offstage, metaphorical spaces – poised ready to impinge upon the action.[37]

If we look to the play's 'landscape of persons', however, we find an extended pattern in the management of space that functions in performance like the refractive space of *Edward II*, as a counterweight to the moral tale. But where space in *Edward II* intervenes to set figures apart from each other, the space between figures in *Faustus* typically 'connects'. It draws attention to the relationships between the characters, defining their complementary roles: magician and devil, show-presenter and spectator, master and servant. Such space will often connect characters located at different levels of knowledge or experience or status, and in highlighting the bonds between them, will generate ironies. Mephistopheles, despite being 'bound' to Faustus as servant to master, always has more knowledge and more control; Faustus, despite his claims to knowledge and magical power, cannot escape his attachment to Mephistopheles. The connectedness of space persists even when Faustus sees separately as particular

individual. When he stands with the Angels in a conventional grouping, the spaces within the 'landscape' continue to indicate to the
audience the connections between them. The Angels embody the
opposed voices of his inner conflict, even as Faustus perceives and
interprets quite separately.

Memorable examples of 'connecting' space are to be found in the
play's ceremonies or 'ritual shows' (Hattaway's term), but also in
less ceremonial passages of action: in the conversations between
Faustus and Mephistopheles, for instance, or between Faustus and
the Scholars; and in the earnest pleading of the Old Man while
Mephistopheles offers a dagger. One special kind of connecting
space in *Faustus* is what might be termed the 'magic' space of the
conjuring and the shows. The space that is marked out between the
shows and the onstage spectators establishes bonds even as it
defines. Though the spectator is deferred to as superior – and physical elevation may have been achieved for them by the use of a dais
or 'state' – there are conditions for enjoyment, just as there are
conditions, stated and unstated, in the bond that Faustus signs with
hell.[38] For one thing, the onstage spectators are enjoined by the
presenter to be silent, 'for danger is in words'. And, as the Emperor
discovers, they may not breach the 'magic' space to interact with the
show.[39] The inscribing of space between figures with this 'magical'
force is not limited to the main narrative but can be found also in the
comic scenes, especially in the B-text. It is echoed-parodied there in
Robin's inscription of a magic circle and his injunction to Dick to
avoid the 'magic' space ('Keep out of the circle, I say, lest I send you
into the hostry, with a vengeance', B-text 2.2.13–15); and (again in
the B-text) in the 'charming' of the boisterous clowns who interrupt
Faustus at the court of Vanholt (B-text 4.6).[40] In this, as in other
aspects of staging, the B-text takes up and exploits particular
elements of the A-text.

Towards the end of *Faustus* the nature of the space between the
figures changes, and the audience expectations built up by earlier
spaces are overturned. When Faustus breaches the 'magic' space to
embrace Helen, his action signals the loss of the play's connecting
spaces, the loss of all bonds, all relationships (in effect) except the
bond with hell.[41] In the final soliloquy he is isolated on stage, unable
to bridge the gap between himself and the vision of redeeming blood
– located, as his words and gestures would convince the spectators,
only just beyond the visible, onstage space. And then in his last
moments he must face the encroachment of hell across the last, and
most compelling space in the play's 'landscape of persons': 'Ugly

hell, gape not. Come not, Lucifer! ... / Ah, Mephistopheles!' *Faustus* is no simple moral tale. The connecting space within its 'landscapes' is always potentially refractive, setting repeatedly before the spectators images that challenge or distort the 'vertical and antithetical balance' that other elements of staging reflect. These images offer them alternative perspectives on the action, confronting them with the interconnectedness of experience. They reinforce the sense of mutual participation, the shared delight in watching the show – and awaken an apprehension that humanity cannot be disentangled from damnation.

The rhetoric of theatrical space changed after 1585, as the rhetoric of positioning changed, and as space within the 'landscape of persons' became variously enriched, rhetorical, and refractive. This transformation of the traditional 'landscape of persons' represents a second, alternative response by playwright and player to the new London playhouses. It differs from the one identified as 'Shakespearean' by Bevington in that it exploited the dimensions of the stage platform rather than the framing possibilities of the façade, yet it also afforded a pathway to the 'stance of ironic complexity'. The alternative response, deriving from the 'landscape of persons', looked to the players themselves and not simply to iconographic or scenic appropriateness. Because of this, it retained the playing advantages of the old ways and made new ways possible, offering the players a continuing engagement with the spectators in addition to an increasingly complex interaction between the figures on stage.

Marlowe's plays provide notable examples of this second kind of response, which extended the options available for managing space in the playhouse and changed the relationships between spectators and stage action, providing them with new emotional dimensions to their theatrical experience. Bevington and Shapiro, writing of the difference between *Edward II* and Shakespeare's later *Richard II*, suggest that 'Marlowe's theatrical vision is very much directed to the middle ground of human conflict' (265). The comment is more relevant to *Edward II* than the other plays, yet it points to an important but undervalued feature of Marlowe's management of theatrical space. The impact of his plays on contemporary staging depended not only on their 'astounding' spectacles but also on their development of the 'middle ground of human conflict'. In considering how staging changed late in the sixteenth century, and in making sense of later, Shakespearean staging, we should take into account this second kind of response to performing in playhouses – and the radical examples to be found in the plays of Marlowe.

CHAPTER 8

Till experience change

'From jigging veins of rhyming mother-wits.' In six years, from 1587 to 1593, the new rhetoric of Christopher Marlowe transformed theatrical experience in the London playhouses. But this was less a matter of importing humanist learning, values, and energies into popular drama (the standard explanation) than of enabling spectators to see differently and interpret variously. Marlowe's plays, in effect, changed the ways that a spectator might see and make sense of the action on stage. Their revolutionary impact derived from the use they made of the materials of traditional drama – visual sign and cautionary tale, Vice monologue and psychomachia, even the 'landscape of persons'. Marlowe's popular inheritance underpinned the effects of the newer features that have always attracted more attention: the 'mighty line', the grand heroes, the spectacle, the unconventional ideas.

The focus here has been upon Marlowe as the inheritor of the popular tradition, in dialogue with his contemporary audience and the ways they had 'learned to see and respond' (Williams 178). The importance of this audience has been a basic assumption of this book, which has looked to the ways that spectators in the 1580s and 1590s may have perceived, watched, participated, and responded in the playhouse, and to the ways their expectations and previous experiences may have been challenged or confirmed. In reckoning the 'newness' of Marlowe's plays, I have measured the experiences they construct for their spectators against those afforded by other 'popular' plays between (about) 1565 and 1595 with their 'manifest signes' and 'troublesome raigns', their 'spotting' and pageantry, their keen eye for hypocrisy, their scheming of Vices and villains, and their tally of corpses – deserving as well as undeserving.

This study has been concerned with rewriting a reputation – this is not Marlowe the educated outsider or government spy or any other of the familiar stereotypes – but also with looking afresh at some of the commonplaces of 'development' in sixteenth-century drama. Our critical narratives are overdue for revision. We explain late sixteenth-century change too simply and too often in terms of adding humanist learning to the popular tradition, and then adding the genius of Shakespeare. We focus on the 'medieval' or the 'Shakespearean'; and neglect for the most part the period that falls between them. When we address what happened in the playhouse drama between 1585 and 1595 – the years of radical change – our accounts are inadequate, and not only because many playtexts do not survive. Too often Shakespeare obscures our vision, and we notice only what is relevant to the mature Shakespearean play. The considerable, sophisticated legacy of the late moralities is in general disregarded; when mentioned, this immediate inheritance of Marlowe and Shakespeare and their audiences becomes too often a matter of vague influences or quaint survivals.

The continuities, however, are far from vague or quaint. Plays after 1585 continued, for the most part, to call upon an audience to observe and make sense in traditional ways. They are rich in visual signs that direct attention to – and reinforce – conventional understandings. Their cautionary tales exploit conventional ironies. Their framing rhetoric draws upon the old morality contrast between 'what is' and 'what should be'. Their characters still listen to their opposed voices, and their villains retain the manner and rhetorical baggage of the Vice. To these features, moreover, should be added others that are sometimes assumed to be 'new' at some later stage, or typical of later plays (especially later Shakespearean plays), but which are in fact also characteristic of the late morality: a preoccupation with ambiguous signs and deceptive appearances; a concern with interiority; an acute metadramatic awareness; and a satirical perspective on the authorities and everyday life.

The approach adopted here, with its attention to the rhetoric of plays – and in particular the implications of this rhetoric for the ways that spectators view and interpret – has made it possible to identify continuities more clearly, and to locate change and innovation. The boundaries between 'medieval' and 'modern' drama continue to be under contention. This study has explored the timing of particular changes, as well as reconsidering the nature and directions of change, theatrical and cultural. There is no neat, straight-line 'development' in the drama between 1585 and 1595; rather the accumulation and twisting together of many threads as playwrights continued to experiment with different ways of telling stories on stage and engaging with their audiences. If there is any common direction emerging in the conventional dramatic rhetoric of 1580s and 1590s plays, it might be defined as an impulse to elaborate or complicate. In the popular plays of this period this impulse can be observed in the increasing numbers and complexity of visual signs; in the accumulations of striking detail that provided emotional reinforcement for exemplary rhetoric; in the multiplication of framing perspectives; in the complication of dramatic characters; and, not least, in the enrichment of theatrical space. But an urge to elaborate does not sufficiently explain what happens in late sixteenth-century drama. Complication may be the dominant trend in the rhetoric of character, but it leads to figures such as Volpone rather than inevitably to Richard II or Hamlet.

In the accumulation of different threads it is possible to identify certain radical moments or turning-points or divergings where the threads knot or divide, forming new patterns of dramatic rhetoric. It is at these moments – some mere glimpses, others part of patterns deeply imbedded in the rhetoric of a particular play – that we come to understand the revolutionary nature of Marlowe's rhetoric in the theatre, and its difference from that of earlier and contemporary plays. Marlowe's plays offered their early audiences new theatrical experiences that changed their relationship with the action on stage. They exploited the potential of visual signs for other, non-allegorical purposes, calling upon playhouse spectators to do more than simply read through the visual sign and recognise conventional meanings. They challenged traditional perspectives and values, not so much by substituting 'new' ideas for old but by breaking old rhetorical connections. *Edward II* disengaged the 'manifest signe' from its exemplary lesson, making possible a new kind of tragic understanding. *The Jew of Malta* dismantled the framing rhetoric of the morality, casting the Vice adrift from his special position as authorised interpreter of the playworld. *Doctor Faustus* transformed the rhetoric of dramatic character by introducing the new 'debatable' character, bringing a new sense of 'separate' consciousness to the stage, with a figure that perceives and makes sense differently from either playworld or audience. Watching Faustus, the spectators are called upon to set aside ethics ('Should he?') for psychology ('Why does he?'), and make their own individual sense of the figure before them.

This shift in audience focus points to another notable change in audience experience. For all the spectacle and eloquence and energy that once 'ravish[ed] the gazing Scaffolders', the plays of Marlowe also conferred theatrical power on their audiences. This can be seen in those moments in *Faustus* and *Edward II* where the spectators' attention is directed to moment-by-moment experience on stage. It can be found also, to take another example, as an effect of the *Jew*'s contradictory framing perspectives, which offered spectators not merely several alternative interpretations but more than one *kind* of interpretive narrative to make sense of the world, whether 'real' or theatrical. Marlowe's legacy of empowerment persists in our own responses to a number of sixteenth- and seventeenth-century plays: we are still asking 'why' about their 'debatable' characters even four hundred years after they first appeared on the stage.

It is perhaps especially at the radical moments of Marlowe's plays that we come to understand something of the processes of cultural change. This is a subject that is usually explained in ideological terms, in terms that is of what people were thinking. The early modern drama has been raked over for analogies and reflections of ideas current elsewhere – evidence of 'individualism' or Puritan theology, for example, or comments on social tensions. Much of this commentary, however, does little to define or locate cultural change, which is more than a matter of simply airing contrary opinions on stage. The theatre has always accommodated unconventional and unacceptable voices; but these are not necessarily subversive unless the spectators are led to view their world differently. We need to remember that the stories spectators might tell about what happens on stage are shaped by the rhetoric of performance, whether this is associated with some conscious endeavour on the part of the playwright (as in the claims of the Prologue to *Tamburlaine*); or develops from the interaction between audience and action (as in the 'separate seeing' of Faustus); or emerges in response to different configurations of theatrical space.

Not only opinions but, importantly, perceptions. In exploring change in the late sixteenth-century playhouse, we should keep in mind the realignment in the processing of the visual that accompanied more articulate kinds of cultural change. Each of the radical, memorable moments in Marlowe's plays is associated in some way with a change from the traditional in what was seen, literally, on stage. It was the simply visual, the unmediated element in the experience of Faustus and Edward, that provided early audiences with something that was the least traditional or even expected: the signs of individual, non-representative experience. More generally, the new emphases in theatrical space – especially the emergence of rhetorical and refractive space within the 'landscape of persons' –

offered audiences new emotional dimensions to their experience in the playhouse. When they saw before them the spaces that convey *Edward*'s sense of loss and loneliness, they came to apprehend anew the 'middle ground of human conflict' (Bevington and Shapiro 265). This is new viewing, rather than new philosophy.

This book began with the suggestion that we should consider cultural change at the level of ordinary experience, in this case ordinary theatrical experience. The traditional rhetoric of popular drama had assumed certain ways of looking at action and events; it was enmeshed in particular ways of viewing the world and making sense of experience. Marlowe's new rhetoric made it possible for spectators to change their habits of perception – and perhaps to attempt, or even to arrive at, new ways of seeing. As the Prologue to *1 Tamburlaine* had promised, the early audiences did come to experience differently in the playhouse. And that, as Mephistopheles once reminded Faustus, may also have led them to make sense differently: 'Ay, think so still, till experience change thy mind' (*Faustus* 2.1.131). In the end, the most radical transformation of the traditional in Marlowe's plays consisted not in preaching the virtues of individuality nor in offering exemplars of individual *virtù* but rather in giving individual spectators the chance to make sense with their own individual stories. In this empowering of the audience lay the real subversion, the most notable innovation in the English drama before 1595.

NOTES

Chapter 1: Ways of seeing

1 The texts of Marlowe's works used for references are those of the Revels Plays series. The version of *Doctor Faustus* used in citations is the A-text, but the two versions are discussed separately and/or together as relevant. Shakespeare's plays are cited from the Arden editions unless otherwise stated; and some contemporary plays from the Revels Plays series. For other playtexts, I have used accessible editions: some annotated, some facsimile reprints. Most of the plays before 1587, and some minor ones after this date, exist only in old-spelling editions. I have modernised the spelling of play titles and character names, but have not attempted to modernise the texts except for regularising u/v and i/j.

2 The first quotation is from H. Levin's classic study of the early 1950s, *Christopher Marlowe: The Overreacher*, the next two from publications aimed at a wide readership: Kernan in the *Revels History of Drama*, Volume III (1975); Watson in the *Cambridge Companion to Renaissance Drama* (1990). The phrase 'our contemporary', with its allusion to Kott's study of Shakespeare, is used by Felperin as the title for his discussion of Greenblatt on Marlowe. The point that each age 'reinvents' or appropriates the past in its own particular way is developed by G. Taylor in *Reinventing Shakespeare*, though the recognition that any view of the past is necessarily partial is an older commonplace of criticism.

3 On earlier critical stereotypes and trends for Marlowe, see Dabbs (the nineteenth-century reputation); and Friedenreich's introductory essay to his *Annotated Bibliography* (1979). For trends since 1950, see the introductory or review essays of H. Levin, 'Marlowe Today' (1964); Kimbrough (1973); Post (1977); Levao (1988); as well as Brandt's annotated bibliography (1992).

4
>   As lately lifting up the leaves of worthy writers workes
>   Wherein the Noble acts and deeds of many hidden lurks,
>   Our Author he hath found the Glasse of glory shining bright,
>   Wherein their lives are to be seene, which honour did delight
>   To be a Lanthorne unto those which dayly do desire,
>   *Apollos* Garland by desert, in time for to aspire ...
>   And doubting nought right Courteous all, in your accustomed
>   woont
>   And gentle eares, our Author he, is prest to bide the brunt
>   Of bablers tongues, to whom he thinks, as frustrate all his toile,
>   As peereles caste to filthy Swine, which in the mire doth moile.
>   (*Clyomon and Clamydes*, Prologue 2–7, 14–17)

5 Part of the critical endeavour prompted by the quatercentenary of Marlowe's birth in 1964 was devoted to recovering Marlowe as dramatist rather than poet. The high points of this movement are Brooke's

'Marlowe the Dramatist'; and several contributions to the special issue
of the *Tulane Drama Review*, 8.4 (Summer 1964), in particular, Powell;
Brown, 'Marlowe and the Actors'; and interviews with Grotowski and
Robertson. Since that time, there has been a more general acceptance of
Marlowe's dramatic powers, although with varying degrees of conde-
scension and with the emphasis continuing to be on Marlowe as
polemicist. Discussions that take into account considerations of staging
and/or modern productions include those of Leech, *Marlowe*; Zucker;
Hattaway; and Birringer. Cartelli's *Economy of Theatrical Experience*
discusses the plays from the viewpoint of playhouse experience. Editions
of the playtexts now tend to allocate more space to staging history, and
there are several book-length studies of the staging of particular plays,
including Tydeman on *Doctor Faustus*; Geckle on *Tamburlaine* and
Edward II. A few studies focus on the experimental nature of Marlovian
dramaturgy: Brooke, 'Marlowe the Dramatist'; Waith; Rocklin,
'Experimental Dramatist'.

6 See, for example, Battenhouse; Kocher; Weil; Bartels, 'Fictions of
   Difference'; Greenblatt, *Learning to Curse*. The polemical impulse has
   been persistent: the urge to recruit Marlowe for, or against, one's cause
   dates back to Robert Greene's remarks to the 'Gentlemen readers' of
   Perimedes the Blacksmith (1588) and shows little sign of abating. Where
   Shakespeare is called upon in support of 'Establishment' values (as
   cultural icon, in effect), Marlowe is more often claimed as representing
   the unconventional (the inverse-icon), though the perception of what
   this might amount to has changed. Apart from the two film versions of
   Edward II (Ian McKellen, Derek Jarman), striking instances have been
   Shepherd's attempts to appropriate Marlowe as feminist and Marxist;
   and, at the level of popular culture, Oscar Zarate's comic-book version
   of *Faustus*, which appeared not long after the Falklands crisis of 1983
   and in which Helen appears in the guise of Margaret Thatcher and
   Mephistopheles is attired in a Union Jack shirt. There have perhaps been
   fewer 'psychoanalytical' than 'historical' interpretations, but they have
   been influential nevertheless. Most align playwright with play, and are
   concerned with matters such as insatiable cravings for power (Knights,
   'Strange Case'); deep divisions in personality (Steane); or homosexual
   anxieties (Kuriyama, *Hammer or Anvil*).

7 References to these 'critical commonplaces' in order: H. Levin,
   Overreacher; Kocher; Greenblatt, *Renaissance Self-fashioning*; Sales,
   Marlowe (this draws parallels between Tamburlaine's campaigns and
   those of English commanders such as Essex in Ireland).

8 My comments in this paragraph develop from the discussions of
   Bluestone, *Story to Stage*; R. Levin, 'Feminist Thematics', 'Leaking
   Relativism', 'Unthinkable Thoughts'; and Pechter, 'New Historicism',
   What Was Shakespeare?

9 I am using 'see' to refer to the whole process of perception in the theatre,
   including hearing, as well as to 'viewpoint' or 'perspective'. At the same
   time, I follow the emphasis of writers such as Dessen in arguing for the
   importance of what was actually seen on the playhouse stage.

10 The constructing of audience perspectives is emphasised by several
   writers, including Cartelli, *Economy of Theatrical Experience* (organis-

ing 'the central fantasy content'); and Shepherd (ideological implications).

11 See the studies of Elton; Manley; Serpieri; C. Taylor.

12 Many discussions of the relationship between theatre and society since the 1970s have stressed the political (Orgel, 'Making Greatness Familiar'; Mullaney) or commercial aspects (Yachnin; Gurr, *Playgoing* 116–17). Most contemporary comments, on the other hand, saw the relationship in moral and religious terms. Compare two typical views, both from 1592. Nashe advocates plays as morally cleansing since 'all coosonages, all cunning drifts over-guylded with outward holinesse, all stratagems of warre, all the cankerwormes that breede on the rust of peace, are most lively anatomiz'd' (*Pierce Penilesse* 88); while William Webbe, Lord Mayor of London, issues a routine complaint: 'the youth ... [of the city] is greatly corrupted & their manners infected with many evill & ungodly qualities by reason of the wanton & prophane divises represented on the stages' (letter to John Whitgift, Archbishop of Canterbury, 25 February 1591 [1592], Rutter 54). But plays could also be seen as valuable to public policy: in Robert Wilson's *The Three Lords and Three Ladies of London* they are not only 'for recreation of the mind' (1344) but become part of the defiant, morale-building civic display as London awaits the Armada:

> Lord *Pomp*, let nothing that's magnificall
> Or that may tend to *Londons* graceful state
> Be unperfourm'd, as showes and solemne feastes,
> Watches in armour, triumphes, Cresset-lightes,
> Bonefiers, belles, and peales of ordinance.
> And [Lord] *pleasure*, see that plaies be published,
> Mai-games and maskes, with mirth and minstrelsie,
> Pageants and school-feastes, beares, and puppit plaies.
>
> (*Three Lords* 1319–26)

13 Playtexts for these Vices, in order: *Cambises*; *The Three Ladies of London*; *The Conflict of Conscience*.

14 The term as used here owes something to Robert Weimann's important study, *Shakespeare and the Popular Tradition in the Theater*, though I would disagree at a number of points with his account of the transition from the moralities to Shakespeare. Brooke earlier referred to the 'popular dramatic tradition' in arguing Marlowe's exploitation of existing genres ('Marlowe the Dramatist' 105).

15 On other dramatic traditions see, for example, the studies of Boas, *University Drama* (academic drama); Hunter, *Lyly* (court); Clemen, *Tragedy before Shakespeare*, and Altman (classical and rhetorical).

16 Canon and chronology: my discussion will be centred on the major plays in the Marlowe canon, with only occasional reference to the two minor plays. *Dido Queen of Carthage* was probably written earlier than 1587, and its principal address is to elite (courtly, academic, boy-player) dramatic traditions rather than to the popular stage. *The Massacre at Paris* is late and 'public', but has considerable textual difficulties. A definitive chronology of Marlowe's plays has not been established; and the sequence of material in this book is not intended to imply one. My

interest here is less in development from play to play than in relationships within a dramatic tradition. At the same time, I do assume a
particular chronological sequence: that *Faustus* is 'late' rather than
'early', and certainly later than the *Jew*. In assuming this, I am relying
largely upon the kinds of changes *Faustus* makes to the popular tradition and upon the complexity of the theatrical experience it offers its
audience. For detailed discussion of the date of *Faustus* see the
Introductions of Greg, Bowers, Keefer, Bevington and Rasmussen; and
the articles of Kuriyama, 'Dr. Greg and *Doctor Faustus*'; Keefer, 'Verbal
Magic'; Ericksen. Ormerod and Wortham provide a useful introductory
summary in their edition of the A-text. More generally, there is no exact
chronology for playtexts in the period 1565 to 1595; and I rely for the
most part on the scholarly guesses of modern editors. In any case it is
probably more useful to think in terms of approximate markers. In very
general terms, the extant plays written or printed after about 1565 are
less likely to be simply 'educational' or elite entertainment, and more
likely to be suitable for the new professional theatres in London – and
hence within the possible experience of the 1580s playwrights and
popular audiences. The important exceptions, of course, are the printings of classical plays (editions of Seneca, for instance) and of plays from
the boys' theatre (of Lyly, in particular). The year 1587 marks a sudden
flush of new playwrights and new printings and, perhaps more importantly, of innovative dramaturgy: this is the period of Marlowe and his
contemporaries. The next convenient marker is about 1594 or 1595. By
this time, Marlowe was dead, as were Greene and Kyd; regular playing
in London had resumed after much disruption by plague in 1592 and
1593; and Shakespeare was writing *Richard II* or *Romeo and Juliet*
rather than *Richard III* or *Titus Andronicus*.

Chapter 2: Approaches and contexts

1 'Rhetoric' is used in this general sense in this book. 'Rhetorical' and
  'rhetorically', on the other hand, are used in two senses: (1) pertaining
  to the basic, neutral sense, as in 'rhetorical pattern'; (2) with suggestions
  of excess or display. The meaning of any particular example should be
  apparent from its context.
2 'Rhetoric' in the basic sense was by no means the only way that the
  sixteenth century saw the term. 'Rhetoric' was also commonly associated with extravagance and insincerity. Indeed Marlowe's only use of
  the word is in Hero's protest to Leander: 'Who taught thee Rhetoric
  to deceive a maid?' (I.338). Traditionally, Drama was seen as an
  aspect of Rhetoric, as one of the kinds of poetry. A morality play
  performed on a booth stage is used to represent Rhetoric in Brueghel's
  1560 engraving *Temperance* (Klein 245; note also Southern 508–9).
  Sidney's objections in the *Apology* to contemporary plays (133–7) are
  essentially rhetorical ones: they breached the conventions of rhetorical
  practice, 'observing rules neither of honest civility nor of skilful Poetry'
  (133). For a useful introduction to sixteenth-century rhetoric in theory
  and practice see Donker and Muldrow; for educational practice and
  sixteenth-century plays, Altman. Other studies of interest include those

of Dixon; Vickers, *Defence of Rhetoric*; Howell; N. Rhodes; Donawerth (on Shakespeare).

3 Discussions of verbal rhetoric in sixteenth-century drama include: on Shakespeare's 'images', Spurgeon; and, for Marlowe, Marion Smith; Meehan. On Shakespeare's 'style', Doran. On Marlowe's 'style', J. Cunningham (Introduction 51); Kernan (255–6); Levenson; Morris; Peet; Van Hook.

4 See Elam, *Semiotics of Theatre and Drama*; Pavis, *Dictionnaire du théâtre*, *Languages of Stage*; Ubersfeld, *Lire le théâtre*, *L'école du spectateur*.

5 Leith and Myerson propose a rhetorical model for discourse generally, based on the assumption that language is essentially a kind of social action, not merely referring to itself but always part of a dialogue, always part (that is) of the social world.

6 See Ong, *Ramus*; Manley.

7 In this attention to roles, 'dramatic rhetoric' coincides generally with Robert Hapgood's 'theatre poetry', which guides the activities and responses of the 'theatre ensemble' (actors, playgoers, even readers). See also Howard on Shakespeare's 'art of orchestration'.

8 On the urge to construct meaning, see Carlson, *Theatre Semiotics* 7; Beckerman, 'Theatrical Perception' 167.

9 See also Pavis, *Languages of Stage* (defining differences between text and performance); Berger ('imaginary audition'); Coursen (responding to Berger, text as 'secondary' and 'derivative').

10 See, for example, McGann; Orgel, 'What is a Text?'; Werstine; Maguire. On the texts of *Faustus*, Warren; Marcus.

11 There are many useful studies of sixteenth-century cultural and theatrical practices. A selection: Beckerman, *Shakespeare at Globe*; Bevington, *Action Is Eloquence*; Bradbrook, *Common Player*, *Themes and Conventions*; Braunmuller, 'Arts of Dramatist'; Brown, *Plays in Performance*; Chambers; Craik, *Tudor Interlude*; Dessen, *Elizabethan Stage Conventions*; Drew-Bear; Fleischer; Foakes, *Illustrations of English Stage*; Graves; Gurr, *Shakespearean Stage*, *Playgoing*; Hattaway; *Henslowe's Diary*; Hunter, 'Flatcaps and Bluecoats'; Kernodle; Knutson, 'Repertory System', 'Shakespeare's Playhouse World'; Linthicum; H. McMillin, *Staging of Elizabethan Plays at the Rose Theatre* (in some ways more reliable than the study of the same title by E. Rhodes); Reynolds; Rutter; M. Shapiro; Slater; Southern; Styan, *Shakespeare's Stagecraft*; Thomson; Wickham, *Early English Stages*. Problems in assessing the available evidence have been discussed by a number of writers. On the need to recognise the rhetorical context of evidence see the collection edited by Pechter, *Textual and Theatrical Shakespeare* (1996), especially essays by Bristol, 'How Good Does Evidence Have to Be?'; Dessen, 'Recovering Elizabethan Staging'; Osborne.

12 For additional discussion of the problems of interpreting stage directions, see Dessen, 'Shakespeare and Theatrical Conventions'; Rocklin, '*Producible Interpretation*'.

13 Most discussions of this aspect deal only with modern productions of Shakespeare. See, for example, Michael Scott; Dessen, *Elizabethan Stage*

Conventions, 'Modern Productions'; Berry; G. Taylor, *To Analyze Delight*; Kennedy.

14 Kennedy (34–42) situates Poel in the context of other nineteenth-century experiments in 'Elizabethanism'. For a useful account of Poel's productions, see Speaight.

15 The term 'deictic' has more specialised applications both in emblem theory (see Daly) and (especially) in semiotics. Daly refers briefly to the use of 'deictic formulae' ('Look at me') in connection with emblematic moments in both German baroque and English Renaissance drama (143, 147–8). Elam (138–40) and Serpieri (122–3) comment on the deictic as a basic function of performance language, with deictic expressions important in establishing relationships between speakers and immediate contexts for the action.

16 Useful studies of conventional devices are provided by Dessen, *Elizabethan Stage Conventions, Viewer's Eye*; Craik, *Tudor Interlude*; Hunter, 'Flatcaps and Bluecoats'.

17 The insistence on variability is by no means the only view among performance critics of Renaissance plays. Some performance approaches to Shakespeare are just as 'closed' as many non-performance readings. On the diverse nature of performance criticism see Thompson and Thompson's historical survey; Worthen.

18 A similar point is made by Shepherd (xiv), and by Cartelli (*Economy of Theatrical Experience* 1–5). Hunter suggests a need to correct 'the usual illusion that Shakespeare's art is not only a supreme artistic achievement but also a supreme historical cause' (*English Drama* 4).

19 Most comparisons between Marlowe and Shakespeare are narrowly based on 'ideas' and verbal rhetoric (see, for example, Sanders; J. Shapiro). Cartelli suggests that we correct the stereotypes by attending to 'the distinctiveness of Marlowe's and Shakespeare's respective approaches to their audiences' (*Economy of Theatrical Experience* 5). See also Brooks; Duane; Dutton.

20 The approach through experience and expectations has been attempted intermittently, though with differences of scope or emphasis. Notable instances include Bradbrook, *Themes and Conventions*; Southern; Hunter, *English Drama* (expectations of genre).

21 Attempts to describe the emotional response of audiences date back to Aristotle and his analysis of tragic performance: the concept of *catharsis*, for example, or the effects of *peripateia* or *anagnoresis*. Many modern discussions of response (of pleasure in particular) derive from Freudian theory. Cartelli refers to Freudian notions of pleasure, fantasy, and resistance to establish general conditions for audience behaviour and response. See also, for example, Ubersfeld, 'Pleasure of Spectator'; and on 'anxiety' Greenblatt, *Shakespearean Negotiations* 134–5.

22 A prayer for the queen is not uncommon. Plays before 1580 ending this way include *Common Conditions, Like Will to Like, New Custom*, and *Patient and Meek Grissill* (Houle).

23 Despite their popularity – they comprise one-third of all plays recorded 1570–1585 – only three 'romances' have survived: *Clyomon and Clamydes, Common Conditions, The Rare Triumphs of Love and Fortune*. In addition, there are references to twenty-seven 'lost' plays of

this kind (Littleton 195–8). For useful accounts of surviving plays before 1587 see *Revels History II*; Southern; Houle.

24 Cameron (44) claims even more plays for Wilson, including *The Rare Triumphs of Love and Fortune*, *Fair Em*, *A Knack to Know a Knave*, and *Mucedorus*.

25 For extracts from the prologue to *Clyomon and Clamydes*, see above, Ch. 1, n. 4.

26 McMillin and MacLean identify the verse 'medley' (a mixture of verse styles) as a distinctive feature of the plays of the Queen's Men (143–54). Some of the plays from 1587 onwards, such as *Locrine*, are probably revisions of earlier plays, updated in line with the new fashion for blank verse (on this, see Berek); others, including *Faustus*, preserve traces of older dramatic 'business' (see Pettit; Bradbrook, 'Eldritch Tradition').

27 The play was apparently written in 1581 for Leicester's Men, but the text shows signs of abridgement to meet changed circumstances, perhaps when the company lost players with the formation of the Queen's Men in 1583. In the first printed version (1584) two boys only are required to act the 'three ladies'; in the final scene they must share the role of Love, with Lucre instructed to leave the stage '*to make ready for Love quickly, and come with Dilligence*' (1914–16). A missing scene may be referred to by Gosson in *Plays Confuted*; he mentions a debate where Love is against plays because 'they expose her tricks', but Conscience approves of them (see Bradbrook, *Common Player* 183). The other significant popular printing of the early 1580s was *The Conflict of Conscience*, but this may not have been written with the public stage in mind. The title-page provides a doubling scheme for six players (similar to the numbers available in the earlier itinerant troupes), who might 'shew this Comedie in private houses, or otherwise'.

28 McMillin and MacLean stress the political role of the Queen's Men, in particular their formation in 1583 with the support of both Walsingham and Leicester as 'an avenue for bringing the theatre back into the service of a Protestant ideology which could also be identified as the "truth" of Tudor history' (33). Wilson and the Queen's Men were also actively involved in the Marprelate controversy of 1588–89; see especially McMillin and MacLean 53–5; also Heinemann 174–5; Cameron 4–9.

29 Mithal claims this as an inversion of the morality convention of last minute repentance; but Dessen notes other instances in the late moralities. The sequel, the *Three Lords*, ends more neatly, with Love, Conscience, and Lucre rehabilitated and splendidly married; with Simony departed over the seas and Usury branded so that he can charge ten per cent only and no more. On the other hand, the home-grown social abuses persist: Fraud is arrested and tied to one of the stage posts, but Dissimulation releases him and the two villains slip away.

30 Bradbrook (followed by Heinemann 174) suggests Tarlton played Simplicity, citing the use of a Tarlton catchphrase (*Common Player* 181). Hunter opts for Wilson himself ('Revolution and Continuity' 42).

31 Other examples of the estates morality are *The Tide Tarrieth No Man* (1576); *The Cobbler's Prophecy* (also by Wilson, printed 1594); *A Looking Glass for London and England* (Lodge and Greene, *c.* 1590).

32 The preoccupation with definition is noted by Burns as a feature of

earlier plays (52), but the tendency persists in the late morality, where labelling is always more important than motivating. An insight into traditional thinking about character names is provided by the prologue to the first version of *Conflict of Conscience* (printed 1581), a play which dramatises an actual story of Calvinist despair. The playwright was concerned, the Prologue advises us, that if he used the historical name of 'Frauncis Spera' mentioned on the title-page, the spectators would not apply the lesson to themselves – and so he changed the name of the protagonist to Philologus, lover of talk. To make sure of this in the play's second version printed later the same year, the historical name is omitted altogether: the title-page refers only to 'a miserable worldlinge, termed, by the name of PHILOLOGUS'.

33 On this structure see, for example, Dessen, *Late Moral Plays* 135. Altman identifies two basic structures in sixteenth-century plays: the demonstrative; and the 'exploratory', in which different views of a situation were tested (should the aristocratic heroine marry the poor but virtuous suitor or the rich but less virtuous one?). Both structures depend, nevertheless, on the same traditional habits of perception and interpretation.

34 Jones, 'Dangerous Sport', *Engagement with Knavery*; Happé, '"The Vice" and Popular Theatre'.

Chapter 3: Viewing the sign

1 General studies of the visual sign in the sixteenth century are provided by Daly; Höltgen; Freeman. Bibliographies can be found in Dees; Doebler, 'Bibliography'. Studies of iconography in the drama include those of Dessen; Diehl; Doebler, *Shakespeare's Speaking Pictures*; Wickham; Zucker.

2 Quotation from Richard Mulcaster's account, *The Passage of Our Most Drad Soveraigne Lady Quene Elyzabeth through the Citie of London to Westminster the Daye before her Coronacion* (London, 1558), fol. Ciiiiv (qtd in Kipling 44).

3 *Mankind* is a fifteenth-century morality (1461–85), probably devised for performance by a travelling company of six players. *Apius and Virginia* (most likely a boys' play) dates from *c.* 1564, though the only extant edition is that of 1575. On *Cambises*, see above, Chapter 2.

4 Apart from theatrical practice, evidence for this persistence depends largely on negative examples, on the vehemence of the attacks on playing, for example, or 'idolatrous' Catholic worship (see Diehl's comments on Foxe, 'Observing the Lord's Supper' 153).

5 On Calvin's distinction between *idol* (which tempts to worship) and *figure* (which acts as mnemonic), see (for example) Diehl, 'Observing the Lord's Supper'. Diehl comments that Calvin nevertheless 'conceives of the visible element as a necessary rhetorical tool by which God "exhorteth us to come unto him"' (156). Collinson traces Protestant attitudes to the use of plays, songs, and graphic images, suggesting that Protestant response to visual signs was in two stages, first iconoclasm, and then (from *c.* 1580) iconophobia.

6 On the active involvement of the Protestant establishment with plays

and players see Breitenberg (on *Gorboduc*); White (on the 'alliance between drama and Protestantism' before 1580); and McMillin and MacLean (on the motives underlying the formation of the Queen's Men in 1583, and their policy of staging 'truth and plainness').

7 McMillin and MacLean provide useful commentary on the *Three Lords*: including the play as 'medley' (122–5), as well as its performance style (125–30), and versification (143–8).

8 The printed text provides lengthy stage directions for the battle (over thirty lines in all). Southern offers a reconstruction of the action which involves the yard as well as the stage (568–75, especially fig. 42, p. 571). Heraldic devices were in vogue in 1580s and 1590s plays. Wilson's earlier play, *The Three Ladies of London*, has a satirical verbal description of the 'armes' of Fraud by Simplicity (1634–43). In hanging up shields on stage, Wilson may be following (or have anticipated, depending on the dating) the example of the *Spanish Tragedy* 1.4 (see Hattaway 120; Kohler 47 n. 34). See also the devices on the shields in *Edward II* 2.2; these, however, are not necessarily on stage (see Forker's comment, note to 2.2.11).

9 The Armada was defeated in July 1588. Another indication of dating in the playtext is the tribute (lines 367–73) paid by Wit and Simplicity to Tarlton, who had died on 3 September 1588.

10 The chariot of Sesostres, drawn by four kings, occurs in the first dumb show of the play *Jocasta*; this was written for performance at the Inns of Court in the 1560s, but reprinted in 1587, when Marlowe was quite possibly writing Part Two of *Tamburlaine*. What is not generally noted is the use of a second chariot in the *Jocasta* dumb shows: the dumb show before Act 5 presents 'a plaine Type or figure of unstable fortune' by means of a 'double faced' woman, 'beyng drawen in by .iiij noble personages' and leading two kings with one hand and two slaves with the other; during the show, crowns and garments are exchanged between kings and clowns. As Kipling and others have commented, English 'civic triumphs' also featured chariots: Queen Elizabeth, 'imitating the ancient Romans', celebrated victory over the Armada by riding through London in a 'tryumphant chariot' (Richard Hakluyt's account, qtd Kipling 40).

11 Compare, for example, the following responses to the chariot: a sign of 'increasing insanity' (Ellis-Fermor 40), or the vices associated with Covetousness (Battenhouse 169–70), or ambivalence and control (Waith 78); 'ludicrous: a brace of kings provides an inefficient means of haulage' (Leech, 'Structure of *Tamburlaine*' 39); 'satisfy[ing] a sadistic taste' (Steane 70); 'reflecting sublimated sexual inadequacy and frustration' (Cockcroft 51); 'The greater his efforts to make it [history] fit his own "best wisedome", the more destructive and foolish he appears' (Weil 141).

12 'Emblem' is used in this book as including three related terms: 'device', 'show', and (in a specific context) 'gest'. Wickham uses 'device' in various ways, including: (1) the frame 'around which to construct the play as an entity', and (2) visual components 'through which the author's abstract ideas and arguments can be projected to the audience in forceful, figurative images' (*Early English Stages* 3: 78). Brown notes

that Marlowe speaks of '"shows," a then fashionable word implying a highly developed Renaissance art in which thematic significance was the organizing principle' ('Marlowe and the Actors' 163). Hattaway uses the Brechtian term 'gest' to refer to 'moments when the visual elements of the scene combine with the dialogue in a significant form that reveals the condition of life in the play' (57).

13 For a useful survey of changing critical approaches to the visual element in Renaissance drama see Bevington, *Action Is Eloquence* 5–17. A range of 'emblematic' aspects, including narrative structure, is discussed by Wickham, *Early English Stages* 3:65–115. Studies on particular aspects include Dessen, *Viewer's Eye* (properties and costumes); and Fleischer (stage grouping and rituals).

14 Doebler, 'Bibliography', provides a list of iconographic studies; his full-length study, *Shakespeare's Speaking Pictures*, discusses Shakespeare's plays from this perspective. For the plays of Marlowe the most comprehensive treatment is that of Zucker, with most other commentaries focusing upon single plays or particular emblems. The iconographic approach has prompted a mix of critical reactions from enthusiastic to wary; its problems and limitations are addressed by several scholars, including Steadman; Mehl, 'Emblematic Theatre'; Dundas.

15 See also Belsey's discussion of *The Duchess of Malfi* ('Emblem and Antithesis'). The most extensive treatment of the emblematic as a survival of medieval culture is that of Wickham.

16 Note also the persistence of the traditional idea of *ut pictura poesis*. Most iconographic studies refer to the Neoplatonic stress on the visual: as in Diehl, 'Iconography and Characterization'; Mehl, 'English Renaissance Drama'. On the increasing importance of the visual as a development fostered by printing see Ong, *Orality and Literacy*, 'Allegory to Diagram'. On developments in cartography, allied to perspective painting, see P. Armstrong.

17 In *Viewer's Eye* Dessen traces several notable visual signs from the moralities to the mature plays of Shakespeare. On the iconography of the history plays see Fleischer. On significant gesture and movement see Slater; Bevington, *Action Is Eloquence*, though both of these concentrate on Shakespearean adaptations of tradition. Note also Hunter's comments on visual conventions, including costume, in 'Flatcaps and Bluecoats'. Bosonnet provides a useful survey of the significant 'stage properties' in Marlowe's plays.

18 On this sense of 'dramatic emblem' see Powell 205; Daly 135. Hattaway uses the term, but also includes dumb show as an example of visual emblem (65). The 'dramatic emblem' should be distinguished from the 'device', instances of which are also used on stage. What the audience sees on Policy's shield (picture plus motto) is a 'device'; it becomes one element of a 'dramatic emblem' in performance when Simplicity draws attention to it and explains its significance. The difference is largely one of intended audience. The 'dramatic emblem' assumes a more general audience in the theatre and appeals to issues of general interest, though topical or coterie meanings may also be intended. The 'device' is often aimed at a specific group, even a single individual (a mistress perhaps); and its message may be no more than a personal one. Puttenham's

description of the uses of the 'emblem' as 'to insinuat some secret, wittie, morall and brave purpose presented to the beholder' (108) is sometimes cited as showing the purpose of emblems in general, but the context suggests he is referring to the 'device', especially as used at court and by 'Princely personages'.

19 For a list of studies treating emblematic parallels in dumb show, pageant, and masque see Dees 408-9. Daly discusses emblematic forms generally in English and other literatures (1–53), as well as 'emblematic drama' (134–67).

20 The division into three elements is especially characteristic of sixteenth-century emblem-books, less so of later ones (Freeman 37, 238–9). Of course, not all emblem-book pages adhere to a three-part pattern: purposes and audiences vary. The amplification may be omitted, or the motto; and the role of the reader then becomes to supply what is lacking. In addition, the three parts are not always clearly differentiated in function (illustration, explanation, interpretation). Thus the 'message' incorporated in the motto may be restated in the closing lines of the verse, or augmented by supplementary material placed in the margins of the page (often Greek or Latin tags). The type of an emblem-book page described here is that found in Whitney's collection, *A Choice of Emblems and Other Devices*, published 1586. The analogies between emblem-book pages of this kind and the dramatic emblems of the *Tamburlaine* plays are discussed in more detail in my 'Transforming the Emblematic'; figure 1 of this article shows the emblem '*Vincit qui patitur*' (Whitney 220).

21 In the edition used for this quotation (Pelican Shakespeare), the wording of the stage directions is based on the folio version of the play, with additional material in brackets derived from the 1595 Quarto of *The True Tragedie of Richard Duke of York*. In the *True Tragedie* the son–father entries occur at the same time, establishing immediately a symmetrical stage picture; in the Folio they are separated by the Son's speech and the King's commentary.

22 The dramatic functions of emblems are discussed in: Mehl, 'English Renaissance Drama'; Diehl, 'Inversion, Parody, and Irony', 'Iconography and Characterization'; and (for Marlowe's plays) Powell; Zucker.

23 Similar instances of the deictic initiate other dramatic emblems in both Parts: the 'footstool', for example, with 'Now clear the triple region of the air / And let the majesty of heaven behold / Their scourge and terror tread on emperors' (1 *Tamburlaine* 4.2.30–2); or Tamburlaine's lesson on fortitude: 'And see him lance his flesh to teach you all' (2 *Tamburlaine* 3.2.114). The most memorable instance is of course the exhortation of the king-horses: 'Holla, ye pampered jades of Asia!' (2 *Tamburlaine* 4.3.1).

24 Other dramatic emblems in the *Tamburlaine* plays conclude similarly, with a 'motto' marking the end of the emblem before the action recommences: 'Thus am I right the scourge of highest Jove, / And see the figure of my dignity / By which I hold my name and majesty' (2 *Tamburlaine* 4.3.24–6).

25 *De casibus* tragedy is a medieval form which presents the 'fall' of an

important person from prosperity or high estate (Watson 317). It is often associated with images of Fortune's wheel, and with a rejection of the world in the *contemptus mundi* tradition (Potter 240–1).

26 On the iconographic significances of the *Tamburlaine* emblems see J. Cunningham, Introduction 44–51, 63–6; and Zucker 53–4. On traditional representations of kings and Fortune see Fleischer 32, 41–3.

27 See, for example, Thurn, 'Sights of Power' 15; Cole 103. On a more general ambivalence, Bartels, 'Double Vision' 21.

28 For other comments which suggest some containment of ironies, see Weil 124; Mulryne and Fender 63–4; and Barber 68 ('the play's basic limitation ... [is] its overriding of irony'). Despite the frequency of ironic 'readings', modern productions have cut or omitted 'ironic' sections, especially in Part Two (the Olympia episode, for example). On modern productions of the plays see Leslie; Geckle 47–88.

29 The 'jades of Asia' became a popular catchphrase in less than dignified contexts; on this see Sales, *Marlowe* 51–2.

30 On the response of other playwrights to the *Tamburlaine* rhetoric see (for example) Brooke, 'Provocative Agent'; J. Shapiro; Hunter, *English Drama* 49–68. McMillin and MacLean argue of *Selimus* that the 'mediocre blank verse' is used to represent a stage in the conqueror's 'moral degeneration' (159).

31 The text used is the A-text version in Bevington and Rasmussen (Revels Plays edition). The two versions agree generally for this passage (indeed for most of this scene). Apart from variations in spelling, 'Ah' for 'O', the 1616 substitution of 'heaven' for the 1604 'God' (78), and a few lines printed as prose, the main differences are: (1) changes in person: 'I ... my ... mine' (A-text 54–5) becomes 'Faustus ... his ... his'; 'thee' (A-text 78) alters to 'me'; (2) a change in tense and/or intentionality: 'will' (A-text 61) to 'do'.

32 The arm-cutting may also suggest initiation ritual and/or blood sacrifice. On the iconographic possibilities of the passage see Zucker 157–8; Brockbank 42; Barber 114–17. On possible emblematic costuming, see Hattaway 169, 171. The blood-letting is suggested by, but is more spectacular than, the description in the source, *The Historie of the Damnable Life, and Deserved Death of Doctor John Faustus* [*Damnable Life*]; this mentions only: 'he tooke a small penknife, and prickt a vaine in his left hand'; and 'How Doctor Faustus set his blood in a saucer on warme ashes, and writ as followeth' (7).

33 Greenblatt makes a similar point, applying the 'experiment' to Faustus's whole career as perhaps 'a test of the proposition that hell is a fable' (*Renaissance Self-fashioning* 290 n. 5).

34 Similar stage business is also found in Lodge and Greene's *Looking Glass* (c. 1590). The conscience-stricken Usurer carries a knife and halter on to the stage; then '*The evill angell tempteth him, offering the knife and rope*' (p. 217); but he hears 'a voice amidst mine eares' and repents.

35 Melton's description is incidental and late (1620), but quite possibly indicates earlier practice as well. Michael Bristol suggests audience feelings of 'complicity' in the farcical scenes, commenting that 'this vocabulary of devilment – firecrackers, thrashing, horns, animal masks,

drenchings – is a collectively sanctioned practice of physically abusive mummery useful for settling old scores and for punishing unamiable or arrogant individuals' (*Carnival and Theater*, 154). Another kind of appeal may have operated with the shows of Helen: in early performances her appearance may have owed something to the conventional eroticism of the *Damnable Life*, where the 'Lady' has a purple gown, golden hair, cherry lips, rose cheeks, white neck, and 'amorous cole-black eyes' (65) – just as the appearance of Elizabeth Taylor in the Richard Burton film of *Faustus* appealed, supposedly, to mid-twentieth-century fantasies.

36 For descriptions of response to the emblematic as ambivalent or divided see, for example, Belsey, 'Emblem and Antithesis' 216; Diehl, 'Inversion, Parody, and Irony' 201–2. For response as detached or critical or even 'alienated' see, for example, Mulryne and Fender 64; Hattaway 95–6.

37 A striking example of the lasting emotional impact of emblematic action can be found in one of the rare accounts of sixteenth-century performance. Many years after seeing a morality play called *The Cradle of Security*, R. Willis recalled how three ladies (Pride, Covetousness, and Luxury) induced a prince (who did 'personate in the morall, the wicked of the world') 'to lie down in a cradle upon the stage, where these three ladies joining in a sweet song rocked him asleep, that he snorted again, and in the mean time closely conveyed under the cloths where withal he was covered, a vizard like a swine's snout upon his face, with three wire chains fastened thereunto, the other end whereof being holden severally by those three ladies, who fall to singing again, and then discovered his face, that the spectators might see how they had transformed him.' Willis comments: 'This sight took such impression in me, that when I came towards man's estate it was as fresh in my memory, as if I had seen it newly acted.' From *Mount Tabor, or Private Exercises of a Penitent Sinner* (London, 1639), 111–13, qtd in Dessen, *Viewer's Eye* 17–18. The playtext does not survive. Dessen suggests that Willis saw the performance in the 1560s or 1570s. Willis's memory of the event may have been shaped, as Pearlman suggests, by his later reading and by his late-in-life repentance; these factors do not, however, detract from the lasting impact of the experience, nor from his involvement in – rather than detachment from – the emblematic performance.

Chapter 4: Lessons of history

1 Beard continued to revise and expand the book, with new editions appearing in 1612, 1631, and (posthumously) 1647. Beard is also remembered as the schoolmaster of Oliver Cromwell. He is usually described as a 'Puritan' but this is challenged by John Morrill in his account of Cromwell's early years (for this reference I am indebted to Patrick Collinson in discussion at Cambridge, June 1993). Morrill notes that Beard was 'a greedy pluralist' (27) and at one time chaplain to James I (30).

2 I have omitted stage directions not in the 1594 quarto.

3 Others who suggest that the murder was not seen on stage include Charlton and Waller (1933); and Merchant (1967). These comments

could well reflect staging practices at the times they were made rather than staging conventions and possibilities in the sixteenth-century play-house.

4 Holinshed's account includes two interpretations of Edward's death: one relatively sympathetic to Edward, which saw his suffering as excessive; the other his own judicious assessment, which nevertheless suggests the operation of poetic justice. Holinshed views Edward's career as an exemplum, with his death and suffering the consequence of his own actions: 'in that he wanted [lacked] judgement and prudent discretion to make choise of sage and discreet councellors'. He draws the moral: 'So that thereby it appeareth of what importance it is to be trained up in youth with good and honest companie' (587–8). If only Edward had received a better education!

5 Those who argue for a double effect (poetic justice, but abhorrent) include Cole 184–6; Brooke, 'Marlowe the Dramatist' 103–4; Thurn, 'Sovereignty, Disorder' 136.

6 Not all instances of violence illustrate deserved punishment. In *Apius and Virginia* (printed 1575), Virginius beheads his daughter to prevent her dishonour; the stage direction reads '*Here tye a handcarcher aboute hir eyes, and then strike of hir heade*' (834.1). In *Titus Andronicus* Virginia's story provides a precedent for putting Lavinia out of her misery: 'Because the girl should not survive her fame' (5.3.41). In *3 Henry VI*, the children (Rutland and Edward, Prince of Wales) are slaughtered in revenge for the deeds of their elders.

7 For useful general surveys of the concept, forms, and uses of the exemplum refer to Wimsatt; Donker and Muldrow; on the moral and educative purposes of sixteenth-century rhetoric generally see (for example) N. Rhodes.

8 On the exemplary method in sixteenth-century education and its connections with the drama see Altman; Riggs. Much of the study of classical texts (including dramatic ones) in the schools involved finding notable passages and citing them – often quite detached from their contexts – as illustrations of ideas worth remembering; these exempla then provided material for the commonplace book every student was expected to compile. The process was one that relied upon recognition of conventional wisdom, with exempla identified and sorted according to conventional 'topics'.

9 The *Art* was first printed in 1589. Puttenham is reciting commonplace views of history, morality, and exempla; for the same arguments applied to early 1590s drama (much of which had 'historical' content of some kind, whether native or exotic) see Nashe's comments on the death of Talbot, cited below.

10 'Mirror' was also used to refer to a comprehensive collection of material or stories. On the 'mirror' as an important feature of medieval and Renaissance literature see Wimsatt 137–63. William Baldwin's 'Dedication' to the 1559 version of *The Mirror for Magistrates* typifies the processes of seeing involved: 'For here as in a loking glas, you shall see (if any vice be in you) howe the like hath bene punished in other heretofore, whereby admonished, I trust it will be a good occasion to move you to the soner amendement' (65–6). An actual mirror is used as

a stage property in the morality *The Conflict of Conscience* (1581) to reflect the spiritual condition of the protagonist Philologus, first as a 'gladsome Glasse', the instrument of temptation – 'Naught els but pleasure, pompe, and wealth, heerein to mee appeare' (1689); later as the 'Glasse of deadly desperation' (1985), the catalyst to despair (2002–4). Philologus – and the audience – are directed how to interpret the mirror by the characters Sensual Suggestion and Horror.

11 Kaplan notes that the flaying incident had a long history as an exemplum. The spectators may of course have applied the lessons of the play differently, according to their own perspectives on 'tyranny': perhaps as endorsing 'loyal Anglican doctrines about the duties of kings and their subjects' (W. Armstrong 289); or as promoting the views of radical Protestants, offering first 'a veiled but unmistakable critique of Mary' but also a 'warning to Elizabeth not to repeat the errors of her father', including his double-dealing with religion (Hill 430). See also Johnson, Introduction.

12 Plays with debates on exempla include both Parts of *Tamburlaine* (though the discussion is often curtailed by the redefining rhetoric of the hero), the *Spanish Tragedy* (though this is less episodic than most), the *Three Lords*, *Alphonsus*, *Troublesome Reign*, and Shakespeare's three *Henry VI* plays.

13 As with *Tamburlaine*, the Gentlemen Readers were not forgotten in this process of edification. The readers of the two-part *Troublesome Reign* were supplied with two 'addresses', which provide a particular interpretative frame ('Christ's true faith', 'base treason', 'fond rashness', 'monkish falseness', and so on) for the exempla that follow.

14 The *Tamburlaine* plays contain almost all the references in Marlowe's plays to a 'mirror', 'glass', or 'image', with most of them occurring in Part One. In Part Two, the unsatisfactory son Agydas is referred to as 'Image of sloth and picture of a slave' (4.1.91); and Zenocrate's picture has some exemplary effect (3.2). The Epilogue to *Faustus* offers Faustus's entire career as a cautionary tale: 'regard his hellish fall, / Whose fiendful fortune may exhort the wise'.

15 On the influence of *Tamburlaine* and the Marlowe–Shakespeare dialogue, see Berek; Brooke, 'Reflecting Gems', 'Provocative Agent'; Brooks; Bradbrook, 'Shakespeare's Recollections'; Riggs on the early histories; Shapiro. For a more recent discussion of the relationship, dating the whole first tetralogy before *Edward II*, see Forker, Introduction 17–41. The textual parallels between *Edward II* and the *Henry VI* plays, including the early printed versions, *The First Part of the Contention* and *The True Tragedy of Richard Duke of York*, are noted and discussed in Charlton and Waller's edition of *Edward II* and Cairncross's editions of *2 Henry VI* and *3 Henry VI*. The *Massacre* also has textual parallels with the *Henry VI* plays (as well as with *Edward*); Maguire comments: 'Parallels with Shakespeare's *Henry 6* seem to have been part of the original verbal and structural design' (281).

16 On the iconographic dimension to the action of *Edward II* see Bevington and Shapiro; Dessen; Fleischer; Merchant; Zucker. In considering the effect of the play on its early audiences, we need to include a sense of ritualised action, even in incidents where order is disturbed. Modern

productions, on the other hand, have tended to emphasise the personal and individual at the expense of the ceremonial, which has in turn influenced critical commentary. A notable instance is the 1969 Prospect Theatre Company production, directed by Toby Robertson with Ian McKellen as Edward, and filmed by the BBC in 1970.

17 Deats suggests that at least half of the classical parallels alluded to in the play are associated with disorder of some kind ('Myth and Metamorphosis' 306). On '*quam male*', see also Kelsall 48.

18 Though the terms of the confrontation suggest traditional values, their actual political stances could well represent something more radical. Summers, for example, defines Edward's rule in terms of 'the secular autocracy of the Italian Renaissance' (*Politics of Power* 163). For other views of the political issues involved, see Cohen; Fleischer; Hattaway; Robertson; Ribner; Voss.

19 The issue of homosexuality in the play has elicited a range of critical responses from uneasiness to crusading zeal. Sixteenth-century spectators may also have responded in differing ways: see, for example, Summers, 'Sex, Politics, and Self-realization' 222–3; Jardine 22–4. A regular playgoer may perhaps have noticed the parallels between the language of Edward and Gaveston and the language of the adulterous Queen Margaret and Suffolk in 2 *Henry VI* (note, for instance, the scene of leave-taking, 2 *Henry VI* 3.2.339–412, with its talk of banishment from self, dying, the soul, and Elysium, as a possible source of the phrasing and verbal imagery in the scenes between Edward and Gaveston). Modern productions of the play have featured the homosexual element (note the interview between Robertson and Geckle, in Geckle 96–7), especially after theatrical censorship ended in England in 1968. One element of this emphasis can be a visual linking of Lightborn with Gaveston, thereby insisting that the audience take notice of 'poetic justice' (see, for example, Robertson 179; Brown, 'Marlowe and the Actors' 171; Hattaway 159). For the stage history of *Edward II* until 1986 see Geckle; for an overview from the 1590s to 1992 see Forker, Introduction 99–116.

20 On Edward's lack of capacity to understand, see Altman 365; McElroy 206 n. 5.

21 Clemen, 'Some Aspects of Style'; Braunmuller, 'Early Shakespearian Tragedy'.

22 Honigmann (Arden edition, 1954) dates *King John* early, at 1590–91; the more usual dating is 1596–97 (lviii). The parallel scene in *Troublesome Reign* relies much less on drawing attention to visible detail, resorting instead to cliché and declamation: 'You rolling eyes … / Send forth the terror of your Mover's frown, / To wreak my wrong upon the murtherers / That rob me of your fair reflecting view' (*1 Troublesome Reign* 1495–9).

23 These changing political slogans are accompanied by several notable shifts in the vocabulary of confrontation. Political arguments in the first half of the play are conducted in the language of rank and hierarchy. From the scene of Gaveston's capture (2.5) the important terms become 'right', 'honour', and 'justice' – although 'pride' and 'treachery' remain at issue. 'Right' and 'justice' do not occur before Gaveston's capture,

nor after Edward's abdication. 'Right' in particular is linked with the legitimising of claims for power, as in Edward's 'royal right'. Other words that alter markedly in their reference during the play are 'God'/'god' and 'Nature' (these are also used in political slogan-making) and, in more general contexts, 'heaven', 'hell', and 'die'/'death'.

24 McElroy identifies anticlimax as characteristic of Edward's speeches (220–3).

25 The repetitive style of the play is noted generally but responded to variously: Sanders claims 'neurosis' (141); McElroy, 'inventiveness' (208).

Chapter 5: Framing the action

1 The morality tradition of social criticism persisted more strongly than Shakespeare-centred criticism often recognises. It outlasted the morality-style narrative, and is especially notable in plays before 1595, contemporary with those of Marlowe: *Troublesome Reign* (clerical abuses, nobility), *Famous Victories* (lawcourts), the *Henry VI* plays. See Riggs 32 for a list of such plays to 1590; also Heinemann 173–7.

2 As Mithal comments (133, note to line 1280), the purchase of such foreign 'trash' cost England £100,000 each year. A number of late moralities included 'comic and sinister foreigners'; for a list of such plays see Potter 197.

3 The communal wisdom of proverbs is more prominent in the *Jew* than any 'Machiavellian' precepts. Proverbs and biblical allusions (Bawcutt glosses about ninety) greatly outnumber the verbal echoes of Machiavelli or his opponents (Bawcutt glosses fewer than twenty). Some instances of the latter may also be proverbial in origin (e.g., 1.2.209: 'Great injuries are not so soon forgot'). The confrontation between Barabas and the Knights (1.2.95–155), despite its demonstration of Machiavellian 'policy', is conducted in theological and proverbial terms; Bawcutt glosses only one possible echo of Machiavelli (147–9). Most examples of all categories (proverbial, biblical, 'Machiavellian') occur in the speeches of Barabas, but he does in any case speak almost half the lines of the play (49 per cent, according to H. Levin, *Overreacher* 211).

4 For accounts of this critical debate see Friedenreich, '*Jew* and its Critics'; Bawcutt, Introduction 16–20. For the play as essentially 'Christian' see, for example, Cole; Hunter, 'Theology of *Jew*'; Beecher. For the 'Machiavellian' or 'atheist' alternative see H. Levin, *Overreacher*; Steane. On the play's 'Machiavellian' ideas as reflecting the diversity of sixteenth-century response refer to Bawcutt, 'Machiavelli and Marlowe's *Jew*'. For other useful discussions of the Machiavellian aspect see Summers, *Politics of Power*; Minshull, '"Sound Machevill"'; Margaret Scott.

5 See, for example, Greenblatt, *Learning to Curse*; Bartels, 'Fictions of Difference'.

6 Older criticism characterised the play as inconsistent, as comprising two acts of tragedy (the Marlovian part) followed by three acts of farce and/or textual corruption. See, for example, Boas; for the opposing view, H. Levin, *Overreacher* 96. The *Jew*'s first audiences may well have accepted the play as a 'tragedy' in the older sense: it was first printed as

such (see the 1633 title-page); and its special place in the playhouse repertory may also have been as a 'tragedy' (Knutson, 'Repertory System').

7 Studies discussing the *Jew* with reference to the Vice tradition include Spivack; Cole; Craik, Introduction; Rocklin, 'Experimental Dramatist'.

8 Apart from Spivack, other useful studies of the Vice convention, especially its dramatic functions, include Wierum; Happé, 'The Vice: A Checklist', '"The Vice" and Popular Theatre'. Weimann sees the didactic function as secondary, linking the Vice and his 'sport' primarily with an alternative 'ritual heritage of ... amoral inversion' (156–60).

9 On the tradition of direct address see Johnson, 'Audience Involvement', who cites examples from *Fulgens and Lucrece* (1490s) to *The Three Lords and Three Ladies of London* (late 1580s).

10 See, for example, Brooke, 'Marlowe the Dramatist'; Cartelli, 'Endless Play'; Rocklin, 'Experimental Dramatist'; and the performance history of James L. Smith.

11 Like several other late moralities the *Three Ladies* has more than one figure functioning as Vice. Dissimulation himself declines in importance as commentator in the course of the play as other Vices take over, becoming more of an allegorical character (he eventually marries Lady Love/Lust, even though he is only in love 'from the teeth forward'). This change, however, has no effect on the singlemindedness of the play's framing rhetoric.

12 Modern productions have tended to dress Barabas soberly, a significant exception being the 1965 Royal Shakespeare Company (RSC) version at Stratford, where Eric Porter's Barabas was suave and self-assured in 'an elaborate and rich gown, a mantle of thick-piled fur, a decoration around his shoulders, and large jewelled rings on each hand' (J. Smith 20).

13 Prologues were not of course limited to defining the issues of the play. They might also: explain the story so far (*Conflict of Conscience*); summarise the story to be enacted (*Apius and Virginia*); and/or promise good 'honest' entertainment with a mixture of gravity and mirth (*Virtuous and Godly Susanna*).

14 At end of the play this sequence of movements may well be reversed, providing the play with a symmetrical visual frame. Barabas returns to the façade to fall into the cauldron, while Ferneze closes the play as Machevil had opened it, from a framing platform position, calling upon all to 'note' the fatal device.

15 Despite the wishful thinking of some commentators, Wilson was not necessarily 'enlightened' about Jews: in the sequel play Simony claims that 'thy [Usury's] parentes were both Jewes, though thou wert borne in London' (*Three Lords* 1442). On the *Jew* as satire see the studies of (among others) H. Levin, Rothstein, Sanders, Weil.

16 The blurring of differences between Barabas and the Christians can also be seen in the equivocal use of terms such as 'profession', 'promise', and 'faith' (Bawcutt, Introduction 20). Note also Freer's comment on the play's use of proverbs (and of expressions that sound like proverbs) as suggesting 'an overwhelming number of appeals to infinitely conflicting authorities' (157).

17 Henke (2: 243) cites line 370 as 'alluding specifically to sexual grap-
   pling'. That being 'metamorphosed to a nun' should somehow be similar
   to the rape of Proserpina recalls the comments of the Friars, and anticipates later allusions to the illegitimate fruits of the nunnery. Individual
   words and phrases here (though their examples are not taken from this
   particular passage) are glossed by Henke 2: 290, 258; Partridge 196,
   197–8, 176; Colman 218, 211.
18 J. Smith quotes from the RSC prompt copy to describe what happened
   on stage in that production; the following (J. Smith 15) gives an idea of
   the farcical action (the prompt copy is referred to as 'PC'): 'Jacomo
   enters, and executes a series of "double takes" on seeing the body (163).
   Then he grabs Barnardine's staff (171), "swings it round Right. Barn.
   drops down. Jacomo swings back" (PC), strikes the body as it falls, and
   "looks down at Barnardine very pleased" (PC). As the scene continues,
   Ithamore "smears 'blood'" (PC) on the corpse (175), "shows head to
   Jac. Jac. drops stick" (PC), tries to escape, and is finally hustled off by
   Barabas and Ithamore who "shake hands" (PC) behind the friar's back
   (202).'
19 One contemporary parallel with the *Jew*'s absurdities may be found in
   the farcical action of Shakespeare's early comedy, *The Comedy of
   Errors* (probably later than the *Jew*, perhaps 1591–92; not recorded
   until 1594). *Errors* draws attention to its literary origins in Plautine
   comedy where the *Jew* recalls its popular theatrical origins. Both plays
   depend, nevertheless, on coincidence and improbabilities, on self-righteous sermonising and stereotyped social relationships, on playworlds
   with their own rules and narrative logic. At the same time, *Errors* is
   contained more neatly inside its narrative frame, with all difficulties
   resolved in the final scene.
20 Bevington also notes the change but suggests that Barabas returns to his
   'original nature' (*Mankind to Marlowe* 225–6).
21 Several commentators note that this speech refers to various popular
   myths against the Jews: see Cole 140; Sanders 339–51.
22 On these changes within the Vice convention, see Spivack; Dessen, *Late
   Moral Plays*.
23 To the extent that any of these villains are unambiguously reprehensible, they may also be patterned on the 'Machiavellian' figures in the
   Spanish Tragedy, which may well have preceded the *Jew*. Another
   descendant of the Vice, who still functions as a (secondary) interpreter
   of the playworld, is Mephistopheles; Leech labels him 'a metamorphosis
   of the Vice' (*Marlowe* 108).
24 Weimann argues that the player Richard Tarlton 'completely secularized
   the Vice', dissociating the role from its didactic functions (187). The
   Clown-figure in the *Three Ladies*, however, though possibly played by
   Tarlton, continues to be quite separate in function and viewpoint from
   the Vices of the play, as is the Clown-figure in the play's sequel, staged
   after Tarlton's death in 1588.
25 Modern productions usually deal with the *Jew*'s excess of perspectives
   by trimming supposedly inconsistent elements, thereby limiting the
   options available to their audiences. When the play was first revived in
   1818 by Edmund Kean the Jew was presented as a 'tragic hero, the

honest Israelite unjustly victimised' – but only after extensive expurgat-
ing and 'modernising'. The omissions included Machevil's Prologue, the
poisoned porridge and flowers, and the fall into the cauldron, with
Barabas shot down instead (Maclure 70–7; J. Smith 4–5, 7–10). The
pruning and adapting have continued. The 1964 RSC production, for
example, altered the balance between Barabas and Ferneze by cutting
references to Barabas's 'policy' and reassigning Ferneze's aggressive
statements to Del Bosco, so that, while Barabas appealed to the audience's sympathies as a 'romantic gangster', Ferneze became a
'whimpering weakling' (J. Smith 19–21). A similar approach has been
taken to *Titus Andronicus*, which was first performed within five years
of the *Jew*, and which has a similar excess of perspectives; on cuts made
in modern productions to suppress 'inappropriate laughter' see Hirsh
66–72.

Chapter 6: Looking at Angels

1 References in this paragraph, in order: Kernan 257; Watson 312;
  Greenblatt, *Renaissance Self-fashioning* 200; Goldman, 'Histrionics of
  Ravishment' 22, 40; Goldman, 'Performer and Role' 92; Leech,
  Marlowe 216; Hunter, 'Revolution and Continuity' 39; Hall 1.3.16–17;
  Jonson, *Timber* 542; Gurr, *Playgoing* 136–7. Most of these comments
  also draw comparisons, even if only implicitly, between characters in
  Marlowe and Shakespeare; on this see also States 47; Danson,
  'Continuity and Character'; Muir 147–8.
2 For the term 'imaginary interiority' see Belsey, *Subject of Tragedy* 48.
3 'Debatability' does not imply that any individual spectator or reader will
  feel impelled to engage in self-debate about a character's motives. Nor
  does it preclude a group consensus, based upon prevailing notions of
  psychology.
4 These examples, as well as others, are discussed in more detail in Burns.
5 White comments similarly, remarking that he discovered this lack of
  distinction between realistic and allegorical figures when he produced
  Enough Is as Good as a Feast (210 n. 28).
6 Shepherd suggests competing models of the individual in the 1580s:
  Protestant; conservative (human nature as influenced by Reason); and
  Machiavellian (emphasis on the anarchic, anti-social human will); these
  were overtaken in the 1590s by a 'non-problematic, depoliticised subjectivity' (83–8, quotation at 83).
7 For other versions of this general approach see Grantley (a duality: in
  Marlowe, '*both* figure *and* character', 227); Sinfield finds an impression
  of 'continuous consciousness' in some Shakespearean characters, though
  the continuity is still 'only … an effect of culture and its multiple
  discourses' (62–3); Hellenger argues that 'Elizabethan reality … was
  essentially social and public' (36), and hence 'social roles were the
  means not of avoiding but of participating in reality' (41). Dollimore
  postpones 'essentialist humanism' to the Enlightenment, but argues for
  a different, 'materialist' subjectivity in the Renaissance (249).
8 Burns identifies the catalyst for the eighteenth-century shift in critical
  thinking as the actor David Garrick and his revolutionary acting style

that presented 'distinct coherent persona[e]' (186). See also Desmet, for a similar view on the persistence of classical rhetoric in Shakespeare; Vickers, for continuing neoclassical influence on the concept of character, even late in the eighteenth century.

9　See also Aers, *Community, Gender, and Individual Identity*; Patterson, 'On the Margin', *Negotiating the Past*.

10　In the modern theatre, the illusion of 'realistic' character is often considered an important element in performance. Burns and Worthen note the influence of Stanislavskian acting techniques; Biggs discusses the problems that arise in acting Marlowe for actors trained this way. The persistence of 'realistic' character interpretation in 'non-academic' criticism is noted by Burns (221–2); and by Shepherd, who comments that the 'depoliticised subjectivity' of Shakespearean characters is 'not necessarily a healthy ... [development], though it goes down a bomb at A level and Stratford' (83).

11　The suggested 'types' include Everyman (Ellis-Fermor); Overreacher (Pinciss, *Literary Creations*); academic (Lindley 15); 'learned fool' (Weil 68).

12　Similarly, West 103–4; Leech, *Marlowe* 111, Jump xlviii.

13　A similar point is made by Brockbank. Outside the playhouse, angels and devils were often considered to be 'real' spiritual beings with defined powers and functions (Cole 234), even 'substantial' beings (West 102). Angels were indeed topical in the late sixteenth century, figures of contemporary interest and debate (Brennan). They were active presences in popular theology and learned poetry alike (the poems of Donne are quite infested with angels). Despite this, angels were infrequent visitors to the stage; and Marlowe's Angels may initially have occasioned some surprise, especially for readers of the *Damnable Life*, which has devils aplenty but no angels to admonish or incite. Antecedents for opposed Good and Evil Angels can be found, but not in the popular drama that comprised the theatrical experience of Marlowe's first audiences. The instance usually cited is *The Castle of Perseverance*, a play of the early fifteenth century; but this is remote in time from *Faustus*, and presents a quite different relationship between Angels and Humanum Genus (Cole 237). Pettit (171) notes the Angel scenes in *Faustus* as examples of 'formulaic dramaturgy', citing as one antecedent the good counsellor and bad counsellor scene as in *Gorboduc*.

14　The offering of rope and dagger is a stage business cliché of the Vices. On costume, Craik, *Tudor Interlude* 52–3. On staging possibilities as well see Dessen, *Viewer's Eye* 137–39; Hattaway 170–6. The Angels may have entered and left through '*several* [i.e. different] *doors*', like the Angels of the B-text 'judgement' scene, but they are unlikely to have been remote framing figures, stationed 'above' or relegated to the back of the stage, though such staging is not impossible. The term 'buzzeth' in their third appearance ('Who buzzeth in mine ears I am a spirit?' 2.3.14) may even suggest, as Dessen comments, 'an intimate physical relationship' (*Viewer's Eye* 138).

15　The label 'psychomachia' itself derives from the influential epic poem of Prudentius (*c.* AD 400), which presents an allegorical battle between virtues and vices. For brief accounts of this see Houle 174; Spivack 78–91.

16 Spivack argues that the psychomachia is overtaken by the theatrical energies of the Vice. Bevington, *Mankind to Marlowe*, traces the persistence of the 'psychomachia plot' with its 'sequential, progressive, and alternating form' (261). Dessen identifies another kind of persistence: individual scenes of 'stage psychomachia', demonstrating moments of decision (*Viewer's Eye* 129–47, *Late Moral Plays* 141); see also Sanders 217.

17 Allegorical conflicts, in order, from *Conflict of Conscience* (1581), *Tide Tarrieth No Man* (1576), *Three Lords* (1588).

18 The play dates from *c.* 1564, though the only extant edition is that of 1575. It was probably written for acting by boys (see Happé, *Tudor Interludes* 273), but observes the same conventions for presenting character as adult plays.

19 Craik suggests that Conscience is located behind some kind of scenery, a 'house' perhaps. A position 'above' is also not impossible, though (as Craik comments) unlikely (*Tudor Interlude* 121 n. 16).

20 *Tide Tarrieth* is printed as 'compiled by' George Wapull. The title-page gives instructions for doubling ('Foure persons may easily play it'), and describes the play, a collection of exempla illustrating the proverb, as 'A moste pleasant and merry commody, right pythie, and full of delight'.

21 *Looking Glass* is recorded as played at the Rose in 1592, but is usually dated about 1590, not long before the first performances of *Faustus*, or (as most studies of the dating of *Faustus* since the 1970s suggest) not long after. Whatever the sequence, however, it provides an instructive foil. *Looking Glass* also uses two angelic figures, an Evil Angel and a heavenly-messenger Angel, but they are never on stage together. The Usurer scene in *Looking Glass* may derive from several in *Faustus* (or be reworked there), but the differences are none the less significant. The visual rhetoric of the scene in *Looking Glass* perhaps owes more to the conventions of dumb show: the Evil Angel does not speak even though he is seen – and recognised – by both audience and Usurer.

22 'Subjectivity' in earlier plays was also indicated by various conventional devices. Shepherd identifies several of these in plays of the 1580s and 1590s: individual figures that are visually separate from pageant or tableau; 'moments of individual feeling [that] are marked as discontinuities in the spoken, as speechlessness or silence' (76); moments when the 'gaze [of the character] cannot be shared by the audience', as when Richard III acts out his response to 'the fearful shadow that pursues him' (77).

23 In 'Faustus and the Angels', which includes an earlier version of some material in this chapter, I also adopted a more traditional approach, discussing the play in terms of 'the tragic consequences of ... [Faustus's] failure to perceive' (19).

24 The traditional 'theatrical metaphor' of 'seeing and not-seeing', with examples ranging from the moralities to Shakespeare, is explored by Dessen, *Elizabethan Stage Conventions* 130–55. That Faustus's imperfect awareness was notable and worth exploiting theatrically may be confirmed by the changed emphases in the B-text. This develops the

visual ironies of faulty awareness by introducing devils to watch the action, probably from 'above', in scenes 1.3 and 5.2.

25 In the preceding scene, Philologus does not see the figure of 'Spirit', since he is captivated by the glass Suggestion offers, and its images of 'pleasure, pompe, and wealth' (1689); but he still hears and fully understands Spirit's message: 'Alas, what voice is this I heere, so dolefully to sounde, / Into mine eares, and warneth mee, in time yet to beware' (1681–2).

26 On this effect in the bond-signing scene, see above, Chapter 3. Other instances in *Faustus* where the attention of the audience is drawn to individual moments of experience include the second encounter with Helen, and Faustus's farewell to the Scholars (here, as elsewhere, his detachment from others is suggested in terms of some physical impact): 'I would lift up my hands, but see, they hold them, they hold them' (5.7.33–4).

27 Presenting inner conflict or decision-making through voices external to the character, though less common in later plays, always remained an option for the sixteenth- and seventeenth-century playwright. Dessen points to possible instances in later plays, including *The Revenger's Tragedy* and *Antony and Cleopatra* (*Viewer's Eye* 139–56). Other influences in the persistence of opposed voices were literary and educational. See (for example) Altman; Braunmuller, 'Early Shakespearean Tragedy' 121.

28 Mooney focuses on continuities in speech and stage positioning (80–6), applying Weimann's concept of *Figurenposition* (see below, Chapter 7).

29 *Titus Andronicus* is most probably later than *Faustus*: it was recorded as 'ne' by Henslowe in January 1594 and printed later that year.

30 The question of silence is perhaps more complex than Shepherd suggests, with the use of silence to denote extreme emotion persisting in plays after 1590. Some instances of the aside, for example, exploit the convention by using the device of silence to indicate two emotions at once. See, for example, York's aside in *2 Henry VI* 5.1: in this, the opening words, 'Scarce can I speak' (23), are used both to indicate his 'deep melancholy' to those on stage, and as a rhetorical marker to emphasise the strength of his anger to the offstage audience (before he elaborates on the latter emotion for eight articulate lines).

31 For the staging and iconography of the Old Man scene, see Tweedie; S. McMillin, 'Figure of Silence'.

32 The parallel scene in *Troublesome Reign* puts greater emphasis on deserved punishment: 'O, plague / Inflicted on thee for thy grievous sins!' (*2 Troublesome Reign* 1096–7). As well as the 'raging' of fever, this John suffers like Richard of Gloucester, and in a somewhat similar style: 'I see – I see, a thousand thousand men / Come to accuse me for my wrong on earth!' (1108–9).

33 Edward's occasional 'debatability' is associated with moments of strong emotion. The most notable instance occurs in his death scene, where his speech registers moment-by-moment experience. Elsewhere, he is shown as indulging in a deal of conventional lamentation, but this is contained for the most part within a series of exemplary frames.

34 The point is a critical commonplace. See, for example, McAlindon on the 'semantic duality of certain key words' (129); Shepherd on the

uncertain 'authority' of books and writing (96–7). Bevington and Rasmussen offer an extensive survey of *Faustus* criticism, commenting that: 'Increasingly … the most persuasive criticism about *Doctor Faustus* has spoken of its "complementary" aspects, of "multiplicity of vision", "ambivalent effect", "dualism", "dilemma", "paradox", "oxymoron", "divided response", "double view" and the like' (Introduction 31). Bluestone comments similarly in his earlier but also wide-ranging survey, '*Libido Speculandi*' (1969).

35 See, for example, Bevington and Rasmussen, Introduction 24–5, 31–2.

36 For a detailed discussion of the ambiguities of Lucifer's response to Faustus's prayer see Bluestone, '*Libido speculandi*' 65–9.

37 *Richard II* was possibly written *c.* 1595. The play was entered in the Stationers' Register in August 1597 and a quarto version (omitting the deposition scene) published that year. See Ure xiii–xiv, xxix–xxx.

38 The Revels Plays editor, M. L. Wine, considers Alice Arden to be a triumph of 'realistic portraiture', because no explanation is offered for the strength of her passion (Introduction lxxii). But in terms of the traditional rhetoric of character, passion – as much as evil – is its own explanation. And for all her vitality Alice shows little awareness of anything beyond the series of conventional roles she is seen to assume and exemplify: virtuous wife, besotted lover, remorse-stricken murderer.

Chapter 7: Managing the space

1 The distinction between the two kinds of theatrical space, visible and imagined, has been developed (but labelled variously) in several studies of theatrical space: Pavis (*Dictionnaire du théâtre* 146–7) contrasts the visible space of performance ('*espace scénique*') with the metaphorical, abstract space of the text ('*espace dramatique*'); Issacharoff (215) contrasts 'mimetic' (or shown) space with 'diagetic' (or reported) space; Scolnicov (14) contrasts 'theatrical space within' (or perceived, visible) with 'theatrical space without' (or conceived). For Pavis, visible space includes '*espace scénique*' (stage setting), '*espace scénographique*' (stage and house), and '*espace ludique*' (created by the movements of the actors).

2 Compare, for example, Molly Smith and Karen Cunningham on the staging of public executions in Kyd and Marlowe respectively. The former suggests that Kyd ingeniously transfers 'the spectacle of public execution *with all its ambiguities* from the socio-political to the cultural worlds' (229) (my italics); the latter attributes the ambiguities to 'the fundamentally ambiguous perspective of the theater' (214). See also Sales, 'Stage, Scaffold'.

3 On significant costume in the interludes see Craik, *Tudor Interlude* 49–92. The primacy of the player may not have been the case in other, non-dramatic performances (entertainments, pageants) and perhaps in some court performances, where the players could well have been overshadowed by scenic devices. An increasing number of the playwrights, especially after 1595, may have been aware of new theatre designs from the Continent which altered the balance between player and playing space. These designs used painted flats observing the laws of perspec-

tive, and/or installed the monarch as the central focus of the show. Their influence before 1642 was apparent in court masques rather than the playhouses: perspective staging was in any case expensive and needed several days to prepare (Gurr, *Shakespearean Stage* 200–2). On the important, non-dramatic ends served by the masque see Orgel, *Illusion of Power*.

4 Elam (56–67) provides a useful survey of proxemics, drawing upon the studies of Edward T. Hall. Hall divides spatial 'syntax' into the fixed (architecture), semi-fixed (fixed props, lighting), and informal (constituted by the actors and audience, and the domain of proxemics).

5 The point is made by (among others) Thomson 60; Hattaway 56–9. Hattaway also suggests a degree of improvisation (54–5). See also Pettit, who notes the persistence of 'formulaic dramaturgy', which combines routine action with improvised dialogue.

6 Churches were also used. White comments that 'playing in churches continued to be a common occurrence through most of Elizabeth's reign, including several recorded performances by such nationally renowned troupes as Leicester's Men and the Queen's Players' (138).

7 The Fortune contract (1600) refers to the Globe stage as a pattern to follow and specifies a stage measuring 13 m (43 ft) across and projecting 8.4 m (27 ft 6 in) into the yard (Gurr, *Shakespearean Stage* 137–8, 146). The first Rose stage (1587) was 11.4 m (37 ft 6 in) at its widest and about 4.7 m (15 ft 6 in) deep maximum; the second Rose stage (1592) may have been 5.2 m (17 ft) deep (Gurr, *Shakespearean Stage* 128–30; Orrell and Gurr 649). The Rose stage was thus similar in size though not in shape to the stages of the private indoor theatres and of at least one stage at court. For the dimensions of these see Gurr, *Shakespearean Stage* 157 (Blackfriars), 162 (Cockpit-Phoenix), 170 (Cockpit-in-Court). The performance space at the Rose had particular features. The part-excavation of the foundations suggests that no attempt was made to increase the stage area when the theatre was extended and refurbished in 1592; that the façade was not straight but three-sided, following the shape of the bays; that the stage posts were set at or near the front of the platform (see Orrell and Gurr; Foakes, 'Discovery of Rose'; Eccles).

8 On the variety of provincial venues used by the Queen's Men see McMillin and MacLean 67–83.

9 The last instance refers to Southern's suggested staging for *The Three Lords and Three Ladies of London* (568–75, 584–91). Note also Nicoll's suggestions for 'passing over the stage', including the use of the playhouse yard. Southern offers some possibilities for raised platforms in hall staging (see especially the diagrams, figs 32–6, pp. 430–6). See also Weimann 101–2; Craik, *Tudor Interlude* 10–11. Sprinchorn argues for a raised rear stage in the playhouse, to be used for the 'state'.

10 *Clyomon and Clamydes* may have been performed in one version or another from *c.* 1570 to 1599. The play is generally dated 1570–83, with Littleton suggesting 1576, close in date to the similar play *Common Conditions*. It was not printed until 1599, with the claim on the title-page: 'As it hath bene sundry times Acted by her Majesties Players'. McMillin and MacLean argue from the printing date and

casting patterns that this version of the play was used for performances after 1594 (109–10). These may well have been in the provinces, since at this time the Queen's Men appear to have left the London theatres to others (49–53, 89, 149). The Queen's Men, in any case, persevered with traditional styles of versification and staging, including the fourteener (124–54).

11 Studies of the façade and its possibilities include (especially) Bevington, *Action Is Eloquence*; also Kernodle; Zucker (for Marlowe's plays). On the possibilities of the platform see Beckerman, *Shakespeare at Globe*; Styan, *Shakespeare's Stagecraft*.

12 Southern qualifies his comments by conceding that the differences may be 'purely accidental' (545).

13 Each of these instances also 'quotes' its predecessors, in verbal as well as visual terms. Note also *Volpone* 2.2.229.1, where Celia at her window throws down her handkerchief after Volpone's performance as a mountebank.

14 *Clyomon and Clamydes* is not discussed by Southern. For possible playhouse staging see Littleton 31–2. For court or hall staging, see Chambers 39, 42, 45.

15 *Horestes* may have been only the first of many productions at court featuring some kind of upper level: Chambers notes that siege scenes were popular there, with half the plays staged between 1579 and 1585 requiring a 'battlement' (see comments on the staging of *Horestes*, Chambers 38–9, 44–5). Southern (494–506) discusses possible hall staging, suggesting the use of a traverse curtain and ladder for the siege scene.

16 Certain items of stage business were more theatrical than 'real life' in origin, and thus especially available for various rhetorical effects, including parody. *Tamburlaine* was a notable source: Zenocrate's death bed was copied, with variations, as were the assorted triumphs and crownings (Fleischer 90; Gurr, *Shakespearean Stage* 189). Another source of memorable and much-imitated stage business was Kyd's *Spanish Tragedy*, with revenge plays developing their own codes of behaviour, their own theatrical practices and conventions, which belonged as much to the theatrical world as to the 'real' one, if not more.

17 On the stage 'state' and its real-life counterparts see Gurr, '"State" of Shakespeare's Audiences'; he suggests that the dais for the stage throne was elevated by at least three steps (164).

18 Littleton comments that the term 'place' as used several times in the play derives from the *platea* of medieval staging, which is located at the same level as the standing audience (162–3). It may thus suggest two levels in the playing area, perhaps in an early hall-staging before the play was acquired by the Queen's Men, or the use of the yard or pit in the playhouse (on this see Weimann 211–12; Southern). It may also of course simply indicate an area of the platform close to the audience.

19 In Shakespeare's version of the story in *King John* the five moons are mentioned as ominous signs that follow the news of Arthur's death (4.2.183–202). Bevington instances the banquet as another ceremonial occasion which could demonstrate community and concord, but which

often meant violence and hypocrisy (*Action Is Eloquence* 158–9). One sixteenth-century instance is the banquet in *Cambises*, which is preceded by routine foolery (spilling food), commences with formal courtesies, proceeds with 'musicks hermony' and the telling of a moral tale, but ends with the Queen seized by Crueltie and Murder.

20 The marriage celebrations in the sequel, the *Three Lords*, are similarly interrupted, again by Simplicity; there ensues a farcical game in which Fraud is bound to a post and Simplicity is blindfolded and given a torch. The Vice runs away, Simplicity is jubilant (he believes the fire has quite consumed Fraud), and the Lords are gently amused at his expense. The tone of the action then shifts abruptly to a closing prayer for Queen, nobles, and 'all the rest'.

21 For the costume of 'whifflers', see Littleton 181–2. Comic business is similarly associated with 'clearing' in the opening scene of *Julius Caesar*, or in the scene (5.4) before the grand procession to Elizabeth's christening in *Henry VIII*. These 'clearings' may imitate the Lord Mayor's annual procession of triumph through London streets, which was preceded by fencers and 'wildmen' with fireworks (Bradbrook, *Shakespeare in Context* 95–6).

22 On this scene see also Gibbons 208. The stage direction reads only: '*Enter* King Alexander *the Great, as valiantly set forth as may be, and as many soldiers as can*' (358–9), but this draws upon a shared understanding of the details of how such a triumphal entry might be staged: the sequence and grouping of figures in the procession; their possible costumes, accessories, and properties ('Soldiers *loaden with treasure*' perhaps, as in *1 Tamburlaine*); and the accompanying sound effects (the dialogue later calls upon drums and trumpets for the ceremonial exit).

23 On these variable perspectives see Brown, *Plays in Performance* 133–7; Gurr, 'Bare Island' 40. The range of perspectives may have been smaller at the Rose, with its shallower stage, but was nevertheless still significant. The implications of the Rose excavations for theatrical space are yet to be fully explored. Thomson comments that the dimensions of the stage suggest 'a rather different actor-audience relationship, with the actors in flatter lines playing *in front of* a greater proportion of the audience than has been generally assumed in recent years' (40).

24 Other figures that might occupy positions close to the audience were Prologues or Presenters, but these traditional commentators were not usually part of the dramatic action.

25 Space in the 'landscape' of the *Jew* may also separate different levels of action. When for example Barabas is thrown over the walls of the city, the movement across space reframes the action: not simply from city to outside the walls but also from 'realistic' to fantastic.

26 The need to pay more attention to the 'space between' players is urged in my article 'Bridges "through the moving air"'. Holland uses the term differently, to refer to whole stage sets which are situated between other imagined places, and which become spaces of transition and uncertainty.

27 See, for example, Hattaway 101–2. Opinions differ on the placement of Revenge and the Ghost of Andrea. Adams (225) and Tweedie (224) suggest on the platform; Hattaway (115–16) and Kohler (30), above.

28 Stroup counts seven ceremonial entry processions in Part One, fifteen in
Part Two (he does not include in these figures the entry of a group
'without fanfare'). The other play of Marlowe with a large number of
processional entries is *Massacre*, with twelve out of its twenty-three
scenes opening this way.

29 Tamburlaine may first have been envisaged as dominating a 'landscape
of persons' rather than as framed by any playhouse façade.
J. Cunningham suggests that Part One was written with performance in
innyard or open space in mind: it has no specific indication of upper-
level scenes, although Part Two probably uses an upper level to stage the
sieges of Balsera and Babylon (Introduction 23–4). Wickham, arguing
for minimalist requirements, suggests the use of a scenic property in
staging Part Two instead of an upper level ('*Exeunt to the cave*'
189–90). Zucker, on the other hand, envisages the plays exploiting playhouse architecture, proposing an ornate façade and painted backcloths.

30 Except for the scene of Bajazeth's suicide (*1 Tamburlaine* 5.1), the iron
cage is always part of a Tamburlaine-organised ceremony: it is drawn on
to the stage by two Moors at the rear of the royal procession, to be then
set apart from Tamburlaine's throne (4.2) or the banqueting table (4.4).

31 Hodgdon's examples of 'poetic space' include the 'literal and imaginative distance between Leontes and Hermione' in *The Winter's Tale*, and
the repeated images of separation in *Romeo and Juliet*. See also Styan,
'Stage Space'.

32 Styan in 'Stage Space' also uses the term 'deceiving space' with reference
to the temptation scenes in *Othello*. He is, however, describing the
spaces between actor and audience rather than the spaces between
figures on stage. Note also Gauntlett's comments on the 'temptation
scene' in *Othello* (3.3) as showing the 'displacement' of Othello into the
'marginal downstage space, dominated and defined by Iago' (21).

33 This alternation is of course a common visual patterning in other
contemporary plays, including *Hamlet*. *Edward II* is generally seen as
being structured by contrasts; for definition of these see (for example)
Mulryne and Fender 59–62; Merchant, Introduction xvii.

34 McElroy remarks the 'instability of the stage image, the result of
constant changes in the number and grouping of the characters on stage
and of the extreme fluidity of their exits and entrances' (214). Bevington
and Shapiro comment that *Edward II* has fewer instances of vertical
movement than *Richard II*, where disorder is shown typically by vertical collapse or movement.

35 See, for example, Wymer (a reading based on John Jump's mainly B-text
version, which has devils 'above'). Hattaway offers a more 'horizontal'
perspective on the play's staging, describing the action as a procession
of 'ritual shows' interspersed with farce.

36 On staging differences between A-text and B-text see especially
Bevington and Rasmussen 42–8; for differences in the angel and devil
scenes, see (for example) Dessen, *Elizabethan Stage Conventions* 146–9.
Bluestone ('*Libido Speculandi*' 72) suggests that the Devils may have
used a 'state' rather than an above-stage space. He comments that the
stage direction of 'Devils above' is supplied by modern editors; the text
has only '*Thunder. Enter* LUCIFER *and four Devils.* FAUSTUS *to them*

with this speech' (B-text 1.3.0.1–2); and '*Thunder. Enter* LUCIFER, BEELZEBUB, *and* MEPHISTOPHELES' (B-text 5.2.0.1–2).

37 This pattern of movement may have been repeated for each of Faustus's soliloquies (1.1.1–65; 2.1.1–14; 5.2.65–120). The staging of the first soliloquy is, nevertheless, commonly described in terms of a contrast between physical confinement and boundless aspirations, as by Bluestone, '*Libido Speculandi*' 59; Zucker 151.

38 Both versions of the play suggest that raised seating was used for the onstage spectators. In the A-text, Faustus is instructed to 'sit' to await the arrival of the 'hot whore' (A-text 2.1.150–1). During the Show of Sins the comments of Envy imply a differentiation of levels: 'But must thou sit and I stand? *Come down*, with a vengeance!' (italics added) (A-text 2.3.137–8; B-text 2.3.131–2). There are direct references to a 'state' in the scenes at the courts of Pope and Emperor (for example, B-text 4.1.102.5–6). If the B-text Devils also use a 'state', as Bluestone suggests ('*Libido Speculandi*' 72), then these scenes provide disturbing visual echoes of the shows with their superior spectators and their 'magic' space.

39 In the B-text Faustus 'forewarns' the Emperor not to question the 'shapes' of Alexander and his paramour: 'But in dumb silence let them come and go' (B-text 4.1.92–6). Though the A-text lacks a similar injunction, everyone on stage is silent during the show. Later, before the first appearance of Helen, Faustus advises the Scholars (in both versions) 'Be silent then, for danger is in words'. Even after the figure of Helen leaves, the stage still retains some of the sense of 'magic' space, with Faustus himself remaining silent while the Scholars express their admiration and depart.

40 In the A-text, Robin does not inscribe a magic circle in space, though he refers to magic circles he hopes to find in the conjuring book: 'some circles for my own use. Now will I make all the maidens in our parish dance at my pleasure stark naked before me' (A-text 2.2.3–5).

41 Jan Kott notes the appearances of Helen as instances of dumb show. Faustus's action of kissing Helen 'violates' the show by breaching the conventions, especially lack of physical contact (15), but also suspension of narrative action, and silence except for music. See also Mehl, *Elizabethan Dumb Show*. There is no reason to assume that the kiss was not acted in the early performances – even if the Helen of many modern productions has been converted into something untouchable, unattainable, or fantastic (for details of modern stagings of Helen see Brown, '*Doctor Faustus* at Stratford' 196–8; Tydeman 76–7; Michael Scott 28–30; Jackson 6; Bevington and Rasmussen 58).

REFERENCES

Playtexts

*The following editions have been used in citing playtexts, ordered by short
title. Page references are given for* Looking Glass *and* Tide Tarrieth, *with
line references for all others.*

[*Alphonsus*] Robert Greene. *The Comical History of Alphonsus, King of
Aragon. The Life and Complete Works in Prose and Verse of Robert
Greene M.A.* Ed. Alexander B. Grosart. Vol. 13. 1881–86. 15 vols. New
York: Russell, 1964.

[*Apius and Virginia*] R. B. *A New Tragical Comedy of Apius and Virginia.
Tudor Interludes.* Ed. Peter Happé. Harmondsworth: Penguin, 1972.
270–317.

[*Arden of Faversham*] Anon. *The Tragedy of Master Arden of Faversham.*
Ed. M. L. Wine. Revels Plays. London: Methuen, 1973.

[*Bartholomew Fair*] Ben Jonson. *Bartholomew Fair.* Ed. E. A. Horsman.
Revels Plays. London: Methuen, 1960.

[*Cambises*] Thomas Preston. *A Critical Edition of Thomas Preston's
Cambises.* Ed. Robert Carl Johnson. Salzburg: Institut für Englische
Sprache und Literatur, Universität Salzburg, 1975.

[*Clyomon and Clamydes*] Anon. *Clyomon and Clamydes: A Critical
Edition.* Ed. Betty J. Littleton. The Hague: Mouton, 1968.

[*Conflict of Conscience*] Nathaniel Woodes. *The Conflict of Conscience by
Nathaniel Woodes 1581.* Malone Society Reprints. Oxford: Oxford
University Press, 1952.

[*Dido*] Christopher Marlowe. *Dido Queen of Carthage and the Massacre at
Paris.* Ed. H. J. Oliver. Revels Plays. Manchester: Manchester University
Press, 1968.

[*Edward*] Christopher Marlowe. *Edward the Second.* Ed. Charles R. Forker.
Revels Plays. Manchester: Manchester University Press, 1994.

[*Enough Is as Good as a Feast*] W. Wager. *Enough Is as Good as a Feast.
c.* 1565. Henry E. Huntington Facsimile Reprints. New York: Smith,
1920.

[*Famous Victories*] Anon. *The Famous Victories of Henry the Fifth.
Narrative and Dramatic Sources of Shakespeare.* Ed. Geoffrey Bullough.
Volume IV. London: Routledge, 1962. 299–343.

[*Faustus*] Christopher Marlowe. *Doctor Faustus: A- and B-texts (1604,
1616).* Ed. David Bevington and Eric Rasmussen. Revels Plays.
Manchester: Manchester University Press, 1993.

[*Gorboduc*] Thomas Norton and Thomas Sackville. *Gorboduc or Ferrex
and Porrex. Early English Classical Tragedies.* Ed. J. W. Cunliffe.
Oxford: Clarendon, 1912.

[*Hamlet*] William Shakespeare. *Hamlet.* Ed. Harold Jenkins. Arden
Shakespeare. London: Routledge, 1982.

[*1 Henry VI*] William Shakespeare. *The First Part of King Henry VI.* Ed.
Andrew S. Cairncross. Rev. ed. Arden Shakespeare. London: Methuen,
1962.

[*2 Henry VI*] William Shakespeare. *The Second Part of King Henry VI*. Ed. Andrew S. Cairncross. Arden Shakespeare. London: Methuen, 1957.

[*3 Henry VI*] William Shakespeare. *The Third Part of King Henry VI*. Ed. Andrew S. Cairncross. Arden Shakespeare. London: Methuen, 1964.

[*3 Henry VI*] William Shakespeare. *Henry the Sixth Parts Two and Three*. Ed. Robert K. Turner, Jr, and George Walton Williams. Rev. ed. Pelican Shakespeare. Harmondsworth: Penguin, 1980.

[*Henry VIII*] William Shakespeare. *King Henry VIII*. Ed. R. A. Foakes. Arden Shakespeare. London: Methuen, 1957.

[*Horestes*] John Pickering. *A New Interlude of Vice Containing, the History of Horestes*. 1567. Malone Society Reprints. Oxford: Oxford University Press, 1962.

[*Jew*] Christopher Marlowe. *The Jew of Malta*. Ed. N. W. Bawcutt. Revels Plays. Manchester: Manchester University Press, 1978.

[*Jocasta*] George Gascoigne and Francis Kinwelmersh. *Jocasta*. *Early English Classical Tragedies*. Ed. J. W. Cunliffe. Oxford: Clarendon, 1912.

[*King John*] William Shakespeare. *King John*. Ed. E. A. J. Honigmann. Arden Shakespeare. London: Methuen, 1954.

[*Like Will to Like*] Ulpian Fulwell. *An Interlude Entitled Like Will to Like Quoth the Devil to the Collier*. *Four Tudor Interludes*. Ed. J. A. B. Somerset. London: Athlone, University of London, 1974. 128–64.

[*Looking Glass*] Thomas Lodge and Robert Greene. *A Looking Glass for London and England by Thomas Lodge and Robert Greene: A Critical Edition*. Ed. George Alan Clugston. New York: Garland, 1980.

[*Mankind*] Anon. *Mankind*. *Four Tudor Interludes*. Ed. J. A. B. Somerset. London: Athlone, University of London, 1974. 25–51.

[*Massacre*] Christopher Marlowe. *Dido Queen of Carthage and the Massacre at Paris*. Ed. H. J. Oliver. Revels Plays. Manchester: Manchester University Press, 1968.

[*Richard II*] William Shakespeare. *King Richard II*. Ed. Peter Ure. Arden Shakespeare. London: Methuen, 1956.

[*Richard III*] William Shakespeare. *King Richard III*. Ed. Antony Hammond. Arden Shakespeare. London: Methuen, 1981.

[*Spanish Tragedy*] Thomas Kyd. *The Spanish Tragedy*. Ed. Philip Edwards. Revels Plays. London: Methuen, 1959.

[*Tamburlaine*] Christopher Marlowe. *Tamburlaine the Great*. Ed. J. S. Cunningham. Revels Plays. Manchester: Manchester University Press, 1981.

[*Taming of Shrew*] William Shakespeare. *The Taming of the Shrew*. Ed. Brian Morris. Arden Shakespeare. London: Methuen, 1981.

[*Three Ladies*] Robert Wilson. *An Edition of Robert Wilson's Three Ladies of London and Three Lords and Three Ladies of London*. Ed. H. S. D. Mithal. The Renaissance Imagination 36. New York: Garland, 1988.

[*Three Lords*] Robert Wilson. *An Edition of Robert Wilson's Three Ladies of London and Three Lords and Three Ladies of London*. Ed. H. S. D. Mithal. The Renaissance Imagination 36. New York: Garland, 1988.

[*Tide Tarrieth*] George Wapull. *The Tide Tarrieth No Man*. 1576. *Illustrations of Early English Popular Literature*. Ed. J. Payne Collier. Vol. 2. London: 1863. New York: Blom, 1966.

[*Titus Andronicus*] William Shakespeare. *Titus Andronicus*. Ed. J. C. Maxwell. Arden Shakespeare. London: Methuen, 1953.

[*Troublesome Reign*] Anon. *The Troublesome Reign of John, King of England*. *Six Early Plays*. Ed. E. B. Everitt and R. L. Armstrong. Anglistica 14. Copenhagen: Rosenkilde, 1965.

[*Virtuous and Godly Susanna*] Thomas Garter. *The Most Virtuous and Godly Susanna*. 1578. Malone Society Reprints. Oxford: Oxford University Press, 1936 (1937).

[*Volpone*] Ben Jonson. *Volpone or, The Fox*. Ed. R. B. Parker. Revels Plays. Manchester: Manchester University Press, 1983.

Other works

Adams, Barry B. 'The Audiences of *The Spanish Tragedy*'. *Journal of English and Germanic Philology* 68 (1969): 221–36.

Aers, David. *Community, Gender, and Individual Identity: English Writing 1360–1430*. London: Routledge, 1988.

——'A Whisper in the Ear of Early Modernists; or, Reflections on Literary Critics Writing the "History of the Subject"'. *Culture and History 1300–1600: Essays on English Communities, Identities and Writing*. Ed. David Aers. London: Harvester, 1992. 177–202.

Altman, Joel B. *The Tudor Play of Mind: Rhetorical Inquiry and the Development of Elizabethan Drama*. Berkeley: University of California Press, 1978.

Armstrong, Philip. 'Spheres of Influence: Cartography and the Gaze in Shakespearean Tragedy and History'. *Shakespeare Studies* 23 (1995): 39–70.

Armstrong, William A. 'The Authorship and Political Meaning of *Cambises*'. *English Studies* 36 (1955): 289–99.

Barber, C. L. *Creating Elizabethan Tragedy: The Theater of Marlowe and Kyd*. Ed. Richard P. Wheeler. Chicago: University of Chicago Press, 1988.

Barker, Francis. 'Hamlet's Unfulfilled Interiority'. *New Historicism and Renaissance Drama*. Ed. Richard Wilson and Richard Dutton. London: Longman, 1992. 157–66. Rpt. from *The Tremulous Private Body: Essays in Subjection*. London: Methuen, 1984. 29–40.

Bartels, Emily C. 'Malta, the Jew, and the Fictions of Difference: Colonialist Discourses in Marlowe's *The Jew of Malta*'. *English Literary Renaissance* 20 (1990): 1–16.

——'The Double Vision of the East: Imperialist Self-construction in Marlowe's *Tamburlaine, Part One*'. *Renaissance Drama* ns 23 (1992): 3–24.

Battenhouse, Roy W. *Marlowe's Tamburlaine: A Study in Renaissance Moral Philosophy*. 1941. Nashville: Vanderbilt University Press, 1964.

Bawcutt, N. W. Introduction. *The Jew of Malta*. Revels Plays. Manchester: Manchester University Press, 1978.

——'Machiavelli and Marlowe's *The Jew of Malta*'. *Renaissance Drama* ns 3 (1970): 3–49.

Beard, Thomas. *The Theatre of Gods Judgements: or, A Collection of Histories out of Sacred, Ecclesiasticall, and Prophane Authours,*

Concerning the Admirable Judgements of God upon the Transgressours of His Commandements. London, 1597: STC 1659.

Beckerman, B. *Shakespeare at the Globe 1599–1609.* New York: Macmillan, 1962.

——'Theatrical Perception'. *Theatre Research International* ns 4 (1979): 157–71.

Beckwith, Sarah. 'Ritual, Church and Theatre: Medieval Dramas of the Sacramental Body'. *Culture and History 1300–1600: Essays on English Communities, Identities and Writing.* Ed. David Aers. London: Harvester, 1992. 65–89.

Beecher, Don. '*The Jew of Malta* and the Ritual of the Inverted Moral Order'. *Cahiers Élisabéthains* 12 (October 1977): 45–58.

Belsey, Catherine. 'Emblem and Antithesis in *The Duchess of Malfi*'. *Renaissance Drama* ns 11 (1980): 115–34.

——*The Subject of Tragedy: Identity and Difference in Renaissance Drama.* London: Methuen, 1985.

Berek, Peter. '*Tamburlaine*'s Weak Sons: Imitation as Interpretation Before 1593'. *Renaissance Drama* ns 13 (1982): 55–82.

Berger, Harry. *Imaginary Audition: Shakespeare on Stage and Page.* Berkeley: University of California Press, 1989.

Berry, Ralph. *Shakespeare and the Awareness of the Audience.* London: Macmillan, 1985.

Bevington, David. *Action Is Eloquence: Shakespeare's Language of Gesture.* Cambridge, Mass.: Harvard University Press, 1984.

——*From Mankind to Marlowe: Growth of Structure in the Popular Drama of Tudor England.* Cambridge, Mass.: Harvard University Press, 1962.

Bevington, David and Eric Rasmussen. Introduction. *Doctor Faustus: A- and B-texts (1604, 1616).* Revels Plays. Manchester: Manchester University Press, 1993.

Bevington, David and James Shapiro. '"What are kings, when regiment is gone?": The Decay of Ceremony in *Edward II*'. *'A Poet and a Filthy Play-maker': New Essays on Christopher Marlowe.* Ed. Kenneth Friedenreich, Roma Gill, and Constance B. Kuriyama. New York: AMS, 1988. 263–78.

Biggs, Murray. 'Some Problems of Acting *Edward II*'. *The Arts of Performance in Elizabethan and Early Stuart Drama.* Ed. Murray Biggs, Philip Edwards, Inga-Stina Ewbank, Eugene M. Waith. Edinburgh: Edinburgh University Press, 1991. 192–9.

Birringer, Johannes H. *Marlowe's Doctor Faustus and Tamburlaine: Theological and Theatrical Perspectives.* Frankfurt: Verlag Peter Lang, 1984.

Bluestone, Max. *From Story to Stage: The Dramatic Adaptation of Prose Fiction in the Period of Shakespeare and his Contemporaries.* The Hague: Mouton, 1974.

——'*Libido Speculandi*: Doctrine and Dramaturgy in Contemporary Interpretations of Marlowe's *Doctor Faustus*'. *Reinterpretations of Elizabethan Drama.* Ed. Norman Rabkin. New York: Columbia University Press, 1969. 33–88.

Boas, Frederick S. *Christopher Marlowe: A Biographical and Critical Study.* Oxford: Clarendon, 1953.

——*University Drama in the Tudor Age*. Oxford: Oxford University Press, 1914. New York: Blom, 1966.

Bosonnet, Felix. *The Function of Stage Properties in Christopher Marlowe's Plays*. Bern: Francke Verlag, 1978.

Bowers, Fredson. Textual Introduction. *The Complete Works of Christopher Marlowe*. 2nd edition. Cambridge: Cambridge University Press, 1981. II. 123–59.

Bradbrook, Muriel C. 'Marlowe's *Doctor Faustus* and the Eldritch Tradition'. *Essays on Shakespeare and Elizabethan Drama in Honor of Hardin Craig*. Ed. Richard Hosley. Columbia: University of Missouri Press, 1962. 83–90.

——*The Rise of the Common Player: A Study of Actor and Society in Shakespeare's England*. London: Chatto, 1962.

——*Shakespeare in His Context: The Constellated Globe: The Collected Papers of Muriel Bradbrook Volume IV*. London: Harvester, 1989.

——'Shakespeare's Recollections of Marlowe'. *Shakespeare's Styles: Essays in Honour of Kenneth Muir*. Ed. Philip Edwards, Inga-Stina Ewbank and G. K. Hunter. Cambridge: Cambridge University Press, 1980. 191–204.

——*Themes and Conventions of Elizabethan Tragedy*. 2nd edition. Cambridge: Cambridge University Press, 1980.

Brandt, Bruce E. *Christopher Marlowe in the Eighties: An Annotated Bibliography of Marlowe Criticism from 1978 through 1989*. West Cornwall, CT: Locust Hill, 1992.

Braunmuller, A. R. 'The Arts of the Dramatist'. *The Cambridge Companion to English Renaissance Drama*. Ed. A. R. Braunmuller and Michael Hattaway. Cambridge: Cambridge University Press, 1990. 53–90.

——'Early Shakespearian Tragedy and Its Contemporary Context: Cause and Emotion in *Titus Andronicus*, *Richard III*, and *The Rape of Lucrece*'. *Shakespearian Tragedy*. Ed. Malcolm Bradbury and David Palmer. Stratford-upon-Avon Studies 20. London: Arnold, 1984. 97–128.

Breitenberg, Mark. 'Reading Elizabethan Iconicity: *Gorboduc* and the Semiotics of Reform'. *English Literary Renaissance* 18 (1988): 194–217.

Brennan, Michael G. 'Christopher Marlowe's *Doctor Faustus* and Urbanus Rhegius's *An Homelye ... Of Good and Evill Angels*'. *Notes and Queries* ns 38.4 (December 1991): 466–9.

Bristol, Michael D. *Carnival and Theater: Plebeian Culture and the Structure of Authority in Renaissance England*. New York: Methuen, 1985.

——'How Good Does Evidence Have to Be?' *Textual and Theatrical Shakespeare: Questions of Evidence*. Ed. Edward Pechter. Iowa City: University of Iowa Press, 1996. 22–43.

Brockbank, J. P. *Marlowe: Doctor Faustus*. London: Arnold, 1962.

Brook, Peter. *The Empty Space*. Harmondsworth: Penguin, 1972.

Brooke, Nicholas. 'Marlowe as Provocative Agent in Shakespeare's Early Plays'. *Shakespeare Survey* 14 (1961): 34–44.

——'Marlowe the Dramatist'. *Elizabethan Theatre*. Ed. John Russell Brown and Bernard Harris. Stratford-upon-Avon Studies 9. London: Arnold, 1966. 87–105.

——'The Moral Tragedy of *Doctor Faustus*'. *Cambridge Journal* 5.11

(1952): 662–87. Rpt. in *Critics on Marlowe*. Ed. Judith O'Neill. London: Allen, 1969. 93–114.

——'Reflecting Gems and Dead Bones: Tragedy versus History in *Richard III*'. *Critical Quarterly* 7 (1965): 123–34.

Brooks, Harold F. 'Marlowe and Early Shakespeare'. *Christopher Marlowe*. Ed. Brian Morris. London: Benn, 1968. 67–94.

Brown, John Russell. '*Doctor Faustus* at Stratford-upon Avon, 1968'. *Doctor Faustus*. Ed. Sylvan Barnet. Signet Classic. New York: New American Library, 1969. 194–206.

——'Marlowe and the Actors'. *Tulane Drama Review* 8.4. (Summer 1964): 155–73.

——*Shakespeare's Plays in Performance*. London: Edward Arnold, 1966.

Burns, Edward. *Character: Acting and Being on the Pre-modern Stage*. London: Macmillan, 1990.

Cairncross, Andrew S. Introduction. *William Shakespeare: The Second Part of King Henry VI*. Arden Shakespeare. London: Methuen, 1957.

——Introduction. *William Shakespeare: The Third Part of King Henry VI*. Arden Shakespeare. London: Methuen, 1964.

Cameron, G. M. *Robert Wilson and the Plays of Shakespeare*. Riverton, NZ: Cameron, 1982.

Carlson, Marvin. 'Theatre Audiences and the Reading of Performance'. *Interpreting the Theatrical Past: Essays in the Historiography of Performance*. Ed. Thomas Postlewait and Bruce A. McConaghie. Iowa City: University of Iowa Press, 1989. 82–98.

——*Theatre Semiotics: Signs of Life*. Bloomington: Indiana University Press, 1990.

——'Theatrical Performance: Illustration, Translation, Fulfillment, or Supplement?' *Theatre Journal* 37 (1985): 5–11.

Cartelli, Thomas. 'Endless Play: The False Starts of Marlowe's *Jew of Malta*'. '*A Poet and a Filthy Play-maker': New Essays on Christopher Marlowe*. Ed. Kenneth Friedenreich, Roma Gill, and Constance B. Kuriyama. New York: AMS, 1988. 117–28.

——*Marlowe, Shakespeare, and the Economy of Theatrical Experience*. Philadelphia: University of Pennsylvania Press, 1991.

Chambers, E. K. *The Elizabethan Stage*. Vol. 3. 1923. Oxford: Clarendon, 1951.

Charlton, H. B. and R. D. Waller, eds. Introduction. *Edward II: By Christopher Marlowe*. Rev. F. N. Lees. 2nd edition. Case edition. London: Methuen, 1955.

Clemen, Wolfgang. *English Tragedy before Shakespeare: The Development of Dramatic Speech*. Trans. T. S. Dorsch. London: Methuen, 1961.

——'Some Aspects of Style in the *Henry VI* Plays'. *Shakespeare's Styles: Essays in Honour of Kenneth Muir*. Ed. Philip Edwards, Inga-Stina Ewbank, and G. K. Hunter. Cambridge: Cambridge University Press, 1980. 9–24.

Cockcroft, Robert. 'Emblematic Irony: Some Possible Significances of Tamburlaine's Chariot'. *Renaissance and Modern Studies* 12 (1968): 33–55.

Cohen, Walter. *Drama of a Nation: Public Theater in Renaissance England and Spain*. Ithaca: Cornell University Press, 1985.

Cole, Douglas. *Suffering and Evil in the Plays of Christopher Marlowe.* Princeton, NJ: Princeton University Press, 1962.

Collinson, Patrick. *From Iconoclasm to Iconophobia: The Cultural Impact of the Second English Reformation.* [Reading, Berks]: University of Reading, 1986.

Colman, E. A. M. *The Dramatic Use of Bawdy in Shakespeare.* London: Longman, 1974.

Coursen, H. R. *Shakespearean Performance as Interpretation.* Newark: University of Delaware Press, 1992.

Craik, T. W. Introduction. *The Jew of Malta.* New Mermaids. London: Benn, 1966.

——'The Reconstruction of Stage Action from Early Dramatic Texts'. *Elizabethan Theatre 5* (1973): 76–91.

——*The Tudor Interlude: Stage, Costume, and Acting.* Leicester: Leicester University Press, 1958.

Cunningham, J. S. Introduction. *Tamburlaine the Great.* Revels Plays. Manchester: Manchester University Press, 1981.

Cunningham, J. S. and Roger Warren. '*Tamburlaine the Great* Re-discovered'. *Shakespeare Survey* 31 (1978): 155–62.

Cunningham, Karen. 'Renaissance Execution and Marlovian Elocution: The Drama of Death'. *Publications of the Modern Language Association of America (PMLA)* 105.2 (March 1990): 209–22.

Dabbs, Thomas. *Reforming Marlowe: The Nineteenth-century Canonization of a Renaissance Dramatist.* London: Associated University Presses, 1991.

Daly, Peter. *Literature in the Light of the Emblem: Structural Parallels between the Emblem and Literature in the Sixteenth and Seventeenth Centuries.* Toronto: Toronto University Press, 1979.

[*Damnable Life*] *The Historie of the Damnable Life, and Deserved Death of Doctor John Faustus.* Trans. P. F. London: 1592. Amsterdam: Theatrum Orbis Terrarum, 1969.

Danson, Lawrence. 'Christopher Marlowe: The Questioner'. *English Literary Renaissance* 12 (1982): 3–29.

——'Continuity and Character in Shakespeare and Marlowe'. *Studies in English Literature* 26 (1986): 217–34.

Dawson, Anthony B. 'An Impasse Over the Stage'. *English Literary Renaissance* 21 (1991): 309–27.

De Marinis, Marco. 'Dramaturgy of the Spectator'. *The Drama Review* 31.2 (Summer 1987): 100–14. Trans. Paul Dwyer.

Deats, Sara Munson. 'Marlowe's Fearful Symmetry in *Edward II*'. '*A Poet and a Filthy Play-maker': New Essays on Christopher Marlowe.* Ed. Kenneth Friedenreich, Roma Gill, and Constance B. Kuriyama. New York: AMS, 1988.

——'Myth and Metamorphosis in Marlowe's *Edward II*'. *Texas Studies in Literature and Language* 22.3 (Fall 1980): 304–21.

Dees, James S. 'Recent Studies in the English Emblem'. *English Literary Renaissance* 16 (1986): 391–424.

Desmet, Christy. *Reading Shakespeare's Characters: Rhetoric, Ethics, and Identity.* Amherst: University of Massachusetts Press, 1992.

Dessen, Alan C. *Elizabethan Drama and the Viewer's Eye.* Chapel Hill:

University of North Carolina Press, 1977.
——*Elizabethan Stage Conventions and Modern Interpreters*. Cambridge: Cambridge University Press, 1984.
——'Modern Productions and the Renaissance Scholar'. *Renaissance Drama* ns 18 (1987): 205–23.
——'Recovering Elizabethan Staging: A Reconsideration of the Evidence'. *Textual and Theatrical Shakespeare: Questions of Evidence*. Ed. Edward Pechter. Iowa City: University of Iowa Press, 1996. 44–65.
——*Shakespeare and the Late Moral Plays*. Lincoln: University of Nebraska Press, 1987.
——'Shakespeare and the Theatrical Conventions of His Time'. *The Cambridge Companion to Shakespeare Studies*. Ed. Stanley Wells. Cambridge: Cambridge University Press, 1986.
Diehl, Huston. *Staging Reform, Reforming the Stage: Protestantism and Popular Theater in Early Modern England*. Ithaca: Cornell University Press, 1997.
——'Iconography and Characterization in English Tragedy, 1585–1642'. *Drama in the Renaissance: Comparative and Critical Studies*. Ed. Clifford Davidson, C. J. Gianakaris, John D. Stroupe. New York: AMS, 1986. 11–20.
——'The Iconography of Violence in English Renaissance Tragedy'. *Renaissance Drama* ns 11 (1980): 27–44.
——'Inversion, Parody, and Irony: The Visual Rhetoric of Renaissance English Tragedy'. *Studies in English Literature* 22 (1982): 197–209.
——'Observing the Lord's Supper and the Lord Chamberlain's Men: The Visual Rhetoric of Ritual and Play in Early Modern England'. *Renaissance Drama* ns 22 (1991): 147–74.
Dixon, Peter. *Rhetoric*. Critical Idiom Series. London: Methuen, 1971.
Doebler, John. 'Bibliography for the Study of Iconography in Renaissance English Literature'. *Research Opportunities in Renaissance Drama* 22 (1979): 45–55.
——*Shakespeare's Speaking Pictures: Studies in Iconic Imagery*. Albuquerque: University of New Mexico Press: 1974.
Dollimore, Jonathan. *Radical Tragedy: Religion, Ideology and Power in the Drama of Shakespeare and His Contemporaries*. Brighton, Sussex: Harvester, 1984.
Donawerth, Jane. *Shakespeare and the Sixteenth-century Study of Language*. Chicago: University of Illinois Press, 1984.
Donker, Marjorie and George M. Muldrow. *Dictionary of Literary-rhetorical Conventions of the English Renaissance*. London: Greenwood, 1982.
Doran, Madeleine. *Shakespeare's Dramatic Language*. Madison, Wis.: University of Wisconsin Press, 1976.
Drew-Bear, Annette. 'Face-painting in Renaissance Tragedy'. *Renaissance Drama* ns 12 (1981): 71–93.
Duane, Carol Leventen. 'Marlowe's Mixed Messages: A Model for Shakespeare'. *Medieval and Renaissance Drama in England* 3 (1986): 51–67.
Dundas, Judith. 'Shakespeare's Imagery: Emblem and the Imitation of Nature'. *Shakespeare Studies* 16 (1983): 45–56.

Dutton, Richard. 'Shakespeare and Marlowe: Censorship and Construction'. *Yearbook of English Studies* 23 (1993): 1–29.

Eccles, Christine. *The Rose Theatre*. London: Hern-Walker, 1990.

Elam, Keir. *The Semiotics of Theatre and Drama*. London: Methuen, 1980.

Ellis-Fermor, Una. *Christopher Marlowe*. London: 1927. Hamden, Conn.: Archer, 1967.

Elton, W. R. 'Shakespeare and the Thought of His Age'. *Cambridge Companion to Shakespeare Studies*. Ed. Stanley Wells. Cambridge: Cambridge University Press, 1986.

Ericksen, Roy T. 'The Misplaced Clownage-Scene in *The Tragedie of Doctor Faustus* (1616) and its Implications for the Play's Total Structure'. *English Studies* 62 (1981): 249–58.

Felperin, Howard. *The Uses of the Canon: Elizabethan Literature and Contemporary Theory*. Oxford: Clarendon, 1990.

Fleischer, Martha Hester. *The Iconography of the English History Play*. Salzburg: Institut für Englische Sprache und Literatur, Universität Salzburg, 1974.

Foakes, R. A. 'The Discovery of the Rose Theatre: Some Implications'. *Shakespeare Survey* 43 (1991): 141–8.

——*Illustrations of the English Stage 1580–1642*. London: Scolar, 1985.

Forker, Charles. Introduction. *Edward the Second*. Revels Plays. Manchester: Manchester University Press, 1994.

Forsyth, Neil. 'Heavenly Helen'. *Études de Lettres* 4 (1987): 11–21.

Freeman, Rosemary. *English Emblem Books*. London: Chatto, 1948.

Freer, Coburn. 'Lies and Lying in *The Jew of Malta*'. *'A Poet and a Filthy Play-maker': New Essays on Christopher Marlowe*. Ed. Kenneth Friedenreich, Roma Gill, and Constance B. Kuriyama. New York: AMS, 1988. 143–65.

Friedenreich, Kenneth. *Christopher Marlowe: An Annotated Bibliography of Criticism since 1950*. London: Scarecrow, 1979.

——'*The Jew of Malta* and its Critics: A Paradigm for Marlowe Studies'. *Papers on Language and Literature* 13.3 (Summer 1977): 318–35.

Gauntlett, Mark. 'Playing on the Margins: Theatrical Space in *Othello*'. *Essays in Theatre* 10.1 (November 1991): 17–29.

Geckle, George L. *Tamburlaine and Edward II: Text and Performance*. Atlantic Highlands, NJ: Humanities International, 1988.

Gibbons, Brian. 'Romance and the Heroic Play'. *The Cambridge Companion to English Renaissance Drama*. Ed. A. R. Braunmuller and Michael Hattaway. Cambridge: Cambridge University Press, 1990. 207–36.

Goldberg, Dena. 'Sacrifice in Marlowe's *The Jew of Malta*'. *Studies in English Literature* 32 (1992): 233–45.

Goldman, Michael. 'Marlowe and the Histrionics of Ravishment'. *Two Renaissance Mythmakers*. Ed. Alvin Kernan. Baltimore: Johns Hopkins University Press, 1977. 22–40.

——'Performer and Role in Marlowe and Shakespeare'. *Shakespeare and the Sense of Performance: Essays in the Tradition of Performance Criticism in Honor of Bernard Beckerman*. Ed. Marvin and Ruth Thompson. Delaware: University of Delaware Press, 1989.

Grantley, Darryll. '"What meanes this shew?": Theatricalism, Camp and

Subversion in *Doctor Faustus* and *The Jew of Malta*'. *Christopher Marlowe and English Renaissance Culture*. Ed. Darryll Grantley and Peter Roberts. Aldershot, Hants: Scolar, 1996.

Graves, R. B. 'Elizabethan Lighting Effects and the Convention of Indoor and Outdoor Theatrical Illumination'. *Renaissance Drama* ns 12 (1981): 51–69.

Greenblatt, Stephen. *Learning to Curse: Essays in Early Modern Culture*. New York, Routledge, 1990. 40–58.

——*Renaissance Self-fashioning: From More to Shakespeare*. Chicago: University of Chicago Press, 1980.

——*Shakespearean Negotiations: The Circulation of Energy in Renaissance England*. Oxford: Clarendon, 1988.

Greene, Robert. *Groatsworth of Wit, Bought with a Million of Repentance*. 1592. Bodley Head Quartos. Westport, Conn.: Greenwood, 1970.

——'To the Gentlemen Readers'. *Perimedes the Blacke-smith*. 1588. *The Life and Complete Works in Prose and Verse of Robert Greene M.A.* Ed. Alexander B. Grosart. Vol. 7. 1881–86. 15 vols. New York: Russell, 1964.

Greg, W. W. Introduction. *Marlowe's Doctor Faustus: 1604–1616*. Oxford: Clarendon, 1950. 1–139.

Grotowski, Jerzy. 'Doctor Faustus in Poland'. *Tulane Drama Review* 8.4 (Summer 1984): 120–33.

Gurr, Andrew. 'The Bare Island'. *Shakespeare Survey* 47 (1994): 29–43.

——*Playgoing in Shakespeare's London*. Cambridge: Cambridge University Press, 1987.

——*The Shakespearean Stage 1574–1642*. 3rd edition. Cambridge: Cambridge University Press, 1992.

——'The "State" of Shakespeare's Audiences'. *Shakespeare and the Sense of Performance: Essays in the Tradition of Performance Criticism in Honor of Bernard Beckerman*. Ed. Marvin and Ruth Thompson. Delaware: University of Delaware Press, 1989. 162–79.

Hall, Joseph. *Virgidemiarum. The Poems of Joseph Hall*. Ed. Arnold Davenport. Liverpool: Liverpool University Press, 1969.

Hapgood, Robert. *Shakespeare the Theatre-poet*. Oxford: Clarendon, 1988.

Happé, Peter, ed. *Tudor Interludes*. Harmondsworth: Penguin, 1972.

——'The Vice: A Checklist and an Annotated Bibliography'. *Research Opportunities in Renaissance Drama* 22 (1979): 17–35.

——'"The Vice" and the Popular Theatre, 1547–80'. *Poetry and Drama 1570–1700: Essays in Honour of Harold F. Brooks*. Ed. Antony Coleman and Antony Hammond. London: Methuen, 1981. 13–31.

Hattaway, Michael. *Elizabethan Popular Theatre*. London: Routledge, 1982.

Heinemann, Margot. 'Political Drama'. *The Cambridge Companion to English Renaissance Drama*. Ed. A. R. Braunmuller and Michael Hattaway. Cambridge: Cambridge University Press, 1990.

Hellenger, Robert R. 'Elizabethan Dramatic Conventions and Elizabethan Reality'. *Renaissance Drama* ns 12 (1981): 27–49.

Henke, James T. *Renaissance Dramatic Bawdy (Exclusive of Shakespeare): An Annotated Glossary and Critical Essays*. 2 vols. Salzburg: Institut für Englische Sprache und Literatur, Universität Salzburg, 1974.

Henslowe's Diary. Ed. R. A. Foakes and R. T. Rickert. Cambridge: Cambridge University Press, 1961.

Hill, Eugene D. 'The First Elizabethan Tragedy: A Contextual Reading of *Cambises'. Studies in Philology* 89 (1992): 404–33.

Hilton, Julian. *Performance.* London: Macmillan, 1987.

Hirsh, James. 'Laughter at *Titus Andronicus'. Essays in Theatre* 7.1 (November 1988): 59–74.

Hodgdon, Barbara. 'In Search of the Performance Present'. *Shakespeare: The Theatrical Dimension.* Ed. Philip C. Maguire and David L. Samuelson. New York: AMS, 1979. 29–49.

Holinshed's Chronicles of England, Scotland, and Ireland. Vol. 2. London: 1807. New York: AMS, 1965. Rpt. of Raphael Holinshed. *The Third Volume of Chronicles.* 1586.

Holland, Peter. 'Space: The Final Frontier'. *The Play out of Context.* Ed. Hanna Scolnicov and Peter Holland. Cambridge: Cambridge University Press, 1989, 45–62.

Höltgen, Karl Josef. *Aspects of the Emblem: Studies in the English Emblem Tradition and the European Context.* Kassel: Reichenberger, 1986.

Honigmann, E. A. J. Introduction. *King John.* Arden Shakespeare. London: Methuen, 1954.

Houle, Peter J. *The English Morality and Related Drama: A Bibliographical Survey.* Hamden, Conn.: Archon, 1972.

Howard, Jean E. *Shakespeare's Art of Orchestration.* Urbana, Ill.: University of Illinois Press, 1984.

Howell, W. S. *Logic and Rhetoric in England, 1500–1700.* New York: Russell, 1961.

Hunter, G. K. 'The Beginnings of Elizabethan Drama: Revolution and Continuity'. *Renaissance Drama* ns 17 (1986): 29–52.

——*English Drama 1586–1642: The Age of Shakespeare.* Oxford History of English Literature VI. Oxford: Clarendon, 1997.

——'Flatcaps and Bluecoats: Visual Signals on the Elizabethan Stage'. *Essays and Studies* ns 33 (1980): 16–47.

——*John Lyly: The Humanist as Courtier.* London: Routledge, 1962.

——'The Theology of Marlowe's *The Jew of Malta'. Journal of the Warburg and Courtauld Institutes* 27 (1964): 211–40.

Issacharoff, Michael. 'Space and Reference in Drama'. *Poetics Today* 2.3 (1981): 211–24.

Jackson, Russell. '*Doctor Faustus* in Manchester'. *Critical Quarterly* 23.4 (Winter 1981): 3–9.

Jardine, Lisa. *Still Harping on Daughters: Women and Drama in the Age of Shakespeare.* Brighton, Sussex: Harvester, 1983.

Johnson, Robert Carl. 'Audience Involvement in the Tudor Interlude'. *Theatre Notebook* 24.3 (Spring 1970): 101–11.

——Introduction. *A Critical Edition of Thomas Preston's* Cambises. Salzburg: Institut für Englische Sprache und Literatur, Universität Salzburg, 1975.

Jones, Robert C. 'Dangerous Sport: The Audience's Engagement with Vice in the Moral Interludes'. *Renaissance Drama* ns 6 (1973): 45–64.

——*Engagement with Knavery: Point of View in Richard III, The Jew of*

Malta, Volpone, and The Revenger's Tragedy. Durham: Duke University Press, 1986.

Jonson, Ben. *Timber, or, Discoveries*. 1640. *Ben Jonson*. Ed. Ian Donaldson. Oxford Authors. Oxford: Oxford University Press, 1985.

Jump, John D. Introduction, *The Tragical History of the Life and Death of Doctor Faustus: Christopher Marlowe*. Revels Plays. London: Methuen–University Paperback, 1968.

Kaplan, Joel H. 'Reopening King Cambises' Vein'. *Essays in Theatre* 5.2 (May 1987): 103–14.

Keefer, Michael H. Introduction. *Christopher Marlowe's Doctor Faustus: A 1604-version Edition*. Peterborough, Ontario: Broadview, 1991.

——'Verbal Magic and the Problem of the A and B Texts of *Doctor Faustus*'. *Journal of English and Germanic Philology* 82 (1983): 324–46.

Kelsall, Malcolm. *Christopher Marlowe*. Leiden: Brill, 1981.

Kennedy, Dennis. *Looking at Shakespeare: A Visual History of Twentieth-century Performance*. Cambridge: Cambridge University Press, 1993.

Kernan, Alvin. 'The Plays and the Playwrights'. *The Revels History of Drama in English: Volume III 1576–1613*. Ed. J. Leeds Barroll, Richard Southern, T. W. Craik, Lois Potter. London: Methuen, 1975. 237–474.

Kernodle, George R. *From Art to Theatre: Form and Convention in the Renaissance*. Chicago: University of Chicago Press, 1944.

Kimbrough, Robert. 'Christopher Marlowe'. *The Predecessors of Shakespeare: A Survey and Bibliography of Recent Studies in English Renaissance Drama*. Ed. Terence P. Logan and Denzell S. Smith. Lincoln: University of Nebraska Press, 1973. 3–55.

King, John N. *Tudor Royal Iconography: Literature and Art in an Age of Religious Crisis*. Princeton, NJ: Princeton University Press, 1989.

Kipling, Gordon. 'Triumphal Drama: Form in English Civic Pageantry'. *Renaissance Drama* ns 8 (1977): 37–56.

Kirschbaum, Leo. 'Marlowe's *Faustus*: A Reconsideration'. *Review of English Studies* 19 (1943): 225–41.

Klein, H. Arthur. *Graphic Worlds of Peter Bruegel the Elder*. New York: Dover, 1963.

Knights, L. C. 'How Many Children Had Lady Macbeth?' *Explorations*. London: Chatto, 1958. 1–39.

——'The Strange Case of Christopher Marlowe'. *Further Explorations*. London: Chatto, 1965. 75–98.

Knutson, Roslyn L. 'Influence of the Repertory System on the Revival and Revision of *The Spanish Tragedy* and *Dr. Faustus*'. *English Literary Renaissance* 18 (1988): 257–74.

——'Telling the Story of Shakespeare's Playhouse World'. *Shakespeare Survey* 44 (1992): 145–56.

Kocher, Paul H. *Christopher Marlowe: A Study of His Thought, Learning, and Character*. 1946. New York: Russell, 1962.

Kohler, Richard C. 'Kyd's Ordered Spectacle: "Behold ... / What 'tis to be subject to destiny"'. *Medieval and Renaissance Drama in England* 3 (1986): 27–49.

Kott, Jan. *The Bottom Translation: Marlowe and Shakespeare and the Carnival Tradition*. Trans. Daniela Miedzyrzecka and Lillian Vallee. Evanston, Ill.: Northwestern University Press, 1987.

Kuriyama, Constance Brown. 'Dr. Greg and *Doctor Faustus*: The Supposed Originality of the 1616 Text'. *English Literary Renaissance* 5 (1975): 171–97.

——*Hammer or Anvil: Psychological Patterns in Christopher Marlowe's Plays*. New Brunswick, NJ: Rutgers University Press, 1980.

Leech, Clifford. *Christopher Marlowe: Poet for the Stage*. Ed. Anne Lancashire. New York: AMS, 1986.

——'The Structure of *Tamburlaine*'. *Tulane Drama Review* 8.4 (Summer 1964): 32–46. [Rpt. and rev. in *Poet for the Stage*.]

Leith, Dick and George Myerson. *The Power of Address: Explorations in Rhetoric*. London: Routledge, 1989.

Leslie, Nancy T. '*Tamburlaine* in the Theater: Tartar, Grand Guignol or Janus?' *Renaissance Drama* ns 4 (1971): 105–20.

Levao, Ronald. 'Recent Studies in Marlowe (1977–1986)'. *English Literary Renaissance* 18 (1988): 329–42.

Levenson, Jill L. '"Working Words": The Verbal Dynamic of *Tamburlaine*'. *'A Poet and a Filthy Play-maker': New Essays on Christopher Marlowe*. Ed. Kenneth Friedenreich, Roma Gill, and Constance B. Kuriyama. New York: AMS, 1988. 99–115.

Levin, Harry. *Christopher Marlowe: The Overreacher*. London: Faber & Faber, 1954.

——'Marlowe Today'. *Tulane Drama Review* 8.4 (Summer 1964): 22–31.

Levin, Richard. 'The Contemporary Perception of Marlowe's *Tamburlaine*'. *Medieval and Renaissance Drama in England* 1 (1984): 51–70.

——'Feminist Thematics and Shakespearean Tragedy'. *PMLA* 103.2 (March 1988): 125–38.

——'Leaking Relativism'. *Essays in Criticism* 38 (1988): 267–77.

——*New Readings vs Old Plays: Recent Trends in the Reinterpretation of English Renaissance Drama*. Chicago: University of Chicago Press, 1979.

——'Unthinkable Thoughts in the New Historicizing of English Renaissance Drama'. *New Literary History* 21 (1989–90): 433–47.

Lindley, Arthur. 'The Unbeing of the Overreacher: Proteanism and the Marlovian Hero'. *Modern Language Review* 84 (1989): 1–17.

Linthicum, M. Channing. *Costume in the Drama of Shakespeare and His Contemporaries*. New York: Russell, 1936.

Littleton, Betty J. Introduction. *Clyomon and Clamydes: A Critical Edition*. The Hague: Mouton, 1968.

Lunney, Ruth. 'Bridges "Through the Moving Air": Christopher Marlowe and the "Space Between"'. *Essays in Theatre* 11.1 (November 1992): 17–31.

——'Faustus and the Angels'. *Sydney Studies in English* 16 (1990–91): 3–19.

——'Transforming the Emblematic: The Dramatic Emblem in the Plays of Christopher Marlowe'. *Essays in Theatre* 9.2 (May 1991): 141–58.

McAlindon, T. 'The Ironic Vision: Diction and Theme in Marlowe's *Doctor Faustus*'. *Review of English Studies* ns 32 (1981): 129–41.

McElroy, John F. 'Repetition, Contrariety, and Individualization in *Edward II*'. *Studies in English Literature* 24 (1984): 205–24.

McGann, Jerome. *A Critique of Modern Textual Criticism*. Chicago: University of Chicago Press, 1983.

McGuire, Philip C. Introduction. *Shakespeare: The Theatrical Dimension.* Ed. Philip C. McGuire and David A. Samuelson. New York: AMS, 1979. xvii–xx.

——*Speechless Dialect: Shakespeare's Open Silences.* Berkeley: University of California Press, 1985.

Maclure, Millar. *Marlowe: The Critical Heritage 1588–1896.* London: Routledge, 1979.

McMillin, Harvey Scott Jnr. *The Staging of Elizabethan Plays at the Rose Theatre.* Ann Arbor, Michigan: University Microfilms, 1975.

McMillin, Scott. 'The Queen's Men and the London Theatre of 1583'. *The Elizabethan Theatre* 10 (1988): 1–17.

——'The Figure of Silence in *The Spanish Tragedy*'. *English Literary History* 39 (1972): 27–48.

McMillin, Scott and Sally-Beth MacLean. *The Queen's Men and Their Plays.* Cambridge: Cambridge University Press, 1998.

Maguin, Jean-Marie. '*The Jew of Malta*: Marlowe's Ideological Stance and the Play-world's Ethos'. *Cahiers Élisabéthains* 27 (April 1985): 17–26.

Maguire, Laurie E. *Shakespearean Suspect Texts: The 'Bad' Quartos and Their Contexts.* Cambridge: Cambridge University Press, 1996.

Manley, Lawrence. *Convention: 1500–1750.* Cambridge, Mass.: Harvard University Press, 1980.

Manning, John. 'Whitney's *Choice of Emblemes*: A Reassessment'. *Renaissance Studies* 4.2 (1990): 155–200.

Marcus, Leah S. 'Textual Indeterminacy and Ideological Difference: The Case of *Doctor Faustus*'. *Renaissance Drama* ns 29 (1989): 1–29.

Marlowe, Christopher. *The Poems: Christopher Marlowe.* Ed. Millar Maclure. Manchester, Manchester University Press, 1968.

Meehan, Virginia M. *Christopher Marlowe: Poet and Playwright: Studies in Poetical Method.* The Hague: Mouton, 1974.

Mehl, Dieter. *The Elizabethan Dumb Show: The History of a Dramatic Convention.* London: Shenval, 1965.

——'Emblematic Theatre'. *Anglia* 95 (1977): 130–8.

——'Emblems in English Renaissance Drama'. *Renaissance Drama* ns 2 (1969): 39–57.

Melton, John. *Astrologaster, or the Figure-caster.* 1620. Introduction by Hugh G. Dick. Los Angeles: Augustan Reprint Society, 1975.

Merchant, W. Moelwyn. Introduction. *Edward the Second.* By Christopher Marlowe. London: Benn, 1967. ix–xxv.

Minshull, Catherine. 'Marlowe's "Sound Machevill"'. *Renaissance Drama* ns 13 (1982): 35–53.

——'The Dissident Subtext of Marlowe's "Doctor Faustus"'. *English* 39 (1990): 193–207.

The Mirror for Magistrates. Ed. Lily B. Campbell. 1938. New York: Barnes, 1960.

Mithal, H. S. D., ed. Introduction. *An Edition of Robert Wilson's Three Ladies of London and Three Lords and Three Ladies of London.* New York: Garland, 1988.

Mooney, Michael. *Shakespeare's Dramatic Transactions.* Durham: Duke University Press, 1990.

Morrill, John. 'The Making of Oliver Cromwell'. *Oliver Cromwell and the English Revolution*. Ed. John Morrill. London: Longman, 1990.

Morris, Harry. 'Marlowe's Poetry'. *Tulane Drama Review* 8.4 (Summer 1964): 134–54.

Muir, Kenneth. 'Characterisation in Elizabethan Drama and Its Implications for the Modern Stage'. *The Arts of Performance in Elizabethan and Early Stuart Drama*. Ed. Murray Biggs, Philip Edwards, Inga-Stina Ewbank, Eugene M. Waith. Edinburgh: Edinburgh University Press, 1991. 147–55.

Mullaney, Steven. *The Place of the Stage: License, Play, and Power in Renaissance England*. Chicago: Chicago University Press, 1988.

Mulryne, J. R. and Stephen Fender. 'Marlowe and the Comic Distance'. *Christopher Marlowe*. Ed. Brian Morris. London: Benn, 1968. 49–64.

Nashe, Thomas. *Pierce Penilesse, His Supplication to the Devil*. 1592. Westport, Conn.: Greenwood, 1924.

Nicoll, Allardyce. 'Passing Over the Stage'. *Shakespeare Survey* 12 (1959): 47–55.

O'Connell, Michael. 'The Idolatrous Eye: Iconoclasm, Anti-theatricalism, and the Image of the Elizabethan Theater'. *ELH* 52 (1985): 279–310.

Ong, Walter. J. 'From Allegory to Diagram In the Renaissance Mind: A Study in the Significance of the Allegorical Tableau'. *Journal of Aesthetics and Art Criticism* 17 (1958–59): 423–40.

——*Ramus: Method and the Decay of Dialogue: From the Art of Discourse to the Art of Reason*. Cambridge, Mass.: Harvard University Press, 1958.

——*Orality and Literacy: The Technologizing of the Word*. London: Methuen, 1982.

Orgel, Stephen. *The Illusion of Power: Political Theater in the English Renaissance*. Berkeley: University of California Press, 1975.

——'Making Greatness Familiar'. *Pageantry in the Shakespearean Theater*. Ed. David M. Bergeron. Athens, Ga: University of Georgia Press, 1985. 19–25.

——'What Is a Text?' *Research Opportunities in Renaissance Drama* 24 (1981): 3–6.

Ormerod, David and Christopher Wortham. Introduction. *Dr Faustus: The A-Text*. Nedlands, WA: University of Western Australia Press, 1985.

Orrell, John and Andrew Gurr. 'What the Rose Can Tell Us'. *Times Literary Supplement* 9–15 June 1989: 636.

Osborne, Laurie E. 'The Rhetoric of Evidence'. *Textual and Theatrical Shakespeare: Questions of Evidence*. Ed. Edward Pechter. Iowa City: University of Iowa Press, 1996. 124–43.

Partridge, Eric. *Shakespeare's Bawdy: A Literary and Psychological Essay*. London: Routledge, 1968.

Patterson, Lee. *Negotiating the Past: The Historical Understanding of Medieval Literature*. Madison, Wis.: University of Wisconsin Press, 1987.

——'On the Margin: Postmodernism, Ironic History, and Medieval Studies'. *Speculum* 65 (1990): 87–108.

Pavis, Patrice. *Dictionnaire du théâtre*. Paris: Messidor/Éditions sociales, 1987.

——*Languages of the Stage: Essays in the Semiology of the Theatre*. New York: Performing Arts Journal, 1982.

Pearlman, E. 'R. Willis and *The Cradle of Security* (c. 1572)'. *English Literary Renaissance* 20 (1990): 357–73.

Pechter, Edward. 'The New Historicism and its Discontents'. *PMLA* 102.3 (May 1987): 292–303.

——ed. *Textual and Theatrical Shakespeare: Questions of Evidence.* Iowa City: University of Iowa Press, 1996.

——*What Was Shakespeare? Renaissance Plays and Changing Critical Practice.* Ithaca: Cornell University Press, 1995.

Peet, Donald. 'The Rhetoric of *Tamburlaine*'. *English Literary History* 26 (1959): 137–55.

Pettit, Thomas. 'Formulaic Dramaturgy in *Doctor Faustus*'. *'A Poet and a Filthy Play-maker': New Essays on Christopher Marlowe.* Ed. Kenneth Friedenreich, Roma Gill, and Constance B. Kuriyama. New York: AMS, 1988. 167–91.

Pinciss, G. M. *Literary Creations: Conventional Characters in the Drama of Shakespeare and His Contemporaries.* Woodbridge, Suffolk: Brewer, 1988.

——'Marlowe's Cambridge Years and the Writing of *Doctor Faustus*'. *Studies in English Literature* 33 (1993): 249–64.

Post, Jonathan F. S. 'Recent Studies in Marlowe (1968–1976)'. *English Literary Renaissance* 7 (1977): 382–99.

Postlewait, Thomas. 'Historiography and the Theatrical Event: A Primer with Twelve Cruxes'. *Theatre Journal* 43 (1991): 157–78.

Potter, Lois. 'The Plays and the Playwrights'. *Revels History of Drama in English. Volume II: 1500–1576.* Ed. J. Leeds Barroll, Richard Southern, T. W. Craik, Lois Potter. London: Methuen, 1980. 143–257.

Powell, Jocelyn. 'Marlowe's Spectacle'. *Tulane Drama Review* 8.4 (Summer 1964): 195–210.

Puttenham, George. *The Art of English Poesy.* 1589. Ed. Gladys Doidge Willcock and Alice Walker. Cambridge: Cambridge University Press, 1936.

Rabkin, Norman. *Shakespeare and the Problem of Meaning.* Chicago: University of Chicago Press, 1981.

Revels History of Drama in English: Volume II 1500–1576. Ed. J. Leeds Barroll, Richard Southern, T. W. Craik, Lois Potter. London: Methuen, 1980.

Reynolds, George Fulmer. *The Staging of Plays at the Red Bull Theatre 1605–1625.* 1940. New York: Kraus Reprint, 1966.

Rhodes, Ernest L. *The Staging of Elizabethan Plays at the Rose Theatre 1592–1603.* Ann Arbor, Michigan: University Microfilms, 1975.

Rhodes, Neil. *The Power of Eloquence and English Renaissance Literature.* New York: St Martin's, 1992.

Ribner, Irving. 'Marlowe's *Edward II* and the Tudor History Play'. *Journal of English Literary History* 22 (1955): 243–53.

Riggs, David. *Shakespeare's Heroical Histories: Henry VI and Its Literary Tradition.* Cambridge, Mass.: Harvard University Press, 1971.

Robertson, Toby. 'Directing *Edward II*'. *Tulane Drama Review* 8.4 (Summer 1964): 174–83.

Rocklin, Edward L. 'Marlowe as Experimental Dramatist: The Role of the Audience in *The Jew of Malta*'. *'A Poet and a Filthy Play-maker': New*

Essays on Christopher Marlowe. Ed. Kenneth Friedenreich, Roma Gill, and Constance B. Kuriyama. New York: AMS, 1988. 129–42.

——'*Producible Interpretation*: Literary Criticism and the Performance Possibilities of Playscripts'. *Journal of Dramatic Theory and Criticism* 1 (Spring 1988): 149–74.

Rothstein, Eric. 'Structure as Meaning in *The Jew of Malta*'. *Journal of English and Germanic Philology* 65 (1966): 260–73.

Rubin, Miri. 'The Eucharist and the Construction of Medieval Identities'. *Culture and History 1300–1600: Essays on English Communities, Identities and Writing.* Ed. David Aers. London: Harvester, 1992. 43–63.

Rutter, Carol Chillington. *Documents of the Rose Playhouse.* Revels Plays Companion Library. Manchester: Manchester University Press, 1984.

Sales, Roger. *Christopher Marlowe.* New York: St Martin's, 1991.

——'The Stage, the Scaffold and the Spectators.' *Christopher Marlowe and Renaissance Culture.* Ed. Darryll Grantley and Peter Roberts. Aldershot, Hants: Scolar, 1996.

Sanders, Wilbur. *The Dramatist and the Received Idea: Studies in the Plays of Marlowe and Shakespeare.* Cambridge: Cambridge University Press, 1968.

Scolnicov, Hanna. 'Theatre Space, Theatrical Space, and the Theatrical Space Without'. *Themes in Drama* 9 (1987): 11–26.

Scott, Margaret. 'Machiavelli and the Machiavel'. *Renaissance Drama* ns 15 (1984): 147–74.

Scott, Michael. *Renaissance Drama and a Modern Audience.* London: Macmillan, 1982.

Serpieri, Alessandro. 'Reading the Signs: Towards a Semiotics of Shakespearean Drama'. *Alternative Shakespeares.* Ed. John Drakakis. London: Methuen, 1985. Trans. Keir Elam. 119–43.

Shapiro, James. *Rival Playwrights: Marlowe, Jonson, Shakespeare.* New York: Columbia University Press, 1991.

Shapiro, Michael. 'Annotated Bibliography on Original Staging in Elizabethan Plays'. *Research Opportunities in Renaisssance Drama* 24 (1981): 23–49.

Shepherd, Simon. *Marlowe and the Politics of Elizabethan Theatre.* Brighton, Sussex: Harvester, 1986.

Sidney, Philip. *An Apology for Poetry or The Defence of Poesy.* Ed. Geoffrey Shepherd. Manchester: Manchester University Press, 1973.

Siemon, James R. *Shakespearean Iconoclasm.* Berkeley: University of California Press, 1985.

Sinfield, Alan. *Faultlines: Cultural Materialism and the Politics of Dissident Reading.* Berkeley: University of California Press, 1992.

Slater, Ann Pasternak. *Shakespeare the Director.* Brighton, Sussex: Harvester, 1982.

Smith, James L. '*The Jew of Malta* in the Theatre'. *Christopher Marlowe.* Ed. Brian Morris. London: Benn, 1968. 3–23.

Smith, Marion Bodwell. *Marlowe's Imagery and the Marlowe Canon.* 1940. Folcroft, Pa: Folcroft Library Editions, 1973.

Smith, Molly. 'The Theater and the Scaffold: Death as Spectacle in *The Spanish Tragedy*'. *Studies in English Literature* 32 (1992): 217–32.

Smith, Warren D. 'Stage Business in Shakespeare's Dialogue'. *Shakespeare Quarterly* 4 (1953): 311–16.

Southern, Richard. *The Staging of Plays before Shakespeare*. London: Faber, 1973.

Speaight, Robert. *William Poel and the Elizabethan Revival*. London: Heinemann, 1951.

Spivack, Bernard. *Shakespeare and the Allegory of Evil: The History of a Metaphor in Relation to His Major Villains*. New York: Columbia University Press, 1958.

Sprinchorn, Evert. 'An Intermediate Stage Level in the Elizabethan Theatre'. *Theatre Notebook* 46 (1992): 73–94.

Spurgeon, Caroline. *Shakespeare's Imagery and What It Tells Us*. Cambridge: Cambridge University Press, 1958.

States, Bert O. *Hamlet and the Concept of Character*. Baltimore: Johns Hopkins University Press, 1992.

Steadman, John M. 'Iconography and Renaissance Drama: Ethical and Mythological Themes'. *Research Opportunities in Renaissance Drama* 13–14 (1970–71): 73–122.

Steane, J. B. *Marlowe: A Critical Study*. Cambridge: Cambridge University Press, 1964.

Stroup, Thomas B. 'Ritual in Marlowe's Plays'. *Comparative Drama* 7(1973): 198–221.

Styan, J. L. *Shakespeare's Stagecraft*. Cambridge: Cambridge University Press, 1967.

——'Stage Space and the Shakespeare Experience'. *Shakespeare and the Sense of Performance: Essays in the Tradition of Performance Criticism in Honor of Bernard Beckerman*. Ed. Marvin and Ruth Thompson. Newark: University of Delaware Press, 1989. 195–209.

Summers, Claude J. *Christopher Marlowe and the Politics of Power*. Salzburg: Institut für Englische Sprache und Literatur, Universität Salzburg, 1974.

——'Sex, Politics, and Self-Realization in *Edward II*'. *'A Poet and a Filthy Play-maker': New Essays on Christopher Marlowe*. Ed. Kenneth Friedenreich, Roma Gill, and Constance B. Kuriyama. New York: AMS, 1988. 221–40.

Taylor, Charles. *Sources of the Self: The Making of the Modern Identity*. Cambridge: Cambridge University Press, 1989.

Taylor, Gary. *Reinventing Shakespeare: A Cultural History from the Restoration to the Present*. New York: Weidenfeld, 1989.

——*To Analyze Delight: A Hedonist Criticism of Shakespeare*. Newark: University of Delaware Press, 1985.

Thompson, Marvin and Ruth Thompson. 'Performance Criticism; From Granville-Barker to Bernard Beckerman and Beyond'. *Shakespeare and the Sense of Performance: Essays in the Tradition of Performance Criticism in Honor of Bernard Beckerman*. Newark: University of Delaware Press, 1989. 13–23.

Thomson, Peter. *Shakespeare's Theatre*. 2nd edition. London: Routledge, 1992.

Thurn, David H. 'Sights of Power in *Tamburlaine*'. *English Literary Renaissance* 19 (1989): 3–21.

——'Sovereignty, Disorder, and Fetishism in Marlowe's *Edward II*'. *Renaissance Drama* ns 21 (1990): 115–41.

Tweedie, Eleanor M. '"Action Is Eloquence": The Staging of Thomas Kyd's *Spanish Tragedy*'. *Studies in English Literature* 16 (1976): 223–39.

Tydeman, William. *Doctor Faustus: Text and Performance*. London: Macmillan, 1984.

Ubersfeld, Anne. *L'école du spectateur: Lire le théâtre 2*. Paris: Éditions sociales, 1981.

——*Lire le théâtre*. Paris: Éditions sociales, 1982.

——'The Pleasure of the Spectator'. Trans. Pierre Bouillaguet and Charles Jose. *Modern Drama* 25 (1982): 127–39.

Ure, Peter. Introduction. *King Richard II*. Arden Shakespeare. London: Macmillan, 1984.

Van Hook, J. W. 'The Rhetoric of Marlowe's Orations'. *'A Poet and a Filthy Play-maker': New Essays on Christopher Marlowe*. Ed. Kenneth Friedenreich, Roma Gill, and Constance B. Kuriyama. New York: Press, 1988. 49–61.

Vickers, Brian. 'The Emergence of Character Criticism, 1774–1800'. *Shakespeare Survey* 34 (1981): 11–21.

——*In Defence of Rhetoric*. Oxford: Clarendon, 1988.

Voss, James. '*Edward II*: Marlowe's Historical Tragedy'. *English Studies* 63 (1982): 517–30.

Waith, Eugene. 'Marlowe and the Jades of Asia'. *Studies in English Literature* 5 (1965): 229–45.

Warren, Michael J. '*Doctor Faustus*: The Old Man and the Text'. *English Literary Renaissance* 11 (1981): 111–47.

Watson, Robert N. 'Tragedy'. *The Cambridge Companion to English Renaissance Drama*. Ed. A. R. Braunmuller and Michael Hattaway. Cambridge: Cambridge University Press, 1990. 301–51.

Weil, Judith. *Christopher Marlowe: Merlin's Prophet*. Cambridge: Cambridge University Press, 1977.

Weimann, Robert. *Shakespeare and the Popular Tradition in the Theater: Studies in the Social Dimension of Dramatic Form and Function*. Ed. Robert Schwartz. 1978. Baltimore: Johns Hopkins University Press, 1987.

Werstine, Paul. 'Narratives About Printed Shakespeare Texts: "Foul Papers" and "Bad" Quartos'. *Shakespeare Quarterly* 41 (1990): 65–86.

West, Robert Hunter. *The Invisible World: A Study of Pneumatology in Elizabethan Drama*. Athens, Ga: University of Georgia Press, 1939.

White, Paul Whitfield. *Theatre and Reformation: Protestantism, Patronage, and Playing in Tudor England*. Cambridge: Cambridge University Press, 1993.

Whitney, Geffrey. *A Choice of Emblems and Other Devices*. Leyden: 1586. Amsterdam: Theatrum Orbis Terrarum, 1969.

Wickham, Glynne. *Early English Stages: 1300 to 1660*. 3 vols. London: Routledge, 1959–81.

——'*Exeunt to the cave*: Notes on the Staging of Marlowe's Plays'. *Tulane Drama Review* 8.4 (Summer 1964): 184–94.

Wierum, Ann. '"Actors" and "Play Acting" in the Morality Tradition'. *Renaissance Drama* ns 3 (1970): 189–214.

Williams, Raymond. *Drama in Performance*. Revised edition. London: Watts, 1968.

Wimsatt, James I. *Allegory and Mirror: Tradition and Structure in Middle English Literature*. New York: Pegasus, 1970.

Wine, M. L. Introduction. *The Tragedy of Master Arden of Faversham*. Revels Plays. London: Methuen, 1973.

Worthen, W. B. 'Deeper Meanings and Theatrical Technique: The Rhetoric of Performance Criticism'. *Shakespeare Quarterly* 40 (1989): 441–55.

Wymer, Rowland. '"When I Behold the Heavens": A Reading of *Doctor Faustus*'. *English Studies* 67 (1986): 505–10.

Yachnin, Paul. 'The Powerless Theater'. *English Literary Renaissance* 21 (1991): 49–74.

Zarate, Oscar. *Christopher Marlowe: Dr Faustus*. Illus. Oscar Zarate. World Theatre Classics. London: Abacus/Sphere, 1986.

Zucker, David Hard. *Stage and Image in the Plays of Christopher Marlowe*. Salzburg: Institut für Englische Sprache und Literatur, Universität Salzburg, 1972.

INDEX

Note: 'n.' after a page reference indicates the number of a note on that page. Playtexts are indexed by short title, as in the References.